The Indian Vegan Kitchen

The Indian Vegan Kitchen

More Than
150 Quick
and Healthy
Homestyle
Recipes

Madhu Gadia, M.S., R.D.

A Perigee Book

A PERIGEE BOOK
Published by the Penguin Group
Penguin Group (USA) Inc.
375 Hudson Street, New York, New York 10014, USA
Penguin Group (Canada), 90 Eglinton Avenue East, Suite 700, Toronto, Ontario M4P 2Y3, Canada
(a division of Pearson Penguin Canada Inc.)
Penguin Books Ltd., 80 Strand, London WC2R 0RL, England
Penguin Group Ireland, 25 St. Stephen's Green, Dublin 2, Ireland (a division of Penguin Books Ltd.)
Penguin Group (Australia), 250 Camberwell Road, Camberwell, Victoria 3124, Australia
(a division of Pearson Australia Group Pty. Ltd.)
Penguin Books India Pvt. Ltd., 11 Community Centre, Panchsheel Park, New Delhi—110 017, India
Penguin Group (NZ), 67 Apollo Drive, Rosedale, North Shore 0632, New Zealand
(a division of Pearson New Zealand Ltd.)
Penguin Books (South Africa) (Pty.) Ltd., 24 Sturdee Avenue, Rosebank, Johannesburg 2196, South Africa
Penguin Books Ltd., Registered Offices: 80 Strand, London WC2R 0RL, England

While the author has made every effort to provide accurate telephone numbers and Internet addresses at the time of publication, neither the publisher nor the author assumes any responsibility for errors, or for changes that occur after publication. Further, the publisher does not have any control over and does not assume any responsibility for author or third-party websites or their content.

First edition: October 2009

Library of Congress Cataloging-in-Publication Data

Gadia, Madhu.
    The Indian vegan kitchen : more than 150 quick and healthy homestyle recipes / Madhu Gadia.— 1st ed.
        p.   cm.
    Includes index.
    ISBN 978-0-399-53530-7
    1. Vegetarian cookery.   2. Cookery, Indian.   I. Title.
    TX837.G28   2009
    641.5954—dc22   2009020079

PRINTED IN THE UNITED STATES OF AMERICA

10 9 8 7 6 5 4 3 2 1

PUBLISHER'S NOTE: The recipes contained in this book are to be followed exactly as written. The publisher is not responsible for your specific health or allergy needs that may require medical supervision. The publisher is not responsible for any adverse reactions to the recipes contained in this book.

Most Perigee books are available at special quantity discounts for bulk purchases for sales promotions, premiums, fundraising, or educational use. Special books, or book excerpts, can also be created to fit specific needs. For details, write: Special Markets, Penguin Group (USA) Inc., 375 Hudson Street, New York, New York 10014.

Dedicated to
my husband,
Shashi,
and my children,
Manisha and Nitin

Acknowledgments

I AM OVERWHELMED AND overjoyed by the support and encouragement of so many people that words alone cannot express my gratitude. You made writing this book a wonderful journey that I will treasure forever. I read this quote on a Success Poster, and it best describes how I feel toward each and everyone of you: "There is no such thing as a self-made man. You will reach your goals only with the help of others." Thank you for lending me a hand.

First and foremost I want to thank my mother, Satya Vati Gupta, who never tires of talking about food. Even now, after two cookbooks and years of cooking myself, I call her when a new recipe doesn't work, or I'm in need of good old motherly advice on what's for dinner. She has an amazing understanding of Indian cooking and lives and breathes good food. She is the real foodie.

My late father, Vimal Kishore Gupta—I really miss him. He's my hero, the one who taught me the value of family and good, old-fashioned hard work. He always knew the right thing to say to inspire me and make me feel that everything was right in my world.

My husband, Shashi, for his love, support, and encouragement. He pretty much tasted all the recipes in this book, for often that was dinner. I could not have done it without him.

My son, Nitin, whose excitement about Mom's writing a vegan cookbook was contagious. But that's how he is. He popped in and out of the house and willingly tasted the food. He would bring his friends over for taste-testing and tell them all about the dishes and the new cookbook. He brought excitement to the project.

My daughter, Manisha, who was too far to come popping in for taste-testing, but her enthusiasm on the phone was invaluable. She gets excited about my writing as well as the recipes. She is a good writer in her own right and is always willing to give constructive comments.

My son-in-law, Ravi Bewtra, who is always there with encouraging words and positive energy. I am blessed, for now I have two sons.

My brother and sisters: Ajay, Veena, Meenakshi, and Shelly—I can always count on their encouragement, love, and support. I can call them any time for a little gloating or a whining session. My sister-in-law, Anjali, and brothers-in-law, Rajeev Nath, Praveen Bhatia, and Rob McNicol, are equally wonderful and supportive. They all keep me grounded and make my world complete.

My friends in Ames, Iowa: Vandana and Suresh, Amita and Vinay, Simi and Giri, Rema and Shree, Rajshree and Sanjeev, and Rama and Sridhar—I want to thank each and every one of them for their kind words, jokes, and willingness to taste the recipes. They are all from different regions of India and food experts in their own right. They are always willing to share their recipes, expertise, and come and help me at the drop of a hat. You guys rock.

My friend, colleague, and confidant Connie Buss: Thank you for believing in me and for always being there.

My helper, Emily Fifield, for working with me when I needed it. She dropped everything, worked weekends, and made my project a priority for two weeks when I felt overwhelmed with deadlines. She's a quick learner and a conscientious worker—just the kind of person I needed to help me do the nutritional analysis.

My agent, Bob Silverstein of Quicksilver Books, for believing in me and my book proposal. Thank you for bringing this book to light.

My editor, Marian Lizzi, editor-in-chief at Perigee Books, for giving me an opportunity to write this book, for her encouraging words, and for her amazing guidance. Words alone cannot express my gratitude. This book is what it is because of her.

Contents

Introduction

THIS BOOK IS for anyone, vegan or not, looking for great-tasting, authentic, easy-to-follow Indian recipes.

I grew up surrounded with vegetarian food. In India, being vegetarian is considered "normal" and eating meat is the anomaly, at least in my community. Even meat eaters eat vegetarian meals several times a week. Only when I left India did I ever need to ask, "Do you have anything vegetarian?"

Indian vegetarian is clearly defined as a plant-based diet that includes milk and milk products—thus, a lacto-vegetarian way of eating. If you eat anything else, such as eggs or fish, then you must qualify it as an exception—for example, I'm a vegetarian but I eat eggs. Indians are very proud of their vegetarian heritage and lifestyle and celebrate it with fervor.

Today, I have a whole new appreciation for nonvegetarians who choose to become vegetarians or vegans. Initially, when I started writing this cookbook, I thought it would be a breeze, expecting that I would only have to eliminate milk. I soon realized how difficult it is to think—and cook—outside the box. I did not realize how extensively and auto-matically I add milk products in dishes. Once I got over that hurdle, it was a rich experience with amazing results.

Health benefits of eating plant-based meals are well rec-ognized but it did not happen overnight. Working as a di-etitian, I have seen the traditional American diet change over the last couple of decades. I live in the midwest, where meat and potatoes are the staple, and encouraging people to eat more vegetables is a constant challenge. In the mid–1990s, a fellow dietitian observed my vegetarian meal and stated that if she does not have some protein (meat) with a meal, she has a low–blood sugar reaction and does not feel good. I knew what she was saying was scientifically valid, for that's what we were taught, but I knew I had enough protein at that meal as well as throughout the day. A few years later, I was out with the same dietitian when she ordered a vegetarian meal. I looked at her with surprise and she just smiled. In the last few years, several health organizations such as the American Institute of Cancer Research and the American Heart Association have focused on encouraging people to eat more vegetables, fruits, whole grains, and beans. Many health professionals are recommending that people eat vegetarian meals at least once a week. To help Americans reduce their consumption of saturated fat and to help prevent heart disease, stroke, diabetes, and cancer—four of the leading causes of death in America—a national public health campaign called Meatless Monday (a nonprofit organization) is working in conjunction with the Johns Hopkins Bloomberg School of Public Health to make it easier for people to eat at least one vegetarian meal a week. Twenty-eight other public health schools also support the campaign. The program follows the nutrition guidelines of the U.S. Department of Health and Human Services, the U.S. Department of Agriculture, and the American Heart Association.

Although the acceptance of vegetarian meals has increased by leaps and bounds, truly delicious and vibrant plant-based meals can still be hard to come by. Many vegetarian dishes are either bland or laden with cheese, cream, and eggs, making them high in fat and saturated fat and therefore not always healthier than meat-based meals. Although this is certainly beginning to change, a vegetarian or vegan who's looking for variety, flavor, and new options is increasingly turning to ethnic specialties.

Although it includes dairy, the Indian vegetarian diet is naturally close to a vegan diet. Legumes (dal) and whole grains (roti, or whole wheat flatbread) take center stage in a natural, plant-based way of eating. The vegetarian diet among Indians is as ingrained culturally, psychologically, and socially as the nonvegetarian diet is in the rest of the world. Since vegetarianism in India has been a way of life for centuries, the meals are gloriously vegetarian and not a replica of nonvegetarian dishes.

Americans often judge a vegetarian meal by how closely it resembles a nonvegetarian meal (and I understand why). Can the vegetarian meal be nutritionally balanced, appetizing, and hearty without the meat? Is it going to be as gratifying as Mom's meat loaf, mashed potatoes, and green beans *without* the meat loaf? These are the common questions on the minds of those who are trying to eat one vegetarian meal per day, trying to feed a family, are converting to vegetarianism, or are vegans.

Indian vegetarians or vegans are not trying to make a meatless meal look, taste, smell, or feel like a meal with meat. In fact, the Indian objective is dramatically opposite. To Indians, a vegetarian meal (with or without milk) is hearty, appetizing, nutritionally well balanced, satisfying, and has a special flair and distinction of its own.

Holistic Cooking

Indian cooking combines the art and science of preparing food. Ayurveda is a system of traditional medicine native to India. It is a holistic science, which focuses on healing of body, mind, and spirit through food, herbs, and revitalizing therapies. Ayurvedic medicine and therapies in other parts of the world are referred to as alternative medicine. Ayurvedic cooking is about cooking flavorful dishes that promote good health, clean the accumulated toxins (a result of improperly digested food), and rejuvenate the body as each dish is cooked and spiced to achieve maximum digestibility.

This is not an Ayurvedic cookbook, but the use of spices and herbs has the same overlay.

Indians cook naturally, using Ayurvedic principles. Growing up, I often heard things like add more ginger or garam masala to a dish to help aid in digestion or because it's winter. The tradition of natural, Ayurvedic cooking is passed on from generation to generation. You will automatically get all the benefits of Ayurvedic cooking and healing, as the principles are ingrained in Indian cooking.

Indian Vegan Recipes

All of the recipes in this book are gloriously, triumphantly vegan. A majority of the traditional Indian vegetarian recipes are vegan by design. Eggs, hard cheeses, and honey are not a part of a typical Indian vegetarian diet, and therefore not an issue. You will find recipes from appetizers to desserts. Every effort has been made to keep the recipes as authentic as possible—anything less and they never would have passed me, my husband, or my other taste-testers!

Soymilk and other soy products were not used as a replacement for milk or protein except in very few recipes and they are all in the Soy Products section (page 173). I felt that vegans and vegetarians have or can find enough recipes for soy and may be looking for traditional Indian recipes to increase their vegan base repertoire. If you want to substitute soy products for milk, it's easy to do so; just follow the vegetarian recipes in my book *New Indian Home Cooking*.

Serving Indian Meals

Indian dishes can be enjoyed in a variety of ways. Serve one Indian dish with your traditional American meal; for example, try a vegetable curry side with your favorite sandwich, or make a complete Indian meal. Indian meals can be as simple as dal and *chawal* (beans and rice) or as complicated as a *thaali* meal.

Traditionally, Indian meals are served in a *thaali*—a large, rimmed plate. The *thaali* is lined on one side with two to six little bowls (about 4 to 6 ounces each)—called *katori*. Many dishes tend to be in a sauce, and picky Indians want to keep the flavors separate. The small bowls also offer an aesthetically pleasing presentation. The more festive the meal or more important the guest, the greater number of bowls included in the *thaali*. Each bowl is filled with a different item. An elaborate Indian vegetarian *thaali* will have a dal, one to three cooked vegetable dishes, salad, chutney, pickles, yogurt, and dessert all served in bowls with roti, rice, and *papad*.

Don't be overwhelmed! A daily meal consists of one dal, one vegetable, and roti or rice. Chutney, pickles, salad, and *papad* are condiments and can be added to any simple to elaborate meal. This is very similar to a meal of meat, potatoes, green beans, and dinner rolls. Nutritionally speaking, such mixed meals of protein, vegetables, and grain provide a greater variety of nutrients.

Indians subscribe to hospitality to the nth degree. Any time you enter an Indian home, you are expected to eat or drink something; it's about honoring the guest. For more information on Indian hospitality, see Snacks, Chaat, and Beverages (page 51).

Vegan Nutrition

Food—good-tasting and good-for-you—is my passion. As a dietitian, I counsel people on preventing and managing disease. No matter how healthy it is, I know that if food does not taste good, people (patients) will not eat it, at least not forever. Numerous studies indicate that consumers want food that tastes good and is nutritious—in that order. If the dietary changes you make are not permanent, it can be a frustrating experience. And on that note, I recommend to all my clients that, in moderation, all foods can fit into a healthy diet.

One of the reasons you might choose vegan foods is for optimal health. Numerous fears and myths surround vegan diets and its nutritional

adequacy. Writing this book gave me an opportunity to research vegan nutritional concerns. I'm pleased to report that a vegan diet, if planned properly just like any other diet, can meet your nutritional needs throughout your life. The main concerns are to get adequate calcium, vitamin D, vitamin B12, iron, and zinc. As with any diet, remember to include a variety of foods to get the nutrients you need. For detailed nutrition information, see Vegan Diet for Optimal Health (page 31). The nutrition information provided in this book does not constitute medical advice. If you have any medical or nutritional concerns, please see your physician.

How to Best Use This Book

Having a selection of recipes is one thing, but a cookbook is useful only if anyone—from a novice cook to an expert—can follow the recipes with ease and delectable results. The most popular and my favorite comments I received from my previous book, *New Indian Home Cooking*, were: The recipes are easy to follow; the food tastes just like Mom's (Indian children learning to cook); and the dishes are lower in fat and healthier. All the same principles have been applied here.

I have included a handful of features to help you use the book efficiently.

Menus

Start by browsing through the menus; I have planned a month of menus for you. Planning is half the battle in preparing meals. You will find a week of menus in each category; quick meals, any-day meals, breakfast to lunch to dinner menus, and party menus. Enjoy them any which way you like, or create your own.

Recipe Titles: Most recipe titles are in English and have an Indian name. The Indian name most of the time is in Hindi (one of the major Indian languages), and I did the best I could for translation. As you get used to Indian names, you would want to use them, since English translation does not do full justice. For example, *chole* is spicy chickpeas, but really calling *chole* spicy chickpeas undermines its complexity. Do your best; I did.

Time: All recipes give estimated preparation and cook time for your convenience. The actual time may vary based on your familiarity and experience, but nonetheless it will give you a good idea before starting.

Number of Servings and Serving Size: Most of the recipes yield 6 to 8 servings, except chutneys and desserts. The idea is to feed a typical family of four. A person will eat 1 to 2 servings based on what else is served with the meal. Nutritional analysis is based on a single serving as listed. If you eat 2 servings, you will get double the calories, etc. If you're cooking for two, most recipes can be divided in half with ease.

Icons: LF and GF

I have used two symbols for your convenience: Low-Fat (LF) and Gluten-Free (GF).

Every effort has been made to keep the recipes as low-fat as possible; even the recipes that do not have a LF icon are lower in fat than traditional recipes. That is just how I cook. You will find some deep-fat fried recipes. I would equate Indian deep-fat frying to baking. There is minimal baking in Indian cuisine, and deep-fat fried foods can have similar or less fat than baked quick breads and pastries.

Gluten is a protein found in wheat, rye, and barley. A gluten-free diet is recommended for people who have celiac disease or wheat allergy, but it has recently gained popularity among the general population. Corn, millet, buckwheat, vegetables, fruits, and dried beans are naturally gluten-free. The gluten-free recipes included in this book are authentic and delicious.

Using the Nutrition Information

Each recipe includes nutrition information based on a single serving. With each recipe, you will find the amounts per serving for calories, total fat (saturated fat), carbohydrates, protein, fiber, and sodium.

A word about sodium: I use a moderate amount of salt to season food. If you are concerned about sodium intake, reduce or eliminate the salt to taste.

Each recipe was tested and retested for accuracy, taste, and reproducibility. I used nutrition software, nutrition labels, and the USDA National Nutrition Database to calculate the nutritional analysis. When calculating the nutrition information, I made some judgment calls, but the foods were as similar as possible. When ingredient choices appear (such as fresh tomatoes or canned tomatoes), the first one mentioned is used for analysis. If an ingredient is listed as optional, it is not included in the analysis.

Enjoy the recipes, and if you have any questions, feel free to contact me via www.cuisineofindia .com.

Ready to Cook

PUT ON YOUR apron and get started—it's that easy! Other than some quintessential spices, you need very few, if any, special tools or equipment to prepare authentic Indian dishes in your kitchen.

Equipment

If you have the basic kitchen equipment—pots and pans, knives, spatulas, and measuring utensils, you are ready to start.

Most Indian cooking is done on the stovetop using direct heat. The typical four-burner stove is ideal and efficient for Indian cooking. An oven is rarely used in Indian cooking. A clay underground oven (*tandoor*) is used for some cooking in north India, but primarily in the Punjab region. Today, most Indian restaurants showcase the *tandoor*, and it has become a symbol of Indian cooking, but only in restaurants. I have used an oven in place of a *tandoor* to make recipes such as Sesame Seed Naan (page 166).

Basic Tools

Although Indian cooking does not require any special utensils or equipment, the tools listed below will help you save time and energy, and possibly make some foods easier to prepare. You may already have most of these tools or at least a good substitution.

Measuring Cups, Spoons, and Kitchen Scale: All recipes in this book use standard American measuring cups and spoons. You will need an 8-ounce measuring cup or set of cups, and a set of measuring spoons. In recipes where weight is important, it is listed. Use a kitchen scale to measure these ingredients, if necessary. For metric conversions, please see Measurements and Conversions (page 225).

Pots and Pans: Heavy skillets, pots, and pans are crucial for stovetop cooking. A heavy-bottomed pan that allows for even cooking and can withstand long periods of heat is best suited for Indian cooking. A variety of sizes—from 1 quart to 4 quarts—allow for the right pan for most dishes in this book. Thin-gauge stainless steel or aluminum pans can be very frustrating and unforgiving, as they can easily burn your efforts.

Nonstick Frying Pans: You might find a 6-inch and a 10-inch heavy, nonstick frying pan well-situated for preparing some vegetables and onion masalas (cooked spice blends). Nonstick pans allow you to use less oil or fat in cooking, thus saving fat and calories. If you do not like nonstick pans, any heavy frying pan will work equally well.

Wok or _Karahi_: An Indian _karahi_ (pronounced _kar-ha-ee_) is similar to a wok. If you do not have a _karahi_, a wok or a frying pan works well. The _karahi_ is made of a heavy material, often cast iron or aluminum. It is used mainly for deep-fat frying. Less oil is wasted in a _karahi_, due to its construction versus that of an electric fryer. Most Indian frying is done on very high heat, above 350°F. In my experience, an electric wok or fryer is not best suited for flash frying. If the oil is not hot enough, the food tends to soak in more fat

and become greasy. Electric fryers work best for slow- to medium-heat frying.

Iron Griddle or _Tava_: A _tava_ (pronounced _ta-va_) is a slightly concave iron griddle and is best for cooking roti or _paratha_ (flatbreads). Iron maintains temperature and allows for even cooking. Any heavy fry pan can be substituted for a _tava_.

To keep your iron pan from rusting, wipe it dry after washing, and either heat it for a few seconds to make sure it's completely dry, or very lightly oil the surface.

Mortar and Pestle: A stone or metal mortar and pestle works best for grinding small quantities of spices. Buy a relatively heavy mortar and pestle, as light ones tend to slip and take longer to do the job. I use it primarily when I need to crush only 1 or 2 teaspoons of spices. If you do not have a mortar and pestle, do not worry, just put the spices in a heavy plastic bag and crush with a rolling pin. For a larger quantity, a coffee or spice grinder is more efficient.

Pressure Cooker: Almost all Indian cooks I know own a pressure cooker. It is irreplaceable for cooking beans. It saves time and energy (fuel). When beans are your main source of protein, investing and learning to use a pressure cooker is crucial. Once you have worked with a pressure cooker, you will wonder how you ever lived without it. Follow the basic instructions for Using the Pressure Cooker Safely (page 9), and you will find it safe and effective.

Steamer Rack: A flat steamer rack allows air/ steam to circulate and cooks food more evenly. A 6- to 8-inch round metal rack that is ½ to 1 inch high works best, as it fits most pans. If you own a pressure cooker, it likely came with a steamer rack. I use the pressure cooker steamer rack for all my steaming needs. You can also purchase a steamer rack at most kitchen gadget stores.

Other Equipment: The only other equipment that I find helpful is an *idli* maker. But if you don't want to invest in another pan, and don't care about the shape of the *idli* (page 85), you can make them in a cake pan.

USING THE PRESSURE COOKER SAFELY

A pressure cooker cooks food three to ten times faster than using a regular pan. My personal preference is a heavy aluminum or stainless steel 4-quart pressure cooker. Some basic rules for pressure-cooking:

1. Follow the safety rules in the instruction manual of your pressure cooker. A pressure cooker is safe when used properly, but it can be very dangerous if the safety rules are not followed.

2. Prepare foods according to the recipe. Be sure not to overfill the pressure cooker.

3. Seal and place the pressure regulator on the vent pipe, if necessary.

4. Heat on the medium to high setting until full pressure is developed. Each pressure cooker has its own distinctive noise when the pressure is fully developed. In some pressure cookers, the pressure regulator begins to rock, in some it whistles, and in others it just makes a certain noise. Once the pressure is fully developed, the cooking time begins. Lower the heat to maintain a slow, steady pressure and cook for the length of time indicated in the recipe. The time needed to cook the food to the desired consistency may vary based on the pressure cooker. Remember, food cooks much faster in a pressure cooker.

5. Remove the pressure cooker from the burner. If I have time, I let the pressure drop on its own by letting the pressure cooker cool at room temperature. This, of course, causes additional cooking and for some recipes that may be acceptable. If the instructions state to cool cooker at once, cool the cooker under cold running water.

6. After the pressure has dropped completely, open the lid carefully. Do not force the lid off.

7. Lift the cover carefully at arm's length, because some steam will force out as you open the cooker.

8. Again, remember to follow all the safety rules and enjoy the time saving of a pressure cooker.

Small Electric Appliances

If you're a gadget fan and love each gadget's unique feature, by all means enjoy them. You might find the three small appliances listed below helpful in preparing the recipes in this book, of which a blender is the only essential appliance.

Blender: A good powerful blender helps grind all kinds of masala (spice blends), beans, and chutneys effortlessly. In earlier days, people used different types of stones (a similar concept to mortar and pestle) for grinding.

Food Processor: Although not essential, I find a food processor very convenient for grinding dals (beans), grating or chopping a large quantity of vegetables, and making dough for flatbreads.

Coffee Grinder: For coffee drinkers, please don't grind spices in your coffee grinder unless you like spicy coffee! Buy a separate coffee grinder for spices, as it is the most-effective way of grinding whole spices. It grinds them finer than a blender, although a blender can be used followed by a sieve. Wipe the coffee grinder clean before storing.

Techniques

If you're experienced in cooking Indian food, you can skip this section and go straight to the recipes. But for novice cooks, it will help you understand some basic methods of Indian cooking. All you need is the willingness to learn and a little practice. You don't have to master each technique to prepare great-tasting Indian meals at home.

By now you may already know that Indian cooking is more than curry, and definitely takes more than curry powder. Getting the right texture, color, and consistency can depend on using the right technique.

Don't let these methods of cooking intimidate you; they are just new to you. Once you prepare a few of these dishes, you will see a pattern and find Indian cooking a breeze. It's like cooking pasta—one pasta and five sauces equals five dishes.

Remember, if something does not come out perfect or to your liking the first time, hopefully it'll still be good. Make notes in your recipes as to what you might do differently next time.

Preparing Food for Cooking: This may seem like common knowledge, but the way you prepare ingredients has a direct impact on flavor of the finished dish. Whether the onion is finely chopped, coarsely chopped, or ground will all affect the consistency of the curry sauce. Follow the instructions as given.

Measuring Ingredients: Even novice cooks know that a slight variation in quantity can make a difference between a good product and an okay product. Although Indian cooking is very forgiving (unlike baking), measuring and using the ingredients as listed in recipes is imperative to the end results. For all practical purposes, measure to a level cup or spoon.

To reduce the guesswork in quantity, even ingredients such as onion are listed in a measuring cup versus a medium or small onion. These days, the sizes of onions can be one inch or four inches.

Substituting Ingredients: If you do not have an ingredient—especially spices—and are not sure about the substitution, leave it out. You are more likely to get an acceptable product without the ingredient than with an alternate. Spices are potent; a little bit goes a long way and more is not better.

The Cooking Temperature: Since Indian cooking uses the stovetop 99 percent of the time, mastering the heat is fundamental to great cooking. From start to finish, you may need to adjust the cooking temperature of your dish. You may start out heating the pan on high heat for seasoning, then reducing the heat to simmer, and then bumping up the heat again to reduce the sauce to a desired consistency.

Whether you cook with gas or electric doesn't matter; electric stoves just take longer to heat up and cool down. You need to understand and accommodate to your stove.

Seasoning (*Chounk*): Yes, you've heard it before—Indian cooking is all about spices. But more than that, it's about how you season it. *Chounk* is the most common way to season Indian food. Oil or ghee is heated until it is very hot and a slight film develops over the oil, near smoking point. Spices like cumin or mustard seeds are dropped into the hot oil and cooked for only a few seconds until the seeds begin to brown, pop, or change color. This seasoned oil is the *chounk*. One may add the hot, seasoned oil to the food or add the food to the seasoned oil. The *chounk* enhances the flavor of the spices and the food.

Roasting (*Bhun-na*): Roasting or browning of spices and food brings out the taste and flavor of the dish. The food or spices may be dry-roasted or roasted in hot oil. Roasting can affect the finished dish's taste and texture. I remember my mother saying the more you *bhuno* it, the better the flavor.

Simmering: Simmering means cooking food in a liquid that cooks on low heat. In Indian cooking, food is often simmered, closer to a low boil, on medium or low heat, and it may or may not have much liquid in it. For example, vegetables may be cooked on low heat, simmering in its own juices.

Preparing Sauce (*Rasa*): Most Indian sauces are thickened and flavored by spices, garlic, onion, yogurt (if using), or tomatoes. If the sauce is too thin, remove the lid of the pan, increase the heat, and allow the liquid to evaporate to the desired consistency. Thickening also concentrates the flavor and enhances the taste of the dish.

Deep-Fat Frying: Indian food may be stir-fried in oil, sautéed with spices, or fried. Deep-fat frying as a medium for cooking is probably as popular in Indian cooking as baking is in Western cooking. People associate frying with high fat and calories, but it doesn't have to be. Properly cooked fried foods absorb less fat, and can have less fat and calories than foods that have been stir-fried or pan-fried. They may even have less fat than baked pastries. The most important factor in deep-fat frying is to maintain the right temperature for the food. For example, *puri* (fried bread) fried on high heat will soak up less fat than if they were fried on medium heat. Foods can be fried in any type of container. The most common is the wok-like *karahi* (page 8). Nutritionally speaking, you should limit the use of fried foods overall.

SAVE TIME IN THE KITCHEN

In today's fast-paced world, most of us have limited time to cook, but we do want to eat healthy and delicious foods. Every effort has been made to prepare dishes in a time-efficient manner. Here are some universal as well as Indian meal–specific tips to prepare meals in 30 to 45 minutes. Of course, there are dishes and meals that take a longer time and should be prepared when you have the time and feel creative.

1. Keep the ingredients on hand. See Stocking the Pantry for Indian cooking on page 27. Indian cooking uses many dried ingredients, which can be stored for a long time. For perishables, shop only once or twice a week to save time as well as money.

2. Clean and chop vegetables. To save time, I usually clean and chop the whole package of vegetables at one time and refrigerate small portions in sealed plastic bags. If you do not have the time or do not like to mess with chopping vegetables, many grocery stores now carry chopped vegetables, which are convenient and quick to use. The taste of fresh vegetables cannot be duplicated; spend a little extra on fresh ingredients and taste the difference.

3. Use frozen vegetables. Keep a good supply of frozen vegetables; they are a convenient substitute for fresh vegetables. I especially like to keep frozen peas, green beans, mixed vegetables, and spinach on hand.

4. Stock up on canned beans and tomato products. For a quick meal, these are very handy. I have included some recipes using canned beans and tomato sauces.

5. Keep a running grocery list. Encourage family members to add items to the grocery list as needed. This is especially helpful if you have more than one cook in the house.

6. Plan meals for the upcoming week. Sometimes it takes longer to decide what to cook than cooking itself. Add ingredients to the shopping list as you plan your menus.

7. Freeze extras for rainy days. Double the recipe and freeze the extra for those days when nobody can or wants to cook. However, remember not all things freeze well. I have included freezing directions wherever possible.

8. Buy chopped garlic or garlic paste and substitute for fresh, if desired.

9. Freeze ginger or use ginger paste. Preparing ginger can take time. I keep frozen ginger on hand to save time. To freeze ginger, purchase ⅛ to ¼ pound of fresh, tender ginger. Peel and grate or chop the ginger. To grate ginger, grate with the grain to minimize the fiber that comes out. If you have an electric chopper, finely chop the ginger and freeze it. I usually divide the ginger into approximately 1-teaspoon portions, placing them on a plate lined with plastic wrap and freezing it. When it is completely frozen, remove it from the plastic

wrap and store in a sealed plastic bag or container. It will take time initially, but on a daily basis it saves a lot of time.

10. Prepare and freeze onion masala. Chopping, grinding, and cooking the onion masala takes time. I will often prepare and freeze the onion masala portion of a recipe ahead of time. This is very handy when I'm in a hurry or have company. Thaw frozen masala in the refrigerator overnight or in a microwave prior to using. Using frozen masala can save a significant amount of time without altering the taste of the prepared dish.

The World of Spices

Quest for spices has been as adventurous and lucrative as gold, and India has been at the epicenter of the spice trade for hundreds of years. In the free market today, spices are readily available around the world.

I was very pleased to hear that today's average American eats twice the amount of spices as twenty years ago. Availability of spices has changed dramatically. I remember when cumin seeds, the most basic Indian spice, were hard to find and considered exotic. And now, I can find garam masala (an Indian spice blend) in my local grocery store.

Most of the spices listed below are probably available at your local supermarket. Every year, the number of stores that cater to Indian spices and ingredients is increasing. Whole-foods, cooperatives, or health food stores carry an increasing number of Indian spices, dried beans, and other ingredients. Large metropolitan areas such as Chicago or New York have had access to Indian grocery stores for a long time, but now even small- to midsize towns have an Asian (or Indian) store that carries a large selection of Indian ingredients. For convenience, if you still need to order by mail or online, see ordering information on page 29.

Whole or Ground?

Spices are used in all different forms: whole, crushed, ground, roasted, or fried. Each type adds a different texture, taste, and intensity to the dish. Buy whole spices whenever possible, as they have a long shelf life. Fresh-ground spices offer the best flavor.

Spices get their flavor from essential "volatile" oils. Buy ground spices in small quantities, as they lose some of their flavor over time. For best results, once the vacuum seal on a spice jar is broken, use within six months. Mark the date of purchase or the date opened to help you keep track.

Store spices in airtight jars and keep them in a cool, dry cupboard. Do not refrigerate or freeze spices, as the moisture can actually affect their flavor and texture.

A Word About Curry Powder

Curry powder is one spice blend. Most Indians do not use curry powder, and if they do, it is for seasoning a particular dish. Curry powder is often used in America to create curries—a sauce-based yellow dish. I do not use curry powder at all. For each dish, I use individual spices to create a different flavor and taste. No more words about curry powder.

Substituting Spices

Spices and their blends add distinct flavor and taste to each dish. A recipe may call for whole or ground spice. The whole variety is usually more potent than its powdered form. Substituting the spices can alter the taste and character of the dish. If an ingredient is not available, omitting it is usually the better choice.

Glossary of Spices and Other Ingredients

A list of spices, herbs, and other unique ingredients is given below with their description, uses, and benefits. The common Hindi translation of each is included in italics.

SPICES/INGREDIENTS	DESCRIPTION	USES AND BENEFITS
Asafetida or Asafoetida *(Heeng)*	Raw asafetida has a very strong and pungent odor, but when cooked it imparts a pleasing distinct flavor to dishes. It is also known as stinking gum or devil's dung. Whole asafetida has a hard, gummy, or sap-like texture. It is sold in whole form as little rocks or as powder. Asafetida powder is milder and is easier to use. Store in its original container and keep it sealed at all times; otherwise its aroma will contaminate other spices and ingredients.	Asafetida is used extensively in bean and vegetable dishes. It is used most commonly as a digestive aid. It is reputed to lessen flatulence and thus considered a must in beans and cruciferous vegetables such as cauliflower.
Ajwain *(Caram Seeds)*	You are most likely to find *ajwain* in an Indian grocery store, as it is fairly uncommon in other cuisines. The slender brown seeds look like little cumin seeds but have a much stronger flavor. It may be confused with caraway seeds, Bishop's weed, or celery seeds due to its appearance. *Ajwain* is very aromatic and slightly bitter and pungent. Even a small amount will completely dominate the flavor of a dish. Use it sparingly!	*Ajwain* is added to fried breads or flatbreads or snacks, or in seasoning for its unique flavor. *Ajwain* reduces flatulence and other stomach discomforts. It is also used to treat nausea-type symptoms. It is often given to women in the first few weeks after delivery, to aid digestion.

Amchur (Mango Powder)	Made from dried unripe mangoes (a sour variety). It is most commonly used and available as a dried powder.	*Amchur* adds a sweet-sourness to food. If unavailable, lemon or lime juice can be substituted.
Basmati Rice	See Rice and Other Grains (page 137).	
Bay Leaves (Tej Patta)	Dried bay leaves are used most frequently for their fragrance and distinctive flavor. Fresh leaves are rarely used. The whole leaf is removed or pushed aside when eating.	They are frequently used whole in seasoning rice dishes such as *pulao* and *biryani*. The dried leaves are also ground in spice blends. Bay leaves are used as appetite stimulant, diuretic, and in herbal oils to reduce muscular aches and pain.
Beans, Legumes, and Pulses	See Bean, Legumes, and Pulses (Dal) (page 115).	
Gram Flour **Chickpea Flour** (Besan)	This is the flour of chana dal (page 128) and is very versatile. It is sometimes called chickpea flour and made from chickpeas (garbanzo beans). For best results, use *besan* from chana dal, available where Indian groceries are sold.	It is used as a thickener, a batter, or as a binding agent. It is often used like all-purpose flour in Western cooking. It is more nutritious and may absorb less oil than all-purpose flour but will impart a very distinct flavor.
Black Peppercorn (Kali-Mirch)	Cultivated in India, it is one spice that has brought traders, merchants, and armies to India for centuries. The most common variety is black peppercorns, but white peppercorns are also used. For best results, buy whole peppercorns and grind as needed. Black pepper imparts a different flavor than red chiles in food, though both are used extensively. White peppercorns are skinned before drying and appear to be slightly less potent.	Black pepper is ubiquitous in Indian cooking. It is used as a whole peppercorn as well as ground black pepper. It is also a part of many spice blends. Peppercorns are believed to have numerous health benefits such as relieving constipation, nasal congestion, and sinusitis. It is often added to hot tea and soup in winter to help relieve symptoms of a common cold. It definitely tastes and feels good when you have a stuffy nose and can hardly breathe—it seems to help open up the nasal passages.
Black Salt (Kala Namak)	This is an unrefined mineral salt that is mined. In its original form, it is a gray-black rock. When ground, it has a pink-purple color. It has a strong, almost offensive aroma due to its high sulfur content, but the taste is very unique and pleasant. A little bit goes a long way.	Black salt is primarily used in snacks and chaats. It can be part of a spice blend, such as chaat masala (page 24), or sprinkled on top of a fruit salad to add complex flavors. Add a pinch to scrambled tofu to mimic the taste of eggs. It is considered a cooling spice and is used to relieve heartburn and intestinal gas.

Cardamom *(Elaichi)*	There are two different types of cardamom used in Indian cooking: small green pods and large black pods. (The bleached-white cardamom pods are basically the same as green ones.) The green pods are used most frequently for flavoring tea and desserts. The large black pods look like little beetles, are typically cheaper than green pods, have a stronger flavor, and are used in spice blends.	Cardamom pods are often used whole for seasoning as well as in spice blends. Cardamom flavor is as popular in Indian desserts as vanilla is in Western desserts. Cardamom powder loses its flavor quickly and is the least potent form of the spice. Buy the whole pods, remove the seeds, and grind fresh for maximum flavor. Cardamom is used to treat throat infections, lung congestion, and teeth problems. It is also used after meals as a mouth freshener.
Cayenne Pepper	See Chile Peppers.	
Chaat Masala *(page 24)*	This is a hot-and-sour spice blend.	Chaat masala perks up the flavor of uncooked dishes such as yogurt, fruits, and vegetables. It's often sprinkled on top for a little extra flavor. You can purchase chaat masala—or for best results, make your own (page 24).
Chickpea flour	See Gram Flour.	
Chile Peppers **Cayenne Pepper** *(Lal-Mirch)* **Red Whole Chile** *(Sabut-Lal-Mirch)* **Green Chile** *(Hari-Mirch)*	A variety of green and red chile peppers are used in Indian cooking. The chiles can range from mild to very hot, small to large, and dried to fresh. Red chile powder is sold as cayenne pepper in American supermarkets and as chile powder in Indian grocery stores. Do not use "chili powder" sold in American stores, for it is a blend of spices and is used in Spanish or American "chili"—a dish with meat and beans. The hottest part of the chiles is the seeds; remove, if desired. Handle chiles carefully, as they can make the skin tingle and the eyes burn.	Cayenne pepper (red chile powder) and green chiles are used extensively in Indian cooking. It is these chiles that make Indian dishes spicy hot. You can eliminate or reduce the chile peppers in a recipe without compromising the taste; the hotness of food is a personal preference. Chiles—both red and green—contain phytochemicals and are believed to have numerous health benefits such as preventing cancer, reducing heart disease, and reducing chronic pain. Chiles causing stomach ulcers is now considered a myth, as numerous scientific studies have proven that not to be true; but as a caution, if you do have stomach ulcers, use chiles carefully until you know how your body reacts to them.

Cilantro *(Dhania Patta)* **Coriander Leaves**	An aromatic herb that looks similar to parsley but has a distinct flavor. Cilantro is also called Chinese parsley or coriander leaves. The leaves are usually sold in bunches and are readily available in most supermarkets today.	They are used extensively in Indian dishes as a garnish, flavoring, and in condiments (chutney).
Cinnamon *(Dalchini)* **Cinnamon Sticks** **Cinnamon Powder**	Cinnamon is the bark of a tropical tree and is reddish brown in color. Cinnamon is used finely ground or as sticks. Cinnamon sticks have a more pronounced flavor than ground cinnamon.	Cinnamon sticks are often added to hot oil or water to bring out the flavor. Remove the stick just before serving, as it is not to be eaten whole. It is often ground in spice blends such as garam masala, sambhar powder, and chai masala. The benefits of cinnamon are being researched extensively. It has antioxidants and is thought to help digestion and prevent colds and has recently been used in the treatment of type 2 diabetes.
Cloves *(Laung)*	Cloves are dried flower buds with a distinct aroma.	They are used whole or ground in spice blends. Some of the benefits of cloves are: to aid digestion, reduce dental pain, and treat some skin disorders.
Coconut *(Nariyal)*	Coconut palms line the southern coast of India. Both fresh and dried coconut are used in Indian cooking. When buying fresh coconut, make sure it is not moldy or cracked. Shake it to make sure it contains plenty of water. That said, I rarely buy fresh coconut anymore, for Indian grocery stores now carry frozen grated coconut, which can be used as needed. Coconut milk, water, and cream are also readily available and are convenient in recipes. Desiccated coconut is finely grated, almost like sawdust. Desiccated coconut is primarily used for desserts, but it can be substituted for fresh coconut in recipes. Presweetened coconut is not traditionally used in Indian desserts, although I have used it in the dessert recipes for its excellent flavor.	Fresh coconut is used extensively in many south Indian dishes. In north India, dehydrated coconut is more commonly used in desserts. Whole coconut (fresh and dehydrated) is also used for religious and auspicious ceremonies. Coconut and coconut fat have gotten a bad rap over the years for their high saturated fat content. Vegans with very little intake of saturated fat can use it in moderation without health concerns. (Check your blood cholesterol and overall saturated fat intake before using.)

Coriander *(Dhania)* **Ground Coriander** **Coriander Leaves** (see Cilantro)	Coriander seeds and the fresh leaves are used in cooking. The coriander leaves are called cilantro in America. The seeds are slightly smaller than a peppercorn and white to yellowish brown. Whole seeds are used in some recipes, but ground coriander is more commonly used. It is very important to have good ground coriander. When it gets too old, it loses its taste and flavor. I often grind 1–2 cups coriander seeds for freshness.	Ground coriander adds flavor in all types of dishes, as well as thickens sauces. Coriander is used in cooking as a general digestive aid. In Ayurvedic (herbal) medicine, it is used as a diuretic and to treat skin disorders such as acne.
Cumin Seeds *(Jeera)* **Ground Cumin** **Roasted Cumin Powder** (page 25)	These long brown seeds are used in multiple ways. For maximum flavor and taste, dry-roast or fry the cumin seeds in oil. Ground cumin powder is readily available in most supermarkets. Roasted cumin powder is used as seasoning or garnish in uncooked dishes, especially yogurt dishes and chaat.	Cumin seeds are one of the main ingredients in a seasoning (*chounk*). Cumin seeds are also roasted and added to many spice blends. Cumin seeds aid in digestion and are also thought to help in treatment of the common cold.
Curry Leaves *(Meetha Neem)* *Kari* **Leaves**	The curry, or *kari*, plant is widely found in southern India. The small leaves are tender, have mellow flavor, and an incredible aroma. Fresh curry leaves are generally sold on the stem; pull the leaves off the stem just before using to maintain maximum flavor. Fresh curry leaves are now available in many Indian grocery stores in America. When I wrote my last book, *New Indian Home Cooking*, I could only get the leaves in large metropolitan areas such as Chicago, and now I can buy them in Ames, Iowa. If fresh leaves are not available, you can use dried ones (although they have less flavor). The leaves can also be eliminated without sacrificing flavor or taste.	These highly aromatic leaves are used as a seasoning for many dishes from south India. Although they can be eaten, the leaves are typically removed or pushed aside at the time of eating.
Curry Powder	It is a spice blend. Most Indians do not use curry powder in their cooking.	Curry powder will often turn dishes yellow and add the same taste and flavor to all dishes. It is not used in any recipe in this book.
Dal	See Beans, Legumes, and Pulses (page 115).	

ENO	It is also known as "fruit salt." ENO is used like soda or baking powder. It is a mix of sodium bicarbonate, citric acid, and sodium carbonate. In the United States, ENO is only available in Indian grocery stores.	ENO is a preferred rising agent, as it has a fast-acting effervescent action and does not have an aftertaste like sodium bicarbonate. You can substitute baking soda and baking powder instead of ENO, if desired. ENO is also used as an antacid.
Fennel Seeds (Saunf)	From bulbless fennel, these long, greenish-yellow seeds have a mild licorice-like flavor that lingers. The taste is similar to mild anise, but is more aromatic and sweeter. The seeds are used whole, crushed, or ground. Fennel bulb and leaves are typically not used in Indian cooking.	A small amount of fennel seeds adds distinct flavor to a dish. They are also used in pickles and relishes. You will often find Indian restaurants serve fennel seeds after the meal, as a digestive aid and a breath freshener.
Fenugreek Seeds (Methi)	These small, reddish-brown seeds have a strong smell similar to that of burned sugar and have a distinct bitter flavor. Fenugreek leaves and seeds are both used extensively in cooking and herbal medicines.	Fenugreek seeds are often a component of curry powder and other spice blends. They are frequently a flavoring in Indian pickles. Fenugreek seeds are believed to aid in digestion and to increase the production of breast milk in lactating women. They are also available in capsule form as a means to reduce cholesterol and lower blood sugar (however, more studies are needed to substantiate these claims).
Flour (Atta)	See Flatbreads (page 153).	
Garam Masala	Translated, *garam* means "hot," and *masala* means "spices." Garam masala is a blend of spices that are thought to create heat in the body—but not the same as chile hot. There are a variety of garam masala recipes available. I like to grind my own—enough for six months at a time. Often, cooks or families have their own personal recipe for this blend of spices. My family recipe for garam masala is provided for you (page 24). You can also buy prepared garam masala in your local supermarkets as well as Indian grocery stores. If using a store-bought version, try a few different ones. A good garam masala is crucial to the flavor of a prepared dish.	It is a potent spice blend that can alter the taste of a recipe significantly, and should be used sparingly. It is primarily used in north Indian recipes. The benefits lie in the combination of spices used.

Garlic *(Lehsun)*	The bulb of garlic has a characteristic pungent, spicy flavor that mellows and sweetens with cooking.	It is used for both flavoring and medicinal purposes. Garlic is claimed to help prevent heart disease and lower blood sugar, and it has antibacterial and anti-inflammatory qualities.
Ginger *(Adarak)* **Dried Ginger** *(Sonth)*	Young gingerroots are fleshy and juicy with a mild, distinct taste. Dried, ground ginger is a tan-colored, finely ground powder that is used in numerous ways. Dried gingerroots are also sold in Indian grocery stores. I buy ground ginger powder, as it is easier to use.	Ginger is used extensively for its flavor and health benefits. Dried ground ginger is often a component of spice blends. Ginger helps in digestion and is added to brewed tea to prevent and cure the common cold. It has been found to be effective for treating nausea.
Jaggery *(Gur)*	This is raw sugar made from sugarcane. If jaggery is not available, you can substitute dark brown sugar.	Used as sweetener in place of sugar. Jaggery has a high molasses content and is considered to be more nutritious.
Mango Powder	See *Amchur*.	
Masala *(Spices)*	*Masala* means "spices," though the word is used very loosely. It might refer to an individual spice, a blend of spices—such as garam masala—or a combination of ingredients ground together to provide the base for many Indian sauces, such as onion masala. Masala can be wet or dry.	Spices are the backbone of Indian cooking.
Mint *(Pudina)*	Bright green leaves with a strong-scented flavor, this herb can be used fresh or dried.	Fresh mint is used to make chutneys, add flavoring, or garnish many dishes such as cold appetizers and chaat. Used as a medicinal herb to help cure stomachaches and chest pain. It is also used as a digestive aid and a diuretic.
Mustard Seeds *(Rai)*	Mustard seeds used in Indian cooking are the tiny, reddish-brown seeds of a variety of mustard plant. Brown Indian mustard seeds are smaller than the common yellow ones and are much less pungent. When heated, the brown mustard seeds pop and add a smoky flavor. When ground and marinated, they add a pungent and sour taste to the dish.	Mustard seeds are used in seasoning, dry-roasted and ground in spice blends such as sambhar powder, and used whole or ground in pickles. Grinding and marinating intensifies the flavor of mustard seeds.

Negella Seeds *(Kalonji)* **Onion Seeds**	These small, tear-shaped black seeds have an earthy aroma. They are also referred to as onion seeds, which the seeds resemble but are not related to.	They are generally used in pickles. Occasionally, the seeds are used for flavoring vegetables, breads, and fish dishes. *Kalonji* acts as a stimulant to ease constipation and indigestion. It is also used to repel certain insects.
Oil	You can use any vegetable oil for cooking these recipes. My personal preference is canola oil, as it has practically no flavor and is therefore ideal for Indian cooking. It is also high in monounsaturated fats, which makes it heart healthy. I have used olive oil (although not Indian) in some recipes, mostly in salads or for garnishing.	A variety of vegetable oils can be used for preparing recipes in this book.
Papad or Pappadam *(Bean Wafers)*	Dried chip-like snacks that are either dry-roasted or deep-fat fried. The most common *papad* are made with split, hulled beans and are spicy-hot. *Papad* are also made with potato, rice, or tapioca.	Bean *papad* are typically served with meals as a side, just like chips. Other *papad*, such as rice *papad*, are more commonly eaten as snacks.
Paprika *(Degi-Mirch)*	Paprika is a ground red chile with a mild, spicy aroma. An orange-red powder, paprika is ground very fine. Choose paprika with a bright color and a mild flavor. Some paprika has a smoky flavor that changes the flavor of the dish. Be sure to use regular paprika.	Paprika is added to dishes primarily for its beautiful red color. You can substitute mild chile powder (such as ancho), if desired, or eliminate it altogether.
Pounded Rice *(Poha)*	Parboiled, flattened rice. See Rice and Other Grains (page 137).	
Poppy Seeds *(Khus-Khus)*	Poppy seeds are often believed to have a small drug effect, because they come from the same plant as opium. But studies indicate that poppy seeds contain no traces of the drug. Black poppy seeds are most commonly used in the United States, but in Indian cooking white-gray poppy seeds are used exclusively. White-gray seeds have a nutty, sweet taste.	Poppy seeds are used as a seasoning or a thickener. They are added to flatbreads for texture and flavor, and ground into masalas to thicken sauces.

Saffron *(Kesar)*	Saffron threads are bright orange-red dried stamens of the flower and are chiefly used to color food to a golden yellow. Saffron threads also contribute a mild aromatic flavor to food. Saffron is usually expensive and therefore used mostly for special occasions. An ounce of saffron will last you a long time. If saffron is not available, substitute yellow food coloring in desserts or turmeric in curries.	Saffron threads are added primarily to desserts and exotic drinks such as almond milk (*badam ka dudh*) on special occasions. A pinch of saffron adds a lot of color; use it sparingly.
Salt *(Namak)*	Table salt is used in most cooking. Salt, as in any other cuisines, helps bring out the flavor of Indian dishes.	Use in moderation, as desired.
Sambhar Powder (page 24)	This is a blend of spices used in making one particular dish—*sambhar*. As with garam masala, families are partial to their own sambhar powder. You can also purchase sambhar powder at Indian grocery stores.	Used primarily to prepare sambhar, a south Indian bean soup. It is a combination of spices that adds flavor as well as aids in digestion.
Sesame Seeds *(Til)*	Small flat seeds that come in white, rusty red, or black. Sesame seeds add a nutty, sweet flavor especially when toasted. They are used as whole seeds, paste, ground, or as sesame seed oil. Store the seeds in the refrigerator or freezer to prevent rancidity.	Both black and white sesame seeds can be toasted and added as a seasoning or used as a garnish. Roasting brings out a nutty flavor. Sesame seeds are thought to heat the body and thus are most commonly used in cold winter months. Sesame seed desserts are popular primarily in the winter.
Tamarind *(Imli)*	Tamarind is available either dried or as a concentrated paste. It has an acidic, sweet taste. The dried tamarind is soaked in water, squeezed to release the pulp, and strained. The thick pulp or juice is then used in recipes or made into chutneys. The concentrated tamarind paste is convenient; use it sparingly, for it can overpower the dish.	Tamarind is added to dishes for its distinct sweet-sour taste. There is no perfect substitute for tamarind, although you can use *amchur* or lemon juice in some dishes.

Turmeric *(Haldi)*	Turmeric is essential in Indian cooking. It is typically used as a powder, mainly to color food to a bright yellow. It has a mild, earthy flavor.	Turmeric is used for color and health benefits. Turmeric is what makes curries yellow. Turmeric is considered to be a powerful healer. It is used as an antiseptic, anti-inflammatory, and antibacterial. Its health benefits, from preventing cancer to relieving Alzheimer's disease, are being studied. It is also used on auspicious occasions, in prayers, and as a beauty aid.
Silver foil (edible) Gold foil (edible) *(Vark)*	*Vark* is an edible shimmering foil made of pure silver (and occasionally gold). The *vark* is sold between sheets of paper to prevent it from tarnishing. Store in an airtight container or bag. It does not add or change the flavor or taste in any way. It can easily be omitted from any recipe. (Gold foil is rare and very expensive.)	It is used as a decoration on many desserts. It makes the sweets glisten and look elegant.

Homemade Spice Blends and Basic Recipes

Some of my favorite masala recipes are below. Making any one of these is well worth the effort. Store the blends in a cool, dry place in an airtight container and they will last up to a year. A coffee grinder works best to grind the spices. If using a blender, use the small jar, shake frequently, and sieve the spices to obtain a fine blend. Good food begins with good masala!

Garam Masala

MAKES: about 1½ cups

This recipe has been passed on from generation to generation in my family. I only have one garam masala recipe, for I do not mess with perfection.

- ½ cup cumin seeds
- ⅓ cup whole black peppercorns
- ½ cup large cardamom pods or ⅓ cup green cardamom pods
- 1 tablespoon cloves
- 3 cinnamon sticks
- 10 to 12 bay leaves
- 1 tablespoon dried ground ginger

1. Heat a small fry pan on medium heat. Dry-roast the cumin seeds until golden brown. Cool to room temperature.

2. Combine all the spices and grind to a fine powder. If necessary, sift the spices to eliminate any large pieces. Store in an airtight container.

Chaat Masala

MAKES: about ⅓ cup

This is a hot-and-sour spice blend that is sprinkled on snacks and *chaat*. It tastes great and it perks up the flavor of raw vegetables or fruit. I like to keep some in a shaker container to sprinkle as desired. You can find citric acid in health food stores or Indian stores.

- 1 tablespoon cumin seeds
- 2 teaspoons black salt
- 1 tablespoon salt
- 1 tablespoon black peppercorns
- 1 teaspoon ground ginger
- 1 teaspoon citric acid
- 1 tablespoon cayenne pepper

1. Heat a small fry pan on medium heat. Dry-roast the cumin seeds until golden brown. Cool to room temperature.

2. In a spice grinder, combine all the spices and grind to a fine powder. Store in an airtight container, preferably a shaker with lid for convenient use.

Sambhar Powder

MAKES: about ⅓ cup

Homemade sambhar powder has a much fresher taste than store-bought varieties. There are many different variations. You can control the hotness of the blend by adjusting the number of chiles, to taste.

- ¼ cup coriander seeds
- 1 tablespoon cumin seeds
- 1 teaspoon mustard seeds
- 4 to 6 dried red whole chiles, to taste
- ½ teaspoon fenugreek seeds

1-inch cinnamon stick

4 cloves

1. Heat a small fry pan on medium heat. Add all the spices, stir, and roast until the cumin seeds are golden brown. Cool completely.

2. In a spice grinder or blender, grind the spices to a fine powder. Store in an airtight container.

Rasam Powder

MAKES: about ⅓ cup

While some people grind their *rasam* powder fresh for every use, I prefer to make enough for a few uses. You can also purchase *rasam* powder, but it is worth the effort to make your own.

1 teaspoon canola oil

¼ cup coriander seeds

1 tablespoon cumin seeds

¼ teaspoon fenugreek seeds

2 teaspoons peppercorns

4 to 6 dried red whole chiles

1. Heat a small fry pan on medium heat. Add oil and all the spices, stirring to coat. Roast the spices until the cumin seeds are golden brown. Transfer to a plate and cool to room temperature.

2. In a spice grinder or blender, grind the spices to a fine powder. Store in an airtight container.

Roasted Cumin Powder

MAKES: about ¼ cup

This is not a blend, but I use it extensively for flavoring and garnishing many dishes, so I always like to keep some on hand. Roasting cumin seeds brings out their full flavor.

¼ cup cumin seeds

1. Heat a small fry pan on medium heat. Dry-roast the cumin seeds until reddish brown to dark brown. Cool to room temperature.

2. Grind the seeds to a fine powder. Store in an airtight container.

Tamarind Sauce

MAKES: about 2 ½ cups

Reconstituting tamarind takes time and is a little messy. I like to make enough sauce for several uses at a time. Purchase tamarind blocks available in Indian grocery stores, and prepare half a block at a time. Each block is typically seven ounces. Store the remaining half block in a sealed plastic bag; it will keep for months. I usually make the sauce when I want to make tamarind chutney or tamarind rice; both require a lot of tamarind.

The prepared tamarind sauce will keep in the refrigerator for up to one month and can be frozen for later use, if desired.

3½ ounces (½ pack) dried tamarind block

4 cups water

1. Cut or tear the tamarind into about 1-inch pieces. Set aside.

2. In a medium skillet, boil 2 cups of water and add the tamarind pieces. Soak for 1 hour or longer.

3. Mash and squeeze the tamarind with hands. Remove any remaining seeds and discard.

4. In a blender, add the tamarind and 1 cup of water. Grind until well blended.

5. Place a strainer over a bowl and add the tamarind pulp. Using a large spoon, squeeze out all the juice. Slowly add ½ to 1 cup of water, taking out as much of the juice as possible. Discard the strings and membranes.

6. Put the juice back in the skillet and bring to a boil on medium heat. Cook for 5 to 10 minutes, reducing to about 2½ cups of tamarind sauce. Cool to room temperature.

7. Store the tamarind sauce in the refrigerator for up to 1 month and use as needed. If desired, freeze the sauce for up to 1 year. Thaw in refrigerator overnight and use as needed.

·:·

Sprouted Mung Beans

MAKES: about 3 cups

Plan ahead, as it takes about two to three days to soak and sprout the beans. I like to make enough sprouts for a couple of dishes. You can season and eat them with rice or add to salads. Once sprouted, place them in a freezer-safe bag and freeze for up to 6 months; thaw before using.

1½ cups whole mung beans

1. Wash beans in 2 to 3 changes of water. Soak the beans overnight in plenty of water.

2. Drain mung beans. Wrap drained beans in a cloth (an old kitchen towel or a large handkerchief works well) and place in a bowl. Pour ½ cup water over the cloth to keep the beans and cloth moist, and cover with a lid. Keep in a warm place like the oven for 24 to 36 hours. Turn on the oven light. (If your oven has a pilot lamp, the beans will sprout faster.) The mung should have ¼- to ½-inch sprout.

3. Place sprouted mung in a colander and rinse in fresh water. The sprouts are ready to be used.

Stocking the Pantry

This list is for Indian groceries only. Start with the ingredients for particular recipes and build your pantry.

Spices

Indian cooking uses numerous spices and can seem overwhelming to a newcomer. You don't need to purchase every spice in the book to get started. For ease, I have divided the list of spices into two parts: Spice Starter Kit and the Spice Cabinet. You can make numerous dishes with the first six spices in the Spice Starter Kit. As you expand your repertoire of Indian dishes you can expand your pantry. For detailed information about each spice, see Glossary of Spices and Other Ingredients (page 14).

SPICE STARTER KIT

Cayenne pepper (*lal-mirch*)

Cumin seeds (*jeera*)

Garam masala

Ground coriander (*dhania*)

Mustard seeds (*rai*)

Turmeric (*haldi*)

SPICE CABINET

Asafetida (*heeng*)

Ajwain (carom seeds)

Amchur (mango powder)

Bay leaves (*tej patta*)

Black salt (*kala namak*)

Cardamom (*elaichi*)

   Black large cardamom (*badi elaichi*)

Cinnamon sticks (*dalchini*)

   Cinnamon, ground

Cloves (*laung*)

Coriander seeds (*sabut dhania*)

Cumin, ground (*jeera* powder)

Fennel seeds (*saunf*)

Fenugreek seeds (*methi*)

Ginger, ground (*sonth*)

Kalonji (nigella seeds)

Paprika (*degi-mirch*)

Poppy seeds, white (*khus-khus*)

Red chiles, dried whole (*sabut lal mirch*)

Saffron threads (*kesar*)

Sambhar powder

Sesame seeds, white (*til*)

Silver foil (*vark*)

Tamarind, dried (*imli*)

   Tamarind paste

HERBS AND FRESH SEASONINGS

Cilantro (fresh coriander leaves)

Curry leaves (*meetha-neem*)

Garlic (*lehsun*)

Ginger (*adarak*)

Green chiles

Mint (*pudina*)

BEANS, LEGUMES, AND PULSES

For detailed information for each item, see page 115.

Adzuki beans, whole (*chori*)

Bengal gram, whole (*kaale chane*)

   Split, hulled chana (*chana dal*)

Black-eyed peas (*lobhia*)

Black gram, whole (*sabut urad*)

   Split urad, with husk (*chilke-wali urad dal*)

   Split, hulled urad (*urad dal*)

Chickpeas or garbanzo beans (*kabuli chana*)

Kidney beans (*rajmah*)

Lentils, whole (*masoor*)

   Pink lentils (*masoor dal*)

Mung beans, whole (*sabut mung*)

    Split mung, with husk (*chilke-wali urad dal*)

    Split, hulled mung (*mung dal*)

Pigeon peas (split, hulled) (*toor dal*)

CANNED FOODS

Black-eyed peas

Chickpeas (garbanzo beans)

Kidney beans

Tomato sauce, paste, and chopped tomatoes

FLOUR, RICE, AND MISCELLANEOUS

Besan (gram flour or chickpea flour)

ENO

Flour, whole wheat (*roti-atta*, from Indian stores)

    White whole wheat flour, or whole wheat flour

Jaggery (*gur*)

Rice

    Basmati

    Long-grain rice

    Rice noodles

    Poha (pounded rice)

FROZEN FOODS

Green beans

Mixed vegetables

Mustard greens, chopped

Peas

Peas and carrots

Spinach, chopped

Coconut, grated (in Indian stores)

MAIL-ORDER SOURCES

The Internet has made it very easy to locate Indian grocery stores or order online. This is a very short list to get you started.

INDIAN GROCERY STORES

To locate an Indian grocery store near you, visit www.thokalath.com/grocery/index.php.

Patel Brothers
42-92 Main Street

Flushing, NY 11355

(718) 661-1112

www.patelbrothersusa.com

Kamdar Plaza
2646 West Devon Avenue

Chicago, IL 60659

(773) 338-8100

www.kamdarplaza.com

Penzeys Spices
(Sells spices and blends)

Mulitiple locations

800-741-7787

www.penzeys.com

ONLY ONLINE
www.ishopindian.com

www.indiaAuthentic.com

Vegan Diet for Optimal Health

A Nutritionist in the Kitchen

Health and nutrition is probably one of the top reasons you have chosen to cook vegan. I have found, in general, that vegans ask a lot of nutrition questions, tend to be nutrition savvy, and like to understand the benefit of the foods they eat. I am personally always concerned about nutritional adequacy and like to know the facts.

Fears and myths concerning nutritional adequacy often surround vegan diets. Can an all-plant-based diet supply your body with enough nutrients? When assessing the health implications of any diet, there are two key considerations. Is the diet safe and adequate, and does it support optimal health? The answer to both questions is absolutely; a balanced vegan diet is both safe and healthful. The vast majority of health-related studies assure us that well-planned vegan diets can supply adequate nutrition throughout our lives, even during vulnerable times such as pregnancy, lactation, infancy, and childhood.

It is important to recognize that, as with a nonvegetarian diet, including a variety of foods and proper planning of meals is necessary to get all the nutrients you need. These days, it is much easier to be a vegan, as many essential nutrients such as calcium, vitamin D, vitamin B12, iron, and zinc are added to commonly consumed vegan foods.

When planning your vegan diet, give extra attention to the nutrients discussed below.

Protein: Muscle Power

Getting enough protein is a common concern among vegans and vegetarians. Chosen wisely, a plant-based diet with plenty of variety and sufficient calories can provide more than enough protein.

Why Proteins?

As a nutrient, proteins perform many functions, as they are part of every body cell. You need a constant supply of protein to repair, build, and maintain body tissue. The building blocks of protein are known as amino acids. There are two kinds of amino acids—essential and nonessential. Our body makes most of the amino acids naturally; these are known as nonessential amino acids. The ones we cannot produce ourselves are called essential amino acids; these must be obtained through our food choices.

To use protein efficiently for maintaining tissue, it is important that you eat enough calories from carbohydrates and fat. If you consume an inadequate number of calories, protein will be used for energy and thus not be available to do its intended job. And if you eat more protein than you need, the excess protein will be converted to calories—not stored as a reserve supply of protein.

Complete Proteins

It was previously believed that people needed to consciously combine specific plant-based foods at each meal to get complete protein—protein that has all the essential amino acids. Research indicates that if you eat a variety of plant foods—grains, beans, nuts, and vegetables—and enough calories over the course of a day your body will make its own complete protein. By eating a variety of plant proteins, you may get some essential amino acids at lunch and some at dinner, and your body does the matching up for you.

Typical Indian meals are usually served with a variety of food groups such as dal and *chawal* (beans and rice), or roti and *subji* (flatbread with vegetables), with salads and chutneys, naturally providing complementary protein at a specific meal.

How Much Protein Do You Need?

There has been so much emphasis on protein in recent years that people often feel they require a lot more protein than they actually do. According to the U.S. Recommended Dietary Allowances (RDA), adults need 0.8 grams of protein per kilogram of body weight per day. A mixed balanced vegan diet with grains, beans, and vegetables will provide you with adequate protein. To determine your protein needs, see the table below.

WEIGHT IN POUNDS	PROTEIN (GRAMS)
100 (45 kg)	36
140 (64 kg)	51
160 (73 kg)	58
180 (82 kg)	67
200 (91 kg)	73

WHERE'S THE PROTEIN?

Most of the protein in a vegan diet comes from grains, beans, nuts, and vegetables. Fruits provide a negligible amount of protein. In general, you can use the average amount of protein in a particular food category. For example, one serving of grains provides an average of 3 grams of protein. This makes calculations easy and does not require you to look up the protein content of individual foods. Listed below are protein amounts for foods typically found in an Indian meal.

FOOD CATEGORY AND FOODS	SERVING SIZE	PROTEIN (GRAMS)
Grains (Bread, roti, rice, millet— 1-ounce slice or ½ cup cooked)	1 serving	2–3
Vegetables (1 cup raw or ½ cup cooked)	1 serving	1–2
Dried beans, cooked (Chickpeas, lentils, mung beans, pigeon peas)	½ cup	7–8
Soybeans, cooked	½ cup	14
Tofu, firm	½ cup	10
Nuts (Almonds, cashews, pistachios, walnuts)	1 ounce	5–7
Nondairy milks (rice, almond)	1 cup	Less than 1
Soymilk	1 cup	7
Fruits	1 medium	0

Carbs: Energy to Go

Carbohydrates are your most important source of food energy, powering everything from breathing to thinking to running. As with any healthy diet, the carbohydrates in a vegan diet should consist of 55 to 60 percent of total calories. In a 2,000-calorie-per-day diet, that's 1,100 to 1,200 calories from carbohydrates.

Over the last decade or so, carbs have received a bad rap. High protein–low carbohydrate diets have been promoted for quick weight loss. These diets are not balanced and have been unsuccessful in long-term weight loss. If you eat too many total calories, excess calories will be stored as fat—whether they're from carbohydrate protein, or fat.

Worrying about simple and complex carbohydrates can be confusing. Some simple carbohydrate foods are high in fiber and nutrients, such as fruits; and some complex carbohydrate foods, such as processed white flour, are low in fiber. Rather, let's shift the focus to nutrient density and fiber content of foods. Dietary fiber comes primarily from carbohydrates and is loaded with health benefits.

Fiber: Your Body's Broom

In general terms, fiber refers to complex carbohydrates that your body cannot digest or absorb—instead it is eliminated. High-fiber intake is one of the numerous benefits of the all-plant diets. Dietary fiber helps protect us against almost every major chronic disease that plagues modern civilization, including heart disease, cancer, gastrointestinal disorders, diabetes, hypoglycemia, and obesity.

Health experts recommend that most adults should consume 20 to 35 grams of fiber per day. That is 15 to 22 grams of fiber per 1,000 calories consumed. A person on a 2,000-calorie diet should eat 30 to 44 grams of fiber per day.

Which Fiber and Why?

Fibers are the structural components of plants, which gives food its shape. Two types of fiber—insoluble and soluble—are characterized by how they dissolve in water. Both types of fiber are important to your health and can be found in plant-based foods.

Insoluble fiber can be found in whole wheat products, corn, and the skins of many fruits and vegetables. Insoluble fiber is termed "nature's broom," since it helps regulate your bowel movements by reducing the transit time of undigested food through the intestines.

Soluble fiber is found in oats, barley, dried beans and peas, and many fruits and vegetables (such as carrots, apples, and oranges). When soluble fiber combines with water in the digestive tract, it binds to nutrients such as cholesterol and escorts them out of the body.

Both types of fiber have been shown to reduce blood glucose levels in people with diabetes. High-fiber foods digest more slowly than processed foods and thus help regulate blood sugar levels so you don't experience peaks and valleys in your energy levels throughout the day. Eating fiber-rich foods also gives you a sense of fullness, which can help you reduce your total daily caloric intake.

Too much of any food component is not good for you, even fiber. Excessive fiber can make your diet too bulky, which can jeopardize absorption of some nutrients such as calcium, iron, and zinc. In general, vegan diets will not result in excessive intake of fiber unless you add concentrated fiber foods such as wheat bran to whole foods.

Reducing Intestinal Gas

Gas production is a normal, healthy function of the intestines, but unfortunately abdominal bloating can be uncomfortable. Here are some things you can do to help digest fiber-rich foods and minimize side effects:

1. Eat small portions of foods such as beans and cruciferous vegetables (those in the cabbage family), and gradually build up portion size. As your body becomes accustomed to the higher-fiber foods, the bacterial flora of the intestines that digest such foods will increase, thereby raising your tolerance.

2. Drink plenty of liquids to help move the fiber through the intestines.

3. Split and hulled beans (dal) are considered easier to digest than whole beans. For a list of split beans, see page 118.

4. Soak the beans and discard the soaking water. Cook in fresh water. Soaking helps reduce gas from beans, especially whole beans.

5. Drain and rinse canned beans.

6. Avoid overeating in general, as too much undigested food ends up in the colon.

7. Exercise and stress management have also been shown to help with abdominal discomfort, helping move gas along.

8. Flavorings such as ginger, garlic, and onions help digest the foods.

9. Spices such as asafetida, turmeric, and garam masala also aid in digestion. See World of Spices (page 13).

⋅⋅⋅

Fats Matter

Eating vegan does not automatically mean that all your dietary concerns are over, particularly when it comes to the issue of fat—how much, what type, and making sure you're getting the essential fatty acids are all important.

Essential Fatty Acids

The two essential fatty acids, linoleic acid (omega-6) and alpha-linolenic acid, are widely available in foods. In most cases, you get these fatty acids from vegetable oils such as canola, soybean, and corn oils, as well as nuts and seeds. In your body, alpha-linolenic acid converts to omega-3 fatty acid, which has been shown to help prevent heart disease. Eating a variety of foods and balancing your plant-based diet makes it easy to get enough of these fatty acids.

High-Fat or Low-Fat?

The optimal amount of fat in the vegan diet is the same as for other diets; it's the amount of fat needed to ensure good health, promote proper growth and development of children, achieve adequate nutritional intakes, and maximize absorption of nutrients. It is also needed to prevent, treat, or reverse chronic diseases.

Extremely low-fat diets were in vogue in the 1980s and led to mass confusion as to the amount of fat one should eat. Low-fat diets are not recommended for vegans or the general population.

The nutritional analysis of each recipe in this book includes the total fat per serving. Knowing how much fat you need per day helps you keep food choices in perspective.

How Much Fat Do You Need?

Optimal fat for good health and disease prevention is getting 25 to 35 percent of your daily calories from fat.

DAILY CALORIES	FAT GRAMS (30% OF CALORIES)
1200	40
1500	50
1800	60
2000	66
2500	83

Types of Fats

Lipids are fatty substances found in food and our body. There are several kinds of dietary fats, which have been classified into several categories based on their structure.

Unsaturated Fats

There are two types of unsaturated fats: polyunsaturated and monounsaturated. Studies indicate that both of these fats help lower cholesterol levels when used in optimal amounts. Good sources of polyunsaturated fats are safflower, sunflower, corn, and soybean oils. The major monounsaturated fats include canola, olive, and peanut oils. I primarily cook with canola oil for its health benefits and because it has minimal flavor of its own. You can use any vegetable oil of your choice.

Saturated Fats

Saturated fats are generally solid at room temperature. These fats are considered "bad fats," as they are linked to increased risk of heart disease. Most vegans do not need to be concerned about saturated fats, as most plant foods do not contain them. Animal sources, including dairy products, are the main sources of saturated fat in the Western diet. Plant sources include coconut oil, palm oil, and cocoa butter. The latest recommendations on saturated fats are no more than 10 percent of calories from saturated fats, and 7 percent if you have heart disease.

Most vegans can include some tropical fats in their diet. The small amount of saturated fat coming from plant foods such as coconut, nuts, and other fat-rich plant foods will not adversely affect the saturated fat ratio. On the other hand,

for people eating high-fat animal foods, tropical fats add more saturated fat to the diet, thus adding fuel to fire. (Too much saturated fat can also be of concern for people who use tropical oil for all their cooking.) Coconut is extensively used in south Indian dishes. I have included some recipes that use coconut products for variety and flavor.

Cholesterol

A sterol that comes exclusively from animal foods, cholesterol is not a concern in the vegan diet.

Trans Fats

Reducing the intake of trans fats is one of the latest nutritional concerns. Health organizations have asked food manufacturers and the restaurant industry to reduce the use of trans fats.

WHERE'S THE FAT?

The amount of fat and saturated fat in Indian foods used in this book is as follows:

FOODS	AMOUNT	FAT (GRAMS)	SATURATED FAT (GRAMS)
Vegetable oil, canola	1 teaspoon	5	0.3
Vegan margarine, stick	1 teaspoon	4	0.7
Shortening	1 teaspoon	4	2
Nuts and seeds	1 ounce (¼ cup)	15	2
Coconut milk	¼ cup	12	10
Fresh coconut	2-inch square	15	13
Soymilk	1 cup	5	0.5
Tofu, firm	½ cup (1.7 ounces)	6	1

Source: *Bowes & Church's Food Values of Portions Commonly Used*, by Jean A. T. Pennington and Judith Spungen Douglass, Lippincott Williams & Wilkins, 2005.

Hydrogenation (adding hydrogen) is a process that changes liquid vegetable oils to a solid or semi-solid form, such as shortenings and margarine. This process produces trans fatty acids. Once they are in the body, trans fats behave like saturated fats and tend to raise blood cholesterol levels. These days, you will find vegan margarines and shortenings that are trans-fat free. If you use regular shortening or margarine, use them sparingly. Most trans fats appear to come from processed and fast foods.

Balancing Fat Intake

All the types of fats aside, here are some basic take-home points:

1. Aim for 25 to 35 percent of calories from fat for healthy vegan adults (children typically need the higher levels of fat). To translate that into your own needs, see How Much Fat Do You Need? (page 35).

2. Limit intake of foods made with trans fats. Become a label reader and limit the use of products containing shortening and hydrogenated oils. Use commercially fried and baked foods sparingly. More and more restaurants and manufacturers are switching to trans fat–free fats.

3. Use primarily monounsaturated fats such as canola oil, olive oil, nuts, and seeds.

Life-Supporting Vitamins, Minerals, and Phytonutrients

Good health is associated with getting plenty of vitamins, minerals, and phytonutrients.

Today, we know a lot more about the role and benefits of vitamins, minerals, and phytonutrients (plant substances) in maintaining health and in protection from disease such as cancer, heart disease, and osteoporosis. And there are new developments every day as scientists explore and find other substances in food that offer health benefits beyond basic nourishment.

You need more than forty nutrients for optimal health, and the good news is that a carefully planned vegan diet is loaded with most of

DO YOU NEED A SUPPLEMENT?

Planned properly, a vegan diet featuring a variety of foods will provide you with all the vitamins and minerals you need. However, some people, such as pregnant women and adults over fifty, have altered needs and may benefit from supplements. Children, teens, and those on low-calorie diets (fewer than 1,200 calories per day) may also benefit from supplements.

Remember, vitamin and mineral supplements can't replace the nutrients found in whole foods. But they can complement your diet. If you decide to take a supplement, do so wisely: Choose a multivitamin that provides 100 percent or less of the recommended daily allowance. Avoid supplements that provide megadoses. High doses can be toxic and may cause health problems. If your physician has prescribed supplements, follow the recommendations as given.

these. The easiest way to get your vitamins, minerals, and phytonutrients is from a variety of food across food groups, not a cabinet full of supplements.

Vitamins

Vitamins are present in all food groups—grains, vegetables, fruits, dried beans, and nuts. B vitamins (other than B12), are abundant in grains and dried beans, and many grain flours are fortified with these essential vitamins. Vitamins A and C are plentiful in vegetables and fruits, and vitamins E and K are present in plant oils. Thus, the vegan diet tends to be overflowing with these life-supporting substances. Just two vitamins— B12 and D—require your particular attention.

Vitamin B12: Not to Be Ignored

A review of scientific literature shows that vegans require vitamin B12, also called cobalamin, in the form of a supplement or fortified foods. Vitamin B12 helps the body make red blood cells, use fats and proteins, and is part of the structure of every body cell. Although rare, B12 deficiencies can lead to anemia, fatigue, or permanent brain or nerve damage. It's worthwhile for vegans to become B12 experts and take simple steps to avoid deficiency problems.

Fortunately, our bodies recycle and reuse B12 very efficiently; some people are better recyclers than others. The most efficient recyclers can go from 3 years up to 20 years without obvious dietary sources. On the other hand, some individuals run out quickly without a regular supply.

Vitamin B12 is made from fermenting bacteria and can be found in air, water, and soil. It's found in the gastrointestinal tract of host animals (humans included), and is found in all animal products including milk and eggs, which is why both vegetarians and nonvegetarians get plenty of B12.

In centuries past, when foods were fermented (saurkraut or tempeh), airborne bacteria would drift in and enter the fermenting process, making these foods potential sources of vitamin B12. Soil that clings to the produce can also have some vitamin B12. Today, we ferment foods in hygienic conditions and wash foods thoroughly; we cannot count on these same foods to supply us with B12. While our B12 sources from soil, air, water, and fermented foods have declined, we now have the advantage of B12-fortified foods and supplements of known reliability, making it easier to be vegan and be assured of an adequate B12 intake.

The recommended dietary allowance of vitamin B12 for adults is 2.4 micrograms per day, with an increased amount recommended for women who are pregnant or breast-feeding, as well as the elderly. Vegans need to consume a reliable source of B12 two to three times a week. Read food labels to check the vitamin B12 content and make sure you are purchasing foods that are fortified with cyanocobalamin, the form that the body absorbs easily.

To ensure an adequate supply, consider the points below:

- Drink B12-fortified beverages such as juices, soymilk, or rice milk.

- Choose B12-fortified cereals and whole grain products.

- Be aware of seaweed, algae, spirulina, and fermented soy products such as tempeh and miso, as they are not good sources of vitamin B12. The vitamin B12 in these foods is inactive, so it's not a form that the human body can use.

◉ Question nutritional yeast flakes claiming to be a good source of the vitamin, as most yeast is not a good source of vitamin B12.

◉ If you choose to take a supplement, take one that provides 100 percent of the Daily Value (DV) for vitamin B12. Just a small amount of B12 can be absorbed at a time and large doses will just be excreted.

Vitamin D: The Sunshine Vitamin

Vitamin D is a major player in a team of nutrients and hormones that support bone health during growth and throughout life. Your body makes its own vitamin D when the skin is exposed to sunlight. Just five to fifteen minutes of sunlight exposure per day (without sunscreen) on your hands, arms, and face stimulates the production of vitamin D in your body. If you cannot be outside every day, you can get the equivalent benefit by being in sun twenty to forty-five minutes three times per week. If you're darker-skinned, or live in a cloudy or smoggy area, you may need more sun exposure; just don't overdo it. Going for a walk during your lunch break or eating lunch in a sunny area is a great way to get your vitamin D for the day.

Few foods are naturally high in vitamin D, which is why most milk sold in the United States is fortified with vitamin D. Currently, some of the calcium-fortified nondairy milks, juices, and breakfast cereals are also fortified with vitamin D; check nutrition labels. Vegans and people who are not able to be in the sunlight regularly need to be careful to get enough vitamin D through fortified foods or supplements.

Minerals

Like vitamins, minerals help regulate body processes. A vegan diet can provide all the essential minerals in adequate amounts, with some concerns regarding calcium, iron, and zinc.

Bone Up on Calcium

A healthfully planned vegan diet—rich in a variety of fruits, vegetables, nuts, and whole grains—can adequately supply all the calcium needed for optimal bone health. To increase your calcium absorption, be sure to get enough vitamin D and plenty of exercise.

Vegans appear to have similar rates of brittle bone disease (osteoporosis) as compared to meat eaters and milk drinkers. Some studies suggest that vegans may not need as much calcium as rec-

FORTIFIED AND ENRICHED FOODS

Do you sometimes wonder about the difference between fortified and enriched foods? Both terms mean vitamins or minerals were added during processing to make food more nutritious. Enriched means adding back nutrients that were lost during processing, such as B vitamins in grain products. Fortified means adding nutrients that weren't originally present in the food, such as vitamin D in milk.

WHERE'S THE CALCIUM?

Only foods with significant amounts of well-absorbed calcium are listed here. Spinach provides calcium but also has oxalates and may not be as well absorbed.

FOODS	AMOUNT	CALCIUM (MG)
Broccoli, cooked	½ cup	45
Green beans, cooked	½ cup	29
Kale, Mustard greens, cooked	½ cup	90
Okra, cooked	½ cup	88
Potato, sweet	1 medium	32
Garbanzo beans, cooked	1 cup	80
Kidney beans, cooked	1 cup	50
Pigeon peas, cooked	1 cup	70
Soybeans, cooked	1 cup	175
Tofu, calcium set★	½ cup	860
Tofu, not calcium set★	½ cup	100
Almonds	¼ cup (1 ounce)	80
Figs, dried	3	80
Oranges	1 medium	52
Pistachios	¼ cup (1 ounce)	30
Fortified juice★	¾ cup	225
Fortified soymilk★	1 cup	250

★Read the labels

Source: *Bowes & Church's Food Values of Portions Commonly Used*, by Jean A. T. Pennington and Judith Spungen Douglass, Lippincott Williams & Wilkins, 2005.

ommended for the general population, because they seem to absorb and retain more calcium from food. The typically high-protein diet of nonvegetarians may actually decrease calcium absorption and increase its excretion through urine. Vegans should eat adequate plant-based protein, but excess is not beneficial.

So, what is the calcium advice for vegans? Osteoporosis is a devastating disease and everyone—including vegans—needs to make sure they get adequate calcium. Based on our current scientific evidence, vegans should consume the RDA amount of calcium.

For Better Vegan Bones: Adequate calcium intake is a challenge for a majority of people, irrespective of milk intake. In the last few years, the number of calcium-fortified plant foods has increased tremendously, making it easier for everyone—including vegans—to get the calcium they need.

You can easily fulfill your calcium requirements by following these recommendations:

- Eat calcium-rich foods every day such as broccoli, beans, and almonds. See Where's the Calcium? (page 40).

- Make sure the soy or grain beverages and fruit juices you consume are fortified with calcium and Vitamin D. Use calcium-set tofu.

- Spread consumption of calcium-rich foods or supplements over the course of a day, rather than all at once. We absorb calcium more efficiently when a small amount is taken at a time.

- If you're not getting at least 1,000 milligrams of calcium per day (1,200 after age 50), take a calcium supplement. Calcium citrate malate is an excellent choice, as it is the form most readily absorbed. Make sure to include adequate calcium during early childhood years and pregnancy.

- Get adequate vitamin D through sun exposure and fortified foods to help absorb calcium.

- Exercise regularly; include weight-bearing exercises such as walking and lifting weights.

Iron for Energy

You probably know the importance and benefits of iron in your diet to prevent iron-deficiency anemia. But did you know that your body needs iron in the complex process of energy production?

Not getting enough iron in your diet can be an issue whether you are vegan or not. Foods of plant origin contain nonheme iron, which is not as well absorbed as the heme iron found in animal products. But not to worry, you can improve the absorption of nonheme iron, and also get enough iron, with these simple rules:

- Eat a variety of iron-rich plant foods, such as beans, dark-green leafy vegetables, dried fruits, and iron-fortified cereals and breads.

- Include a vitamin C–rich food with every meal. Vitamin C helps your body absorb nonheme iron.

- Use cast-iron cookware. Small amounts of iron pass into the food.

Zinc for Growth

Zinc is essential for growth, for functioning of body processes, and for energy production. Without animal products, zinc can be of concern.

Vegans need to be sure they eat a variety of foods that supply enough zinc.

- Eat a variety of foods with zinc, such as whole wheat bread, whole grains, dried beans, tofu, and nuts.

- Include some sprouted foods, such as sprouted beans, and fermented soy foods, including tempeh.

- Make sure your overall caloric intake is adequate.

- If taking a zinc supplement, be careful not to consume more than the RDA, as it can have harmful effects such as reduced copper absorption or impaired immune responses.

Phytonutrients

Phytochemicals are chemicals that help keep plants healthy. They give fruits and vegetables their unique color, flavor, and texture, and provide us with phytonutrients. Phytochemicals work in many ways, including their oxidative action.

Antioxidants

Antioxidants protect the body from free radicals, which cause damage to the body's cells. They appear to have many valuable health benefits for fighting and preventing illness and disease. Antioxidants have been found to be helpful in lowering cholesterol levels, balancing hormones, and eliminating toxins.

Vegetable and fruits are considered our primary source of phytochemicals. However, many legumes, whole grains, nuts, seeds, herbs, and spices provide impressive amounts of phytochemicals as well. A vegan diet provides you with a variety of these superfoods, which promote health and prevent disease.

Follow the Rainbow

The colorful vegetables and fruits provide you with a "pot of gold" in terms of nutrients. If you consciously eat purple eggplant, blueberries, green leafy vegetables, red tomatoes, oranges, and yellow squashes, you'll easily supply yourself with a full range of vitamins and minerals, as well as phytochemicals and antioxidants. Many of these vital nutrients are only found in plant sources.

Indian Vegan Superfoods

Superfoods are packed with vitamins, minerals, and phytonutrients. The Indian diet emphasizes nutrient-dense foods that have extraordinary health-promoting qualities. Although many foods fit this description, I have selected the top ten superfoods, including herbs and spices, that are a significant part of the typical Indian diet.

1. Almonds

Almonds are the most treasured nuts in the Indian diet. High in unsaturated fats and cholesterol free, they are packed with vitamin E, magnesium, protein, fiber, and calcium. Research shows that eating 1 ounce (about a handful, or 20-25 almonds) of almonds each day may help lower LDL ("bad") cholesterol levels and thereby reduce the risk of heart disease.

2. Canola Oil

Ideal for Indian cooking because of its light flavor and smooth texture, canola oil is one of the healthiest and most versatile cooking oils. Extracted from the canola seed, it has the lowest saturated fat content of any oil commonly consumed in the United States. It's also an excellent source of omega-6 fatty acids and linoleic acid, and it is higher in the omega-3 fatty acid alpha-linolenic acid (ALA) than any other oil commonly used. Studies show that ALA may help protect the heart by its effect on blood pressure, cholesterol, and inflammation.

3. Cauliflower

Cauliflower is showcased in a variety of Indian preparations from the simplest meal to a formal wedding dinner. From the cruciferous vegetable family, cauliflower is high in fiber, folate, vitamin C, and other nutrients. The cruciferous vegetables (also known as the cabbage family), such as cauliflower, broccoli, cabbage, and mustard greens, contain several phytochemicals that may help prevent cancer. These compounds appear to stop enzymes from activating cancer-causing agents in the body, and they increase the activity of enzymes that disable and eliminate carcinogens.

4. Dal (Beans)

Dal is the generic or popular name for all dried beans. Beans are high in protein, fiber, iron, folic acid, and potassium. They are naturally low in fat and are the main source of protein in vegan and vegetarian diets. Beans contain eight flavonoids, plant substances that act as nature's dyes and give many fruits and vegetables their colors. These plant chemicals act as antioxidants that protect against heart disease and certain cancers.

Beans are inexpensive, have a long storage life, and taste delicious. They are versatile and often take center stage as the entrée in an Indian diet. For more on beans, see page 115.

5. Ginger

Fresh and dried ginger are used ubiquitously in Indian dishes. Many Indian cooks seem to know instinctively which foods need more ginger to aid in their digestion. The main constituent of ginger is a substance called gingerol, a strong free radical that acts as an antioxidant. Ginger is known for helping digestion, reducing nausea, and increasing circulation.

Though the benefits of ginger are just beginning to be talked about in the Western world, it is an essential spice in Indian culture and cuisine that is used just as much for flavor as for its medicinal properties. In the winter especially, it is steeped in tea for its flavor and because it is believed to help prevent the common cold.

6. Mango

Mango is the king of fruits in India. In season (May through July), ripe mango is a daily treat. It is also pureed and enjoyed as sauce or soup. Raw mango is preserved, as savory and sweet mango pickles, and as mango powder. Rich in a variety of phytochemicals and nutrients, mango is a model superfruit because it is high in polyphenols and carotenoids. Mango is an excellent source of the antioxidant vitamins A, C, and E as well as vitamins K, B6, and other B vitamins. It is also high in potassium and dietary fiber.

7. Spinach

Spinach is low in calories, high in fiber, and versatile. It is cooked into everything from curry to flatbreads. Iron, calcium, and folate are just some of the nutrients that grace spinach. It has anti-inflammatory properties and is rich in lutein, a carotenoid that scientists have linked to eye health and age-related vision problems.

8. Tea

Recent research shows that tea leaves—black, green, oolong, and white—contain a compound called flavonoids, which have antioxidant effects that protect the body from the effects of aging and help to prevent some chronic diseases. Regular tea consumption not only helps to prevent cancer, heart disease, and other illnesses but also

reduces the risk of stroke, obesity, arthritis, and diabetes.

Chai, a strong brewed black tea with milk and sugar, is the most popular way to drink tea in India. Enjoy 2–4 cups a day of tea or chai and reap the numerous curative and preventative benefits.

9. Turmeric

"Curry" gets its yellow color from turmeric, which is the quintessential spice in Indian cooking. In Ayurvedic practices, turmeric is thought to have many medicinal properties—antiseptic, antibacterial, and anti-inflammation to name a few. Though Western scientists have recognized the medicinal properties of turmeric only recently, researchers have discovered that turmeric has a powerful antioxidant called curcumin, a compound that may help prevent and treat cancer, cardiovascular disease, diabetes, Alzheimer's, Parkinson's, pulmonary disease, inflammatory bowel disease, psoriasis, and arthritis.

10. Whole Wheat Flour

Whole wheat flour is the staple food of northern India and is used to make most of the flatbreads. It is the primary source of energy—the daily bread. Whole grains in general are high in fiber and vitamins compared to refined flours. Fiber is crucial to gastrointestinal health, heart health, and diabetes management.

The Bottom Line

Planning Healthful Vegan Meals

We eat food, not nutrients. Eating foods is just as much about satisfaction, enjoyment, and fun as it is about nutrition and health. Indian vegan foods provide you with variety and choices to meet your nutritional needs and add flavor and taste in your meals. Scientific mumbo-jumbo aside, here are basic guidelines for eating healthfully:

1. Eat a wide variety of foods from all food groups—grains, vegetables, fruits, dried beans, nuts, and seeds. Variety helps ensure sufficient nutrients, phytochemicals, and fiber as well as make meals more exciting.

2. Pay extra attention to make sure you are getting adequate amounts of protein, calcium, iron, zinc, vitamin D, and vitamin B12 from your vegan diet.

3. Eat three meals and one to three snacks each day as needed, to meet your nutritional and caloric needs. Start your day with breakfast, which is the most important meal of the day, providing you with much-needed energy and stamina.

4. Limit the intake of concentrated fats, oils, and added sugars. These foods are high in calories and a poor source of other nutrients.

5. Exercise for thirty minutes at least five days per week. Physical activity is central to energy balance and overall health.

6. When eating an all plant-based diet, it is important to make sure you are getting enough calories to maintain a healthy weight, especially for growing children and teens.

VEGAN AND VEGETARIAN RESOURCES

This is a partial list of resources that you might find helpful:

The Vegetarian Resource Group, www.vrg.org

Veganism in a Nutshell, www.vrg.org/nutshell/vegan

Vegetarian Nutrition Dietetic Practice Group of the American Dietetic Association, www.vegetariannutrition.net

Vegetarian Society of the United Kingdom, www.vegsoc.org

Becoming Vegan: The Complete Guide to Adapting a Healthy Plant-Based Diet, Brenda Davis, R.D., and Vesanto Melina, M.S., R.D. Book Publishing Company, 2000.

For a listing of resources from the Food and Nutrition Information Center (National Agriculture Library), download the Vegetarian Nutrition Resource List at www.nal.usda.gov/fnic/pubs/bibs/gen/vegetarian.pdf.

For more on Indian diet and recipes, go to www.cuisineofindia.com.

A Month of Meals

Menus

Over the years, I have learned—personally as well as from my clients, that planning a meal often takes longer than preparing it. I don't know how many times I've said that if someone would just tell me what to make, I'd make it. But in my family (and probably yours), no one has any suggestions, or worse, they'll tell you the most outrageous thing that cannot be prepared anytime soon.

To help you get started, I have planned a month of menus. There are seven menus in each category, from quick meals to party menus. These are just suggestions; feel free to mix and match and enjoy them any way you like.

Quick Meals

These meals can be prepared in thirty to forty-five minutes. When preparing an Indian meal, I always start with the main dish, which most often is the dal, and then work around it. A balanced Indian meal, whether prepared in a hurry or not, is typically dal, a vegetable, rice, and/or flatbread. You can add other things as desired, but overall you'll have a tasty and nutritious meal as is.

You can replace basmati rice, long-grain rice, or brown rice wherever a recipe calls for rice. Keep in mind that brown rice will take about forty-five minutes to prepare, so start that first.

MENU 1

Black-Eyed Peas and Potatoes (*Aloo-Lobhia*), page 125

Seasoned Zucchini (*Sukhi Lauki*), page 113

Rice, page 139

MENU 2

Quick Kidney Beans (*Rajmah*), page 120

Carrots and Turnips (*Gajar-Shalgum*), page 109

Cucumber-Tomato Salad (*Kheera-Tamatar Salad*), page 193

Rice, page 139

MENU 3

Quick Chickpea Curry (*Kabuli Chane Ki Subji*), page 122

Cabbage-Peanut Salad (*Bund Gobhi-Mungfali Salad*), page 189

Rice, page 139

MENU 4

Pigeon Peas (*Toor Dal*), page 119

Cabbage Mixed Vegetables (*Bund Gobhi Milli Subji*), page 108

Grilled Flatbread (*Roti*), page 157

Rice, page 139

MENU 5

Ginger-Spinach Pink Lentils (*Adrak-Palak Dal*), page 131

Curried Mushrooms and Peas (*Khumb-Matar*), page 104

Rice, page 139

MENU 6

Zucchini-Tomato Dal (*Torai-Tamatar Dal*), page 136

Cumin-Cilantro Edamame (*Hare Soy Ki Subji*), page 180

Rice, page 139

MENU 7

Kale-Tofu Pilaf (*Saag-Tofu Pulao*), page 177

Curried Potato Soup (*Aloo-Tamatar Soup*), page 88

Spicy Papad (*Masala Papad*), page 56

Any-Day Meals

These meals can take thirty to sixty minutes to prepare and may require some preplanning, such as soaking the dal. Also keep in mind that using a pressure cooker to prepare the dal will save a significant amount of time.

MENU 8

Bengal Gram and Bottle Gourd (*Chana Lauki Dal*), page 127

Okra and Onions (*Bhindi-Pyaj*), page 110

Flaxseed Flatbread (*Flaxseed Roti*), page 159

MENU 9

Mung Bean–Tomato Dal (*Sabut Mung-Tamatar Dal*), page 135

Mashed Eggplant (*Baingan Bharta*), page 97

Grilled Flatbread (*Roti*), page 157

MENU 10

Spinach Bengal Gram Dal (*Palak Chana Dal*), page 128

Stuffed Banana Peppers (*Besan Bhari Mirch*), page 95

Millet-Potato Flatbread (*Bajra-Aloo Roti*), page 168

MENU 11

Black Chickpea Curry (*Kaale Chane*), page 123

Curried Onions (*Pyaj Ki Subji*), page 108

Pan-Fried Flatbread (*Paratha*), page 160

MENU 12

Black Bean Pilaf (*Kalli Khichri*), page 143

Mango Soup (*Aam Soup*), page 89

Chickpea Salad (*Kabuli Chana Salad*), page 190

MENU 13

Peas-and-Tofu Curry (*Matar-Tofu*), page 176

Stuffed Okra (*Bharva Bhindi*), page 110

Pan-Fried Flatbread (*Paratha*), page 160

MENU 14

Bean Burgers (*Dal-Vada Burgers*), page 81

Grilled Vegetables (*Bhuni Subji*), page 100

Grilled Corn (*Bhutta*), page 101

Breakfast to Lunch to Dinner

Enjoy these meals any time of the day. Sometimes you just want to eat something fun for dinner that isn't your typical *dal-chawal* (beans-and-rice) meal.

MENU 15

Scrambled Tofu (*Tofu Ki Bhuji*), page 177

Potato-Stuffed Flatbread (*Aloo Paratha*), page 160

MENU 16

Stuffed Mung Bean Pancakes (*Bharva Cheele*), page 80

Tropical Fruit Salad (*Phal Ki Chaat*), page 202

MENU 17

Mung Bean Crepes (*Passhirattu Dosa*), page 83

Madras Potatoes (*Madrasi Aloo*), page 99

Tomato-Coconut Chutney (*Tamatar-Nariyal Chutney*), page 186

MENU 18

Cracked Wheat Snack (*Uppama*), page 78

Mango Yogurt Drink (*Aam Lassi*), page 182

MENU 19

Curried Potatoes (*Sukhe Aloo*), page 100

Fried Bread (*Puri*), page 165

MENU 20

Daikon-Stuffed Flatbread (*Mooli Paratha*), page 163

Almond Spicy Drink (*Thandai*), page 181

MENU 21

Bean-Rice Pancakes (*Adai*), page 84

Coconut Chutney (*Nariyal Chutney*), page 185

Pomegranate Tea (*Anari Chai*), page 75

Party Menus

Having a party or celebrating an occasion gives us an excuse to make and enjoy dishes that we might not take the time to prepare for a routine meal. The menus below are some of my favorite combinations, from drinks to desserts, and are sure to please a crowd.

Be sure to plan ahead, as these menus are time consuming. Don't be afraid to eliminate an item, substitute a dish, or buy the dessert. Remember that you don't want to be exhausted or frustrated when the guests arrive.

When planning a party, I always decide on a menu and grocery shop at least two days before. Over the years, I have learned to streamline my cooking by preparing or partially preparing some of the dishes ahead of time. With a little practice, you'll be dazzling your guests with amazing Indian meals.

MENU 22

Mango Lemonade (*Aam Neembu Pani*), page 73

Black-Eyed Pea Dip (*Sukha Lobhia*), page 55

Spinach and Tofu (*Palak-Tofu*), page 174

Stuffed Baby Eggplant (*Bharva Chote Baingun*), page 96

Cumin Rice (*Jeera Chawal*), page 141

Onion-Stuffed Flatbread (*Pyaj Paratha*), page 162

Crunchy Blossom Pastries (*Chirote*), page 198

Spiced Chai Latte (*Masala Chai*), page 181

MENU 23

Mango Yogurt Drink (*Aam Lassi*), page 182

Cocktail Peanuts (*Mungfali Chaat*), page 54

Potato-Patty Snack (*Aloo-Tikki Chaat*), page 71

Tamarind Chutney (*Imli Chutney*), page 184

Indian Funnel Cakes (*Instant Jalebi*), page 200

Snacks, Chaat, and Beverages

HOSPITALITY IS CENTRAL to Indian culture. The Sanskrit saying "*Atithi Devo Bhava*," meaning "Guest Is God," conveys the respect granted to guests. Most Indians take pride in making a visitor feel comfortable and cared for. A visit is considered incomplete without offering and receiving food.

When you enter an Indian home, you are immediately taken care of. Within a few minutes, you will be offered a glass of water, a ritual that is ingrained among most Indians. Even the children know how to offer water. You bring a glass of water, which is full to the rim (about ¼ inch below), and wait until the guest takes hold of it, and smile or nod before you leave. You put the glass down on the table only per guest's request. There is a gentleness and humbleness to this offering.

A little later, you are offered tea, coffee, or a cold beverage with snacks. If the visit was preplanned, you may be offered three to five or more varieties of snacks. An increasing number of dishes are offered based on the importance of the guest. Even children when visiting their friend's house will be offered some snack.

The snacks offered can be purchased, homemade, or a combination. They are usually prepared ahead of time (for preannounced guests) and then quickly heated before serving. Two or three types of pickles and chutneys may be served with the snack. Pace yourself, for the host will offer the food personally several times—"Please take one more." Don't eat too much, as it is considered improper. (Indians have mastered this fine balance.) My children, when they visit India, are aghast at how much food they are offered. I, on the other hand, love it and have come to expect it. Indians in America will offer the same amount of food or snack but will not push the food on you quite as much.

Snacks

Indians love to snack. The most popular Indian snacks are a blend of taste and textures, such as Hot-Spicy Cereal Mix (page 57). They are crunchy, spicy, hot, and salty, with a hint of sour and sweet, appealing to all your taste buds.

Other than dry snacks, such as *chivra*, there are fresh snacks, which can be served as appetizers, between meals, or as accompaniments. Mixed-Vegetable–Stuffed Pastry (page 62), Eggplant Fritters (page 65), or Kachories are great any time of the day. I have served them for breakfast, teatime, or as appetizers. I'm even known to make a meal out of them for that special don't-want-to-eat-the-same-old-rice-and-beans Sunday dinner.

Chaat

A *chaat* is a food class in itself, unique to India. *Chaat* literally means "to lick"! Chaat was traditionally only available in northern India, but with migration and cultural assimilation, it is now available throughout the country. It's a concoction of various foods smothered with sweet and sour chutneys and spice blends. It can be made of little crispy fried breads (*pani puri*) and filled with Spicy-Sour Drink (page 76), or made with potatoes, like Potato-Patty Snacks (page 71). What makes a food chaat is not what it starts with, but what goes on the top. Chaat never fails to get one's taste buds going. Young or old, everyone loves chaat. A common Indian phrase is "*chaatori hai*," meaning a girl who likes chaat—although in my experience, boys like them equally well. I think it became attached to girls because when women are pregnant, their desire to eat chaat typically increases. This is similar to the pickles-and-pregnant-women myth in America.

Many types of chaat are served with a yogurt topping and thus are not in the scope of this book. Although you can substitute soy yogurt, I chose to skip them, since there are plenty of gloriously vegan varieties to focus on instead. Traditionally, chaat was primarily sold by street vendors, at kiosks. Today, it's available in all types of Indian restaurants, from fast-food joints to fancy dining rooms. There is no substitute for chaat, and once you taste it you'll be hooked. It is best shared with family and friends. I've been known to have just a chaat party; and for my cynical, purist Indian friends who think chaat cannot be a meal, I also make a *pulao* (rice pilaf) so that they feel nourished.

Drinks

Water is the beverage of choice with Indian meals. Alcohol is not accepted or served in most Indian homes. Although alcohol has recently gained popularity in India, especially among the elite class, it is still not adopted as an Indian beverage.

The most popular and uniquely Indian beverage is chai, which has swept the world in the last decade. Chai is brewed tea mixed with hot milk and sugar. Chai can be plain (still mixed with milk and sugar) or brewed with spices, such as masala chai. Coffee (also served with milk and sugar) is also very popular in India, especially in the south. South Indians take their coffee very seriously and as a rule will grind fresh coffee every morning. In northern India, espresso coffee is enjoyed as a delicacy, which is actually similar to cappuccino, and not at all like the European espresso.

Beyond tea and coffee are soft drinks, fruit-flavored cold beverages called sherbet, and lemonade served mostly in the summer. Then there are some very typical Indian drinks like *lassi* (a yogurt drink), which has gained international popularity, and *thandai* (a spicy almond drink). They can be made with soy yogurt (see Soy

PARTY TIME

For events such as a stand-up buffet or a cocktail party for a number of people, browse this whole book, not just this chapter. Consider serving flatbreads cut in small portions, rice *pulao*, and a variety of chutneys as dips and spreads. Just remember, Indian food is saucy and can be messy, so plan to have small plates and forks and spoons available, not just napkins. Be adventurous, and mix a variety of Indian foods with your personal favorites.

Products, page 173). Although Indians drink tea and coffee year-round, cold beverages were traditionally only served in the summer (that's an Ayurvedic medicinal influence). But that too has changed, and today, you can get cold drinks any time of the year.

Spicy Cashews
Masala Kaju

PREP: 5 minutes
COOK: 10 minutes
MAKES: 16 servings
SERVING SIZE: 2 tablespoons

The tang of chaat masala and the heat of black pepper turn these cashews into a gourmet snack. Serve them on special occasions to impress your guests or make a batch for yourself for that snack attack.

1 teaspoon canola or vegetable oil

2 cups (9 ounces) roasted, salted whole cashews

1 teaspoon ground black pepper

1 teaspoon chaat masala (page 24), or purchased

½ teaspoon cornstarch

½ teaspoon sugar

1. In a medium fry pan, heat oil on medium heat. Add the cashews; stir to coat with oil.

2. Sprinkle black pepper, chaat masala, cornstarch, and sugar over cashews; stir to coat. Reduce heat to medium-low.

3. Cook for about 5 minutes, stirring continuously in a lifting and turning motion. Cool completely and store in an airtight container.

NUTRITION INFORMATION PER SERVING:
Calories: 103; Total Fat: 8 g (Saturated Fat: 1.5 g); Carbohydrate: 6 g; Protein: 3 g; Fiber: 1 g; Sodium: 136 mg

Cocktail Peanuts
Mungfali Chaat

PREP: 10 minutes
COOK: 0 minutes
MAKES: 10 servings
SERVING SIZE: 2 tablespoons

At your next SuperBowl party, replace a bowl of nuts with this easy, filling, crowd-pleaser. Use pre-roasted Spanish peanuts for convenience.

1 cup roasted Spanish peanuts

3 tablespoons red onions, finely chopped

¼ cup tomatoes, finely chopped

2 tablespoons cilantro, finely chopped

½ teaspoon chaat masala (page 24), or purchased

¼ teaspoon cayenne pepper, or to taste

½ tablespoon lemon or lime juice

In a small bowl, mix roasted peanuts with chopped onions, tomatoes, and cilantro. Add chaat masala, cayenne pepper, and lemon juice just before serving. Toss well. Transfer to a serving bowl.

NUTRITION INFORMATION PER SERVING:
Calories: 86; Total Fat: 7 g (Saturated Fat: 1 g); Carbohydrate: 3 g; Protein 4 g; Fiber: 1 g; Sodium: 122 mg

Spicy-Coated Peanuts
Masala Mungfali

PREP: 10 minutes
COOK: 20 minutes
MAKES: 24 servings
SERVING SIZE: 2 tablespoons

Surprise your guests with these spicy-coated crunchy peanuts. Have a bowl handy at your next party. Not to worry—although they are fried, they do not absorb much oil.

½ cup besan

1 teaspoon cayenne pepper

1 teaspoon salt

1 teaspoon chaat masala (page 24), or purchased

2 teaspoons fennel seeds, finely crushed

2 cups raw peanuts, with shells

Canola or vegetable oil for frying

1. In a medium mixing bowl, mix besan, cayenne pepper, salt, chaat masala, and crushed fennel seeds. Set aside.

2. Line a baking sheet or a large plate with wax paper. Set aside.

3. Place peanuts in a strainer and wash them under running water.

4. Add the wet peanuts into the besan mixture and stir quickly. The besan mixture will coat the peanuts individually. If there is some mixture left in the bowl, sprinkle the peanuts with some water and stir. Keep doing this until all the besan has been used. Spread the peanuts on the wax paper.

5. Heat about 3 inches oil in a wok/*karahi* or a medium skillet over medium heat. (Or use electric fryer and heat oil to 325°F.) Oil is ready when one coated peanut dropped into the hot oil quickly rises to the top but does not turn brown right away. Adjust heat as needed.

6. Drop a single layer of peanuts into the hot oil. Fry in 2 to 3 batches, depending on the size of your frying pan. Fry for 4 to 5 minutes until the coating turns light brown, turning occasionally. Drain on paper towels.

7. Cool completely. Store in an airtight container.

NUTRITION INFORMATION PER SERVING:
Calories: 84; Total Fat: 7 g (Saturated Fat: 1 g); Carbohydrate: 4 g ; Protein: 3 g; Fiber: 1 g; Sodium: 117 mg

---

GF, LF

Black-Eyed Pea Dip
Sukha Lobhia

PREP: 10 minutes
COOK: 10 minutes
MAKES: 8–10 servings
SERVING SIZE: ¼ cup

Canned or frozen black-eyed peas *(lobhia)* make it simple to prepare this dish any time. For one potluck dinner, I took a big dish of black-eyed peas as a snack. The dish was sitting next to a bowl of corn chips. The next thing I knew, people were dipping the chips in the black-eyed peas and calling it a dip. From then on, I always serve this with chips. Enjoy it as a chaat (snack), a side dish, or as a dip.

1 (16-ounce) can black-eyed peas, or 1½ cups frozen black-eyed peas

1 tablespoon canola or vegetable oil

¼ teaspoon cumin seeds

¼ teaspoon turmeric

¼ teaspoon cayenne pepper, or to taste

1 teaspoon ground coriander

½ teaspoon salt

½ cup water

¼ teaspoon garam masala

2 teaspoons lemon or lime juice

2 tablespoons cilantro (garnish)

½ cup red onions, finely chopped (garnish)

Pita chips (page 56), optional, or gluten-free chips

1. Drain and rinse black-eyed peas. Set aside.

2. Heat oil in a nonstick fry pan on medium-high heat. Add cumin seeds; cook for a few seconds until seeds are golden brown. Add black-eyed peas and stir. Add turmeric, cayenne pepper, coriander, salt, and water. Stir to mix.

3. Bring to a boil. Cover with lid and reduce heat. Simmer for about 10 minutes, until most of the water has been absorbed. Remove from heat.

4. Stir in garam masala and lemon juice. Transfer to a serving platter and garnish with cilantro and finely chopped red onions. Serve as is or with chips, if desired.

NUTRITION INFORMATION PER SERVING:
Calories: 38; Total Fat: 2 g (Saturated Fat: 0 g); Carbohydrate: 5 g; Protein: 1 g; Fiber: 1 g; Sodium: 180 mg

PITA CHIPS

Preheat oven to 375°F. Split 4 pita bread rounds in half horizontally. Cut each half into 6 wedges. Place wedges, cut side up, in a single layer on an ungreased baking sheet. Bake for 7 to 9 minutes or until light brown and crisp. Cool completely on a wire rack. Store in an airtight container for up to 1 week.

LF

Spicy Papad
Masala Papad

PREP: 5 minutes
COOK: 5 minutes
MAKES: 6 servings
SERVING SIZE: 1 papad

If you love *papad* or pappadams, try this variation. All it takes is a few minutes to turn plain *papad* into a crunchy appetizer. These masala *papads* go well with drinks before dinner or as an anytime snack. *Papad* are available in most Indian grocery stores; choose the ones made with dal for this recipe.

Most restaurants today serve *papad* as appetizers. Indians eat *papad* with a meal, very much like potato chips. Many varieties of *papad* are available—plain, mild, or spicy-hot. Most *papad* are made from processed dal/legumes, but there are also potato *papad*, rice *papad*, and other sorts. If served as a snack, they are usually fried; if served with a meal, they are often roasted. I usually microwave my *papad* for convenience; see below.

6 papad (made with beans), purchased
1 tablespoon olive or canola oil
⅓ cup red onions, finely chopped
⅓ cup tomatoes, finely chopped
2 tablespoons coriander, finely chopped
½ teaspoon chaat masala (page 24), or purchased

1. Roast the papad in microwave or over direct fire.★

2. Just before serving, brush one side of the papad with oil.

3. Sprinkle with chopped onion, tomato, and cilantro. Sprinkle chaat masala over all.

4. Serve immediately.

DIRECT FIRE: Roast papad one at a time on a gas or electric stove. On electric stove, use a wire rack. Using tongs, roast papad, turning frequently to avoid burning, until it puffs.

MICROWAVE: Place 2 papad (stacked) on a paper towel or a microwave-safe plate. Microwave for 40–60 seconds on high (time will vary depending on microwave wattage). The papad should puff evenly; if there are brown spots, microwave for less time.

★ Papad can be roasted in two different ways.

NUTRITION INFORMATION PER SERVING:
Calories: 56; Total Fat: 2 g (Saturated Fat: 0 g);
Carbohydrate: 6 g; Protein 2 g; Fiber: 2 g;
Sodium: 238 mg

3. Let cool completely. Store in an airtight container.

NUTRITION INFORMATION PER SERVING:
Calories: 158; Total Fat: 8 g (Saturated Fat: 1 g);
Carbohydrate: 18 g; Protein: 4 g; Fiber: 1 g;
Sodium: 213 mg

GF

Rice-Peanut Snack Mix

Poha Chivra

PREP: 5 minutes
COOK: 10 minutes
MAKES: 8 servings
SERVING SIZE: ¼ cup

*P*oha is pounded rice that puffs up when deep-fried. It is used in a variety of *chivras* or snack mixes. Fried *poha* soaks up a fair amount of oil and tends to burn quickly. I've found that quick-roasting the oiled *poha* is easier, absorbs less oil, and ends up tasting just as good as the fried version.

2 tablespoons canola or vegetable oil

2 cups poha (page 138)

½ cup roasted salted Spanish peanuts

½ teaspoon salt

½ teaspoon chaat masala (page 24), or purchased

¼ teaspoon sugar

¼ teaspoon cayenne pepper, or to taste

1. In a medium skillet, combine oil and poha until it is well coated with oil. Heat the skillet on medium-high heat. Once heated, the poha will cook very quickly. Cook for 2 to 3 minutes, stirring constantly, until the poha starts to puff and turn white. (If the poha starts to turn brown, remove immediately and pour into bowl to avoid further cooking.)

2. Remove from heat and add peanuts, salt, chaat masala, sugar, and cayenne pepper. Mix well.

Hot-Spicy Cereal Mix

Chivra

PREP: 10 minutes
COOK: 30 minutes
MAKES: 20 servings
SERVING SIZE: ¼ cup

*I*f you like hot and spicy savory blends, you will love this. Make sure you have all ingredients measured and ready to assemble before you start.

2 cups corn flakes

½ cup shredded wheat squares

1 cup crispy rice cereal

1 cup potato sticks

½ cup roasted salted cashews

½ cup roasted salted peanuts in the shell, or soy nuts

¼ cup raisins

1 tablespoon sesame seeds

½ teaspoon cayenne pepper, or to taste

½ teaspoon black pepper

1 teaspoon chaat masala (page 24), or purchased

½ teaspoon salt

1 tablespoon sugar

2 tablespoons canola or vegetable oil

½ teaspoon brown mustard seeds

½ teaspoon cumin seeds

8–10 curry leaves, optional

1. In a small bowl, combine corn flakes, shredded wheat squares, rice cereal, potato sticks, cashews, peanuts, and raisins. Set aside.

2. In a separate small bowl, combine sesame seeds, cayenne pepper, black pepper, chaat masala, salt, and sugar. Set aside.

3. Heat oil in a large skillet over medium heat. Add mustard seeds and cumin seeds, cover with lid to keep mustard seeds from popping out, and cook for a few minutes until mustard seeds stop popping. Add the curry leaves, if using, and cook for a few seconds. Remove the pan from heat.

4. Add cereal mixture and stir well. Sprinkle on the spice mixture and stir well. Reduce heat to low and return pan to stove. Stir and cook for 7 to 8 minutes.

5. Cool completely. Store in an airtight container.

NUTRITION INFORMATION PER SERVING:
Calories: 189; Total Fat: 11 g (Saturated Fat: 2 g); Carbohydrate: 20 g; Protein: 5 g; Fiber: 2 g; Sodium: 193 mg

Whole Wheat Crackers
Atte Ki Matri

PREP: 10 minutes
COOK: 35 minutes
MAKES: 12 servings
SERVING SIZE: 2 *matries*

*M*atries resemble crackers. Homemade *matries* are a very popular snack among some families in north India. My mother always has a batch ready when we visit her. and she will also pack a box to go. Typically, *matries* are made of all-purpose flour and shortening. I like to make mine with whole wheat flour and canola oil—higher in fiber and lower in saturated fat. Enjoy them plain, with dip of choice, or with Indian pickles.

1 cup all-purpose flour
1 cup roti-atta, or white whole wheat flour
1 teaspoon salt
1 teaspoon ajwain
5 tablespoons canola or vegetable oil
½ cup water
Canola or vegetable oil for frying

1. In a medium mixing bowl or food processor, combine all-purpose flour, roti-atta, salt, and ajwain. Pour 5 tablespoons oil over the flour and mix well with fingertips or pastry cutter until the flour becomes well coated with oil. Add the water gradually until a stiff dough forms (you may need to add 1 tablespoon more water). Knead for 3 to 5 minutes, until dough becomes smooth and soft.

2. Divide the dough into 2 parts and make two 9- to 10-inch logs. Cover with cloth and let rest for 10 minutes.

3. On a cutting board, cut each log into ½-inch pieces. Using your palms, press each piece into a flat circle. Roll out each dough ball into a circle

2 to 2½ inches wide. Stack 6 circles on top of each other. Using a toothpick, pierce each stack of *matries*, making 4 to 5 holes in each stack.

4. Heat about 3 inches oil in a wok/*karahi* or a medium skillet over medium heat. (Or use electric fryer and heat oil to 325°F.) Oil is ready when a pinch of dough dropped into the hot oil quickly rises to the top but does not turn brown right away. Adjust heat as needed.

5. Carefully drop half of the *matries* (about 12 to 14) into the hot oil. Fry for 8 to 10 minutes, until the *matries* are light brown.

6. Drain *matries* on a paper towel. Cool completely and store in an airtight container.

NUTRITION INFORMATION PER SERVING:
Calories: 154; Total Fat: 10 g (Saturated Fat: 0.5 g); Carbohydrate: 15 g; Protein: 2 g; Fiber: 2 g; Sodium: 195 mg

VARIATION: For traditional *matries*, substitute roti-atta for all-purpose flour—for a total of 2 cups all-purpose flour, and proceed as above.

॰॰॰॰॰॰॰॰॰॰॰॰॰॰॰॰॰॰॰॰॰॰॰॰॰॰॰॰॰॰॰॰॰॰॰॰॰॰॰

Stick Crackers

Nimki

PREP: 10 minutes
COOK: 35 minutes
MAKES: 24 servings
SERVING SIZE: ¼ cup (14–15 pieces)

Enjoy these crackers as a snack any time. Eat them by themselves or with a dab of hot-and-sour Indian pickles or sweet mango chutney. They are also great with hot tea or coffee.

3 cups all-purpose flour
1 teaspoon salt
1 teaspoon ajwain
⅓ cup canola or vegetable oil
¾ cup water
Canola or vegetable oil for frying

1. In a medium mixing bowl or food processor, combine all-purpose flour, salt, and ajwain. Pour the oil over the flour and mix well with fingertips or pastry cutter until the flour becomes well coated with oil. Gradually add ¾ cup water until a stiff dough forms (you may need to add 1 to 2 tablespoons more water). Knead for 3 to 5 minutes, until dough becomes smooth and soft. Divide the dough into 2 parts and flatten each into a large disk. Cover with cloth and let sit for 10 minutes.

2. On a flat surface (a plastic pastry sheet or a wooden board), roll out each disk into a 12-inch circle. With a sharp knife, cut the dough lengthwise into ⅓-inch strips, then cut crosswise about 1½ inches apart.

3. Heat about 3 inches oil in a wok/*karahi* or a medium skillet over medium heat. (Or use electric fryer and heat oil to 325°F.) Oil is ready when a pinch of dough dropped into the hot oil quickly rises to the top but does not turn brown right away. Adjust heat as needed.

4. Using a flat spatula, drop several strips at a time into the hot oil. You should be able to fry all the *nimki* from one circle at a time, depending on the size of your frying pan. Fry for 12 to 14 minutes, until the *nimki* are light brown.

5. Drain on a paper towel. Cool completely and store in an airtight container.

NUTRITION INFORMATION PER SERVING:
Calories: 105; Total Fat: 6 g (Saturated Fat: 0.5 g); Carbohydrate: 12 g; Protein: 2 g; Fiber: 0 g; Sodium: 97 mg

Instant Steamed Cakes

Instant Dhokla

PREP: 10 minutes
COOK: 20 minutes
MAKES: 8 servings
SERVING SIZE: 2 pieces

*D*hokla, a specialty of the Gujarat state, has become popular throughout India. Typically, it is a mix of beans and rice, ground and fermented overnight, and steamed. It's healthy and delicious. Here is a recipe for an instant dhokla that you can prepare anytime—no soaking, grinding, or fermenting required. And the good news is that it turns out just as good as, if not better than, the traditional version.

¾ cup cream of wheat

¾ cup besan

1 teaspoon salt

¼ teaspoon turmeric

1¼ cups water

1 teaspoon ginger, peeled and finely grated

2 teaspoons green chile, finely chopped, or to taste

1 tablespoon lemon or lime juice

2 tablespoons canola or vegetable oil

1 teaspoon ENO or baking powder

SEASONING (CHOUNK)

2 tablespoons canola or vegetable oil

⅛ teaspoon asafetida powder

1 teaspoon mustard seeds

6–8 curry leaves

2 tablespoons chopped cilantro, garnish

2 tablespoons fresh grated coconut, garnish, optional

1. In a medium bowl, combine cream of wheat, besan, salt, and turmeric. Add water and beat with an electric hand mixer on medium speed for 2 to 3 minutes.

2. Add ginger, green chile, lemon juice, and oil. Beat with the mixer for an additional minute.

3. Brush or spray an 8- or 9-inch round metal cake pan with oil. Set aside.

4. Use a large saucepan with a tight lid into which the cake pan will fit. Place a steamer rack or a 1-inch-high ring in the middle of the pan—to raise the surface. Add 1 cup water in the saucepan and heat on medium-high heat.

5. Just before steaming, add ENO to the batter. Stir in a circular motion until blended. Immediately transfer the mixture into the oiled cake pan.

6. Carefully place the cake pan in the saucepan, using tongs for safety, and cover with a lid. Bring water to a full, rolling boil, and reduce heat to medium. Steam for 10 minutes. Remove from the heat and carefully take out the cake pan. Set aside to cool to room temperature.

7. Once cooled, cut *dhokla* into 1-inch squares or diamond shapes. Remove from pan and arrange on a serving platter in a single layer.

8. *Prepare seasoning:* Heat oil in a small fry pan to smoking point. Add asafetida and mustard seeds, covering with a lid to avoid splattering. Fry for a few seconds until mustard seeds stop popping. Remove from the heat, add curry leaves, and cook for a few seconds.

9. Evenly spread the oil seasoning over the *dhokla* pieces. Garnish with cilantro and grated coconut, if desired. Serve with Cilantro Chutney (page 185) and/or Coconut Chutney (page 185).

NUTRITION INFORMATION PER SERVING:
Calories: 156; Total Fat: 8 g (Saturated Fat: 0.5 g); Carbohydrate: 18 g; Protein: 4 g; Fiber: 2 g; Sodium: 358 mg

Mixed Vegetable–Stuffed Pastries

Subji Samosa

PREP: 15 minutes
COOK: 60 minutes
MAKES: 20 servings
SERVING SIZE: 1 samosa

Samosas are one of the most popular Indian snacks. You will find them in most Indian restaurants as appetizers. Potato-stuffed samosas are the most common, although they can be filled with other vegetables, meat, or even sweet fillings. Making samosas can be time-consuming but well worth the effort. If you have the time, try the traditional version below, making your own dough and shell. If you're in a hurry or are looking for another variety, try the frozen pastry dough recipe used in Samosa Puffs (page 62) for all the samosa taste with half the hassle. Serve them for breakfast, snack, or as an appetizer at your next party.

MIXED VEGETABLE FILLING

1 medium potato (about 1 cup), boiled

2 cups frozen mixed vegetables (peas, carrots, corn, and green beans)

1 tablespoon canola or vegetable oil

½ teaspoon cumin seeds

1 tablespoon ginger, peeled and grated

1–2 teaspoons green chiles, finely chopped, to taste

¼ cup water

1 teaspoon salt

2 teaspoons ground coriander

½ teaspoon amchur or 2 teaspoons lemon juice

1 teaspoon garam masala

DOUGH

2 cups all-purpose flour

1 teaspoon salt

3 tablespoons canola or vegetable oil

½ cup water

Canola or vegetable oil for frying

1. *Prepare filling:* Peel boiled potatoes and dice into ¼-inch pieces. Thaw the frozen vegetables in a strainer by rinsing in lukewarm running water. Drain and set aside.

2. Heat oil in a nonstick fry pan on medium-high heat. Add cumin seeds and fry for a few seconds until cumin turns a darker brown. Add ginger and green chiles; stir for a few seconds. Add mixed vegetables, water, and salt, and stir. Cover, reduce heat to medium, and cook for 3 to 4 minutes. Add potatoes, coriander, amchur, and garam masala. Mix thoroughly. Cover with a lid, cook for 1 to 2 minutes, or until heated through. Open lid and stir to mix. Let cool.

3. *Prepare dough:* In a medium bowl or food processor, mix flour, salt, and oil until well blended. Add water and make dough.

4. Turn dough onto a lightly floured surface and knead for about 2 minutes or until dough becomes smooth and soft. Divide dough into 10 equal portions. Roll each dough portion between your palms to make smooth balls.

5. *Assemble samosas:* Pour ¼ cup water into a small bowl; set aside.

6. Roll each ball into a 6-inch circle. Cut in half. Take one half, dip your index finger in water, and run it along the straight edge. Fold in half, overlapping about a ¼-inch straight edge over the other, making a cone. Press to seal the cone.

7. Fill the cone with the vegetable filling. Dip finger in water and run along the inside of the cone mouth and press the lips together to seal the cone. Keep filled samosas between dry towels to avoid drying.

8. Heat about 3 inches oil in a wok/*karahi* or a medium skillet over medium heat. (Or use electric fryer and heat oil to 325°F.) Oil is ready when a pinch of dough dropped into the oil floats up within seconds. (It is important to have the oil the right temperature; if it's too hot, the samosas' crust will brown right away and the inside will not be cooked. If the oil is not hot enough, the samosas might fall apart or get greasy.) Fry 5 to 8 samosas at a time (depending on the size of your *karahi*) until light golden brown, about 5 to 7 minutes on each side.

9. Serve warm with Cilantro Chutney (page 185) or ketchup.

NOTE: Prepared samosas can be refrigerated for up to 3 days or frozen for up to 3 months. If frozen, thaw in refrigerator overnight. To reheat samosas, preheat oven to 350°F and cook for 7 to 9 minutes. Cool slightly before serving.

NUTRITION INFORMATION PER SERVING:
Calories: 109; Total Fat: 5 g (Saturated Fat: 0.5 g); Carbohydrate: 14 g; Protein: 2 g; Fiber: 1 g; Sodium: 244 mg

VARIATION: For all those who love their potato samosas, substitute the potato filling below for the mixed vegetable filling.

POTATO FILLING: Substitute 4 medium boiled potatoes (about 4 cups chopped) and ¾ cup frozen peas, in place of potatoes and mixed vegetables in the Mixed Vegetable Filling. Follow filling directions above.

Quick Vegetable Pastries
Samosa Puffs

PREP: 15 minutes
COOK: 30 minutes
MAKES: 25 servings
SERVING SIZE: 1 puff

There are several benefits of using the frozen pastry sheets as the samosa crust. First, they are less time-consuming and messy to make. They're baked instead of fried. And they have a unique taste, making them an alternate snack all their own.

FILLING
　　1 recipe Mixed Vegetable Filling (page 61)
DOUGH
　　½ package or 1 frozen pastry sheet, thawed

1. Prepare Mixed Vegetable Filling according to recipe. Thaw pastry sheet according to directions.

2. Preheat oven to 400°F.

3. Carefully open the pastry sheet. Lightly dust the counter with all-purpose flour and roll one pastry sheet into a 14 × 14-inch square. Cut the rolled sheet into 5 strips horizontally and vertically, making 25 squares.

4. Place about 1 tablespoon filling in the center of each square; fold one corner of the square over to make a triangle. Press the edges together, sealing the triangles. Stuff all 25 pastries. Place triangles 1 inch apart on an ungreased cookie sheet.

5. Bake for 20 to 25 minutes, until the tops are golden brown. Cool for 10 minutes. Serve warm with chutney or ketchup.

NUTRITION INFORMATION PER SERVING:
Calories: 62 g; Total Fat: 3 g (Saturated Fat: 1 g); Carbohydrate: 7 g; Protein: 1 g; Fiber: 1 g; Sodium: 150 mg

VARIATION: Substitute Potato Filling (see Variation, page 62) for the Mixed Vegetable Filling.

·:·

Mung Bean Fritters
Mung Dal Pakora

SOAK: 2 hours or more
PREP: 15 minutes
COOK: 30 minutes
MAKES: 10 servings
SERVING SIZE: 4–5 fritters

These *pakoras*/fritters are one of my favorites. My neighbor back in India introduced them to me when I was a teenager. The diced potatoes keep the fritters moist and the black pepper adds a distinct flavor and heat. I serve them as appetizers at a party or as a snack with hot tea or coffee.

1 cup (split, hulled) mung dal

½ cup water

1½ cup potatoes, peeled and cut into ¼-inch dice

1–1½ teaspoons black pepper, coarsely ground

1¼ teaspoons salt

2 teaspoons ground coriander

1 teaspoon amchur or 1 tablespoon lemon juice

Canola or vegetable oil for frying

1. Wash mung dal in 3 to 4 changes of water, until the water is relatively clear. Soak dal in cold water for 2 hours or overnight. Rinse again in 1 to 2 changes of water. Strain the dal and discard the water.

2. In a food processor or blender, coarsely grind the drained dal with ½ cup water. Transfer to a mixing bowl.

3. Add the diced potatoes, black pepper, salt, coriander, and amchur. Mix well.

4. Heat 2 inches oil in a *karahi*/wok or skillet on high heat. Oil is ready when a little bit of batter dropped into the oil rises to the top right away (about 375°F).

5. Drop about 1 tablespoon of batter at a time in the hot oil with a spoon or forefingers (if comfortable working with your hands), frying several fritters at a time. Fry for 5 to 7 minutes, until light brown on one side. Turn fritters over and fry on the other side. Drain on paper towels.

6. Serve hot with Cilantro Chutney (page 185).

MAKE AHEAD: You can partially fry all the fritters to light brown color, step 5. Cool and refrigerate in a covered bowl for up to 2 days. Or, freeze them for up to 3 months in a freezer-safe plastic bag. Before serving (thaw if frozen), fry them again on high heat, as in step 5, to golden brown. You can bake them, if desired, in a preheated oven (400°F) in a single layer. Baking makes the fritters a little dry, so take care not to overbake them.

NUTRITION INFORMATION PER SERVING:
Calories: 109; Total Fat: 3 g (Saturated Fat: 0 g); Carbohydrate: 17 g; Protein 6 g, Fiber: 2 g, Sodium: 295 mg

···

Mixed Vegetable Fritters

Subji Pakora

PREP: 15 minutes
COOK: 20 minutes
MAKES: 12 servings
SERVING SIZE: 2–3 fritters

Mixed vegetable fritters/*pakoras* are a popular appetizer in restaurants. In India, they are also a popular street food, sold in kiosks and fried to order. There is nothing like a hot cup of tea and hot *pakoras* on a cold or rainy day. Serve with chutney or ketchup. Besides teatime, my mom also served these for a special Sunday breakfast. I, on the other hand, am known to make a variety of vegetable fritters and call it dinner a couple times a year.

1¾ cups besan

1 cup potatoes, peeled and cut into ¼-inch dice

1½ cups onions, ¼-inch diced

3 cups spinach, coarsely chopped

3 tablespoons cream of rice

¾ cup water

2 teaspoons ground coriander

1 teaspoon cayenne pepper, or to taste

2–3 teaspoons green chiles, finely chopped, to taste

2 teaspoons salt

1 teaspoon amchur or 1 tablespoon lemon juice

Canola or vegetable oil for frying

1. Sift the besan to break any lumps. Set aside.

2. In a mixing bowl, combine potatoes, onions, and spinach. Add besan and cream of rice. Using a large spoon, mix well with water. Add coriander, cayenne pepper, green chiles, salt, and amchur. Mix well to coat vegetables.

3. Heat 3 inches oil in a *karahi*/wok or skillet on high heat. Oil is ready when a little bit of batter dropped in the oil rises to the top right away (about 400°F).

4. Drop about 1 tablespoon of batter at a time in the hot oil with a spoon or forefingers (if comfortable working with your hands), frying several fritters at a time. Fry for 3 to 5 minutes, until golden brown on one side. Turn fritters over and fry on the other side. Drain on paper towels. The fritters will be irregular in shape.

5. Serve hot with chutney of choice.

MAKE AHEAD: You can partially fry all the fritters to light brown color, step 5. Cool and refrigerate in a covered bowl for up to 2 days. Or, freeze them for up to 3 months in a freezer-safe plastic bag. Before serving (thaw if frozen), fry them again on high heat, as in step 5, to golden brown. You can bake them, if desired, in a preheated oven (400°F) in a single layer. Baking makes the fritters a little dry, so take care not to overbake them.

NUTRITION INFORMATION PER SERVING:
Calories: 154; Total Fat: 9 g (Saturated Fat: 0.5 g); Carbohydrate: 15 g; Protein 4 g: Fiber: 2 g; Sodium: 404 mg

Eggplant Fritters

Baingan Pakora

PREP: 10 minutes
COOK: 20 minutes
MAKES: 6 servings
SERVING SIZE: 3 pieces

These are my husband's favorite fritters. If you like eggplant, you'll love these, and if you don't, substitute another vegetable of choice (see Variation).

¾ cup besan

2 tablespoons cream of rice

1 teaspoon ground coriander

½ teaspoon cayenne pepper and/or 1–2 teaspoons green chilies, chopped, to taste

1 teaspoon amchur or 2 teaspoons lemon juice

1 teaspoon salt, divided

½ cup plus 1–2 tablespoons water

1 small eggplant (about 8 ounces)

Canola or vegetable oil for frying

1. Sift besan to break any lumps. In a mixing bowl, combine besan, cream of rice, coriander, cayenne pepper, amchur, and ¾ teaspoon salt. Add ½ cup water and stir well with a large spoon until mixture forms a batter-like consistency.

2. Slice eggplant into ¼-inch-thick circles. If the circles are too wide, cut them in half. Sprinkle with remaining ¼ teaspoon of salt.

3. Heat 3 inches oil in a *karahi*/wok or skillet on high heat. Oil is ready when a little bit of batter dropped in the oil rises to the top right away (about 400°F).

4. Dip several eggplant slices at a time in the batter, making sure they are completely coated. Take out 1 eggplant slice at a time, drain the excess batter on the side of the bowl, and slide it into the hot oil.

Fry several fritters at a time. Fry for 3 to 5 minutes, until golden brown on one side. Turn over and fry the other side. Drain on paper towels.

5. Serve hot with chutney of choice.

NOTE: These fritters do not keep well. The moisture from the eggplant makes them soften as they sit. To reheat, place them in a single layer, in a preheated 400°F oven and bake for 15 to 20 minutes until firm. Do not overbake, as they will become dry.

NUTRITION INFORMATION PER SERVING: Calories: 150; Total Fat: 10 g (Saturated Fat: 1 g); Carbohydrate: 12 g; Protein: 3 g; Fiber: 3 g; Sodium: 396 mg

VARIATION: Substitute thin slices of bell peppers, zucchini, or potatoes in place of eggplant. Or better yet, fry some of each.

Buckwheat-Potato Fritters

Kuttu Pakora

PREP: 5 minutes
COOK: 15 minutes
MAKES: 4 servings
SERVING SIZE: 5 fritters

These fritters are typically eaten during fasting times, when grain is to be avoided. They satisfy and meet the nutritional needs of a fasting person. They are also gluten-free. With all the benefits of buckwheat, why not eat them anytime?

2 medium (8 ounces) potatoes, boiled

⅓ cup buckwheat flour (kuttu atta)

¾ cup water

½ teaspoon salt

¼–½ teaspoon cayenne pepper

Canola or vegetable oil for frying

1. Peel and dice the boiled potatoes into ¼-inch pieces. Set aside.

2. In a medium bowl, mix buckwheat flour with water to make a thick batter. Add salt and cayenne pepper.

3. Gently stir in the boiled potatoes. Let stand for 10 minutes.

4. Heat 3 inches oil in a *karahi*/wok or skillet on high heat. Oil is ready when a little bit of batter dropped in the oil rises to the top right away (about 350°F).

5. Drop about 1 tablespoon of the batter at a time into the hot oil. Fry until golden brown. Drain on paper towels.

6. Serve hot with chutneys of choice.

NOTE: These fritters do not keep well and are best eaten immediately after frying.

NUTRITION INFORMATION PER SERVING: Calories: 177; Total Fat: 7 g (Saturated Fat: 0.5 g); Carbohydrate: 26 g; Protein: 3 g; Fiber: 3 g; Sodium: 298 mg

∙·

Mixed-Bean Cakes
Masala Vadas

SOAK: 2 hours to overnight
PREP: 15 minutes
COOK: 60 minutes
MAKES: 32 servings
SERVING SIZE: 1 vada

Mixed dal/legumes vadas are served like fritters in south India. I call them cakes instead of fritters, as they are very different in texture than *pakoras*/fritters. They can be made plain, with just dals or mixed with vegetables. The wonderful recipe below is from my friend Simi. They are a little tricky to make and may take some practice to get them perfectly round with a hole in the center. Do your best, but they will taste great, no matter what shape you make them.

1 cup (split, hulled) urad dal

½ cup (split, hulled) chana dal

½ cup yellow split peas

1 tablespoon ginger, peeled and chopped

1 tablespoon green chiles or to taste, chopped

½ cup water

½ cup frozen peas

½ cup carrots

½ cup green beans, cut into ¼-inch pieces

1 cup onion, finely chopped

⅛ teaspoon asafetida powder

1 tablespoon salt

½ teaspoon cayenne pepper, or to taste

¼ cup cilantro, finely chopped

Canola or vegetable oil for frying

1. In a mixing bowl, combine urad dal, chana dal, and yellow split peas and wash in 3 to 4 changes of water, until water is relatively clear. Soak for 2 hours or overnight. Rinse again in 1

to 2 changes of water. Strain the dal and discard the water.

2. In a food processor, grind the soaked dal, ginger, green chiles, and water. The mixture should be coarse or grainy. Transfer to a large bowl.

3. Mix in peas, carrots, green beans, and onion. Add asafetida, salt, cayenne pepper, and cilantro.

4. Heat 3 inches oil in a *karahi*/wok or skillet on high heat. Oil is ready when a little bit of batter dropped in the oil rises to the top right away (about 400°F).

5. To make *vadas*, place a small bowl with some cold water next to the batter. I find it easiest to make these *vadas* using a thick plastic sandwich bag. This way you can make one *vada* at a time, pick up the bag, and easily drop each *vada* into the hot oil.

6. Place a sandwich bag flat on the counter and lightly coat the top of the bag with water. Place a heaping tablespoon of batter in the center of the bag. Using your fingers, spread the batter into a circle. Make a hole in the center with one finger. Pick up the bag in your left hand by sliding your fingers under the bag where the *vada* is. Place 4 fingers of right hand lightly over the *vada*, flip over the bag, and remove the bag with left hand. Immediately slide the *vada* into the hot oil. Keep making one *vada* at a time and adding to the oil. You can fry 5 to 6 *vadas* at a time. Fry for 3 to 5 minutes, until golden brown on one side, turn it over, and fry the other side. Drain on paper towels.

7. Serve hot with Coconut Chutney (page 185) or Tomato-Coconut Chutney (page 186).

MAKE AHEAD: You can partially fry all the fritters to light brown color, step 6. Cool and refrigerate in a covered bowl for up to 4 days. Or, freeze them for up to 3 months in a freezer-safe plastic bag. Before serving (thaw if frozen), fry them again on high heat, as in step 6, to golden brown. You can bake them, if desired, in a preheated oven (400°F) in a single layer. Baking makes the fritters a little dry, so take care not to overbake them.

NUTRITION INFORMATION PER SERVING: Calories: 79; Total Fat: 4 g (Saturated Fat: 0.5 g); Carbohydrate: 9 g; Protein: 3 g; Fiber: 2 g; Sodium: 226 mg

Sorghum-Zucchini Cakes

Muthia

PREP: 15 minutes
COOK: 20 minutes
MAKES: 10 servings
SERVING SIZE: 2 pieces

Sorghum flour gives these steamed, savory cakes a unique texture. They are healthy and delicious. It's a two-step process: You first steam the dough mixture and then season and stir-fry until lightly crisp. If available, use bottle gourd (*lauki*), but they are just as good with zucchini, which is readily available year-round. Serve them as an appetizer or a light meal with a bowl of soup.

½ cup sorghum flour (*jawar* flour)

⅓ cup roti-atta, or white whole wheat flour

⅓ cup besan

1 teaspoon salt

¼ teaspoon turmeric

1 teaspoon cumin seeds, lightly crushed

½ teaspoon cayenne pepper, or to taste

1 teaspoon ground coriander

1 teaspoon sugar

2 cups zucchini, grated, or *lauki* (bottle gourd), peeled and grated

2 tablespoons cilantro, finely chopped

1 tablespoon lemon or lime juice

1 tablespoon canola or vegetable oil

SEASONING (*CHOUNK*)

3 tablespoons canola or vegetable oil

½ teaspoon mustard seeds

6–8 curry leaves, chopped

1 tablespoon sesame seeds

1. In a medium bowl, combine sorghum flour, roti-atta, and besan. Add salt, turmeric, cumin seeds, cayenne pepper, coriander, and sugar.

2. Add grated zucchini, cilantro, and lemon juice. Mix well with a large spoon, switching to your hands when the dough becomes difficult to work with (the moisture from zucchini will help make the dough). Mix in the oil. The dough will be soft, almost like a thick cake batter.

3. Brush or spray an 8-inch-round metal cake pan with oil. Spread the dough evenly in the pan. Set aside.

4. Use a large saucepan with a tight lid that the cake pan can fit into. Place a steamer rack or a 1-inch-high ring in the middle of the pan. Add 1 cup water in the saucepan and heat on medium-high heat.

5. Carefully place the cake pan in the pan using tongs and cover with a lid. Bring to a full, rolling boil and reduce heat to medium. Steam for 10 minutes. Remove from heat and carefully take out the cake pan. Set aside and cool to room temperature.

6. Once cooled, cut *muthia* into 1-inch squares. Remove from pan.

7. *Prepare seasoning:* Heat oil in a large fry pan on medium-high heat. Add mustard seeds, cover with a lid (to keep seeds from popping out). Fry for a few seconds until mustard seeds stop popping. Reduce heat to medium, add curry leaves and sesame seeds, and cook for a few seconds. Add the *muthia* pieces in a single layer.

8. Fry the pieces for 4 to 5 minutes on each side until golden brown. Turn the pieces carefully, using a tong or spatula to avoid breaking.

9. Transfer to a serving platter and garnish with all the spices in the pan. Serve with Cilantro Chutney (page 185) or Coconut Chutney (page 185).

NUTRITION INFORMATION PER SERVING:
Calories: 108; Total Fat: 6 g (Saturated Fat: 0.5 g); Carbohydrate: 11 g; Protein: 2 g; Fiber: 2 g; Sodium: 238 mg

Pea-Stuffed Pastries
Matar Kachori

PREP: 10 minutes
COOK: 60 minutes
MAKES: 12 servings
SERVING SIZE: 2 *kachories*

These pastries are basically crispy, stuffed fried breads, served on special occasions as a snack or at a meal. If serving as a snack or appetizer, I make them the size given here, but if serving as fancy bread with a meal, I make them almost twice as big. They are great with chutney or pickles, or dipped in a curry sauce.

FILLING
1 tablespoon canola or vegetable oil
⅛ teaspoon asafetida powder
1 tablespoon ginger, peeled and grated
2 teaspoons green chiles, chopped
3 cups frozen peas, thawed
1 teaspoon ground cumin
1 teaspoon salt
1 teaspoon garam masala
1 teaspoon amchur
1 teaspoon sugar
2 tablespoons fresh or frozen coconut, finely grated

DOUGH
1½ cups all-purpose flour
½ cup roti-atta, or white whole wheat flour
1 teaspoon salt
5 tablespoons canola or vegetable oil
½ cup water
Canola or vegetable oil for frying

1. *Prepare the filling:* Heat oil in a nonstick fry pan on medium-high heat. Add asafetida, ginger, and green chiles and fry for few seconds. Add peas and stir. Add cumin, salt, garam masala, *amchur*, and sugar. Cook for about 2 minutes. Remove from heat.

2. With a fork or a potato masher, lightly mash the peas. Add coconut and stir. Let cool.

3. *Prepare the dough:* In a mixing bowl or food processor, combine all-purpose flour and *atta*. Add salt and oil and blend well. Add water as you mix (you may need to add 1 more tablespoon of water to form soft dough). Knead for 3 to 5 minutes, until dough becomes smooth and soft. Divide dough into 24 balls.

4. *Assemble* kachories: Roll each dough ball into a 2½-inch circle. Place a heaping tablespoon of filling in the center. With your forefingers, crimp the edges of the circle together and seal in the filling. Lightly press the ball on the crimped side to form a flat disk.

5. Keep the filled *kachories* between dry towels to avoid drying.

6. Heat about 3 inches oil in a wok/*karahi* or a medium skillet over medium heat. (Or use electric fryer and heat oil to 325°F.) Oil is ready when a pinch of dough dropped into the oil floats up within seconds. (It is important to have the oil the right temperature because if the oil is too hot, the crust will brown right away and the inside will not be cooked. If the oil is not hot enough, the *kachories* might open and become greasy.) Fry 5 to 6 *kachories* at a time (depending on the size of your pan) until light golden brown, about 4 to 5 minutes on each side. Drain on paper towels. Let cool.

7. Serve at room temperature with Cilantro Chutney (page 185) and/or Tamarind Chutney

(page 184). To store, cool completely and store in an airtight container. Will keep at room temperature for up to three days, or in the refrigerator for up to 1 week.

NOTE: The *kachories* will get slightly soft when stored. To recrisp, preheat oven to 350°F. Place *kachories* in a single layer and heat for 5 to 7 minutes. Cool before serving. The crust becomes crispy as it cools.

NUTRITION INFORMATION PER SERVING: Calories: 221; Total Fat: 14 g (Saturated Fat: 1.5 g); Carbohydrate: 21 g; Protein: 4 g; Fiber: 3 g; Sodium: 425 mg

---

Mung Bean–Stuffed Pastries
Mung Kachori

SOAK: 2 hours to overnight
PREP: 20 minutes
COOK: 30 minutes
MAKES: 12 servings
SERVING SIZE: 2 *kachories*

In this specialty of Rajasthan, mung beans are spiced to taste, stuffed, and fried in a crispy, pastry-like shell. They are sold at kiosks and fast-food restaurants, and served on special occasions and for celebrations at home. I like to keep my stuffing mild and serve them with a variety of chutneys so that guests can enjoy them to their taste preference.

FILLING

1 cup (split, hulled) mung dal

⅓ cup water

Canola or vegetable oil for frying

DOUGH

2 cups all-purpose flour

1 teaspoon salt

¼ cup canola or vegetable oil

½ cup water

½ teaspoon ground cumin

1 teaspoon salt

1 tablespoon coriander seeds, coarsely ground

1 teaspoon fennel seeds, coarsely ground

½ teaspoon cayenne pepper, or to taste

1 teaspoon amchur

1. *Prepare filling:* Wash mung dal in 3 to 4 changes of water, until the water is relatively clear. Soak the dal in cold water for 2 hours or overnight. Rinse again in 1 to 2 changes of water, strain the dal, and discard the water.

2. In a blender, coarsely grind the soaked dal with ⅓ cup water. Transfer to a mixing bowl.

3. Heat 3 inches oil in a *karahi*/wok or skillet on high heat. Oil is ready when a little bit of batter dropped in the oil rises to the top right away (about 400°F).

4. Drop about 1 tablespoon of batter at a time in the hot oil with a spoon, frying several fritters at a time. Fry for 3 to 5 minutes, until light brown on one side. Turn it over, and fry on the other side. Drain on paper towels. Cool the balls slightly and break them open into two. Cool for 5 minutes or more until easy to handle.

5. *In the meantime, prepare dough:* In a mixing bowl or food processor, combine flour, salt, and oil; blend well. Add water as you mix (you may need to add 1 more tablespoon of water to form soft dough). Knead for 3 to 5 minutes until dough becomes smooth and soft. Divide dough into 24 portions. Roll each dough portion between your palms to make smooth balls. Cover with dry towel and set aside.

6. In a food processor, coarsely grind the fried dal balls, using a pulse motion. They should resemble a coarse mixture.

7. Heat a nonstick fry pan on medium–high heat. Add the bean crumbles. Add cumin, salt, coriander, fennel, cayenne pepper, and amchur. Mix well. Fry for 2 to 3 minutes. Remove from heat and cool to room temperature.

8. *Assemble kachories:* Roll each dough ball into a 2- to 3-inch circle. Place about 2 tablespoons of filling in the center, crimp the edges of the circle together, and seal in the filling. Press the ball to form a flat disk.

9. Placing the filled side up, roll the filled disks to a 2- to 3-inch circle again.

10. Keep the filled *kachories* between dry towels to avoid drying.

11. Heat about 3 inches oil in a wok/*karahi* or a medium skillet over medium heat. (Or use electric fryer and heat oil to 325°F.) Oil is ready when a pinch of dough dropped into the oil floats up within seconds. (It is important to have the oil the right temperature because if the oil is too hot, the crust will brown right away and the inside will not be cooked. If the oil is not hot enough, the *kachories* might fall apart or get greasy.) Fry 5 to 6 *kachories* at a time (depending on the size of your pan) until light golden brown, about 4 to 5 minutes on each side. Drain on paper towels. Let cool.

12. Serve at room temperature with Cilantro Chutney (page 185) and/or Tamarind Chutney (page 184). To store, cool to room temperature and store in an airtight container. Will keep at room temperature for up to three days.

NUTRITION INFORMATION PER SERVING: Calories: 270; Total Fat: 16 g (Saturated Fat: 1 g); Carbohydrate: 27 g; Protein: 6 g; Fiber: 1 g; Sodium: 391 mg

---

GF

Potato-Patty Snack
Aloo-Tikki Chaat

PREP: 30 minutes
COOK: 40 minutes
MAKES: 6 servings
SERVING SIZE: 2 *tikkies*

What makes simple potato patties a chaat are the toppings. The sweet, sour, and spicy chutneys, creamy yogurt, a sprinkle of onions and cilantro, and a dash of this and that—every vender has his specialty. *Aloo-tikki* is one of the standard chaats available at most kiosks. When you ordered a plate of *aloo-tikki*, the vendor takes two *tikkies* and swiftly moves them into the hot oil for a few seconds, flips them into a dried leaf bowl (disposable plate) and methodically adds yogurt, chutneys, boiled *chane* (chickpeas), onions, and spices. You have just a few seconds for any special requests, such as "Hold the onions, please," before the chaat is done and in your hands. When I make *tikkies* at home, my son always says, "Mom, yours are better, but the experience of eating it at the kiosk is special." I have to agree.

POTATO PATTIES (*ALOO-TIKKIES*)

5 to 7 medium (2 pounds) white potatoes such as russet or Idaho

1 teaspoon salt

TOPPINGS

1 (15-ounce) can chickpeas or 1½ cups boiled black chana

1 cup soy yogurt, blended, optional

½ cup red onions, finely chopped

3 tablespoons Instant Sweet-and-Sour Chutney (page 187) or Tamarind Chutney (page 184)

Roasted cumin powder, for garnish (page 25)

Cayenne pepper, to taste

Salt, to taste

2–3 tablespoons canola or vegetable oil for frying

1. Wash potatoes. In a large skillet, add potatoes and enough water to about 2 inches above the potatoes. Bring water to a boil on medium-high heat, reduce heat, and boil for 20 to 28 minutes, until the potatoes are done. To check doneness, insert a knife into the potatoes; it should easily pierce the potatoes. Drain the potatoes into a large colander. Cool to room temperature.

2. *In the meantime, set up your chaat assembly station:* Rinse and drain the chickpeas. Whisk the yogurt until smooth, if using. Prepare the chutney, if needed. Have cumin powder and cayenne pepper handy.

3. Peel potatoes and mash with a potato masher to desired consistency. Sprinkle potatoes with salt and mix well with hands. Mixture should come together like dough. Divide potato dough into 12 parts and make round, smooth patties. You may need to oil your hands if potatoes stick to your hands.

4. Preheat electric griddle to 250°F, or heat *tava/iron* griddle on medium heat. Coat the griddle with small amounts of oil. Place the patties about 1 inch apart. Drizzle small amounts of oil around each *tikki*, and cook until brown on one side, about 8 to 10 minutes. Turn patties over, drizzle small amount of oil around each patty, and brown the other side. Using a spatula, slightly flatten each patty.

5. *Assemble tikki-chaat:* Place 2 *tikkies* on a plate; add about 2 tablespoons chickpeas, 2 tablespoons yogurt, if using, 1 tablespoon onion; drizzle with small amount of chutney; and sprinkle with cumin powder, cayenne pepper, and salt, to taste.

NUTRITION INFORMATION PER SERVING: Calories: 339; Total Fat: 9 g (Saturated Fat: 0.5 g); Carbohydrate: 53 g; Protein: 9 g; Fiber: 9 g; Sodium: 601 mg

---

Chickpea-Potato Snack

Chana-Aloo Chaat

PREP: 10 minutes
COOK: 0 minutes
MAKES: 4 servings
SERVING SIZE: ½ cup

My mom would sometimes have this quick snack ready for us when we came home from school. It was always filling, fun, and tasty. Eat it as a snack or as a salad. It's even easier now with canned chickpeas.

1 (16 oz) can chickpeas

1 medium boiled potato (about 1 cup chopped)

2 tablespoons cilantro, finely chopped

2 tablespoons lemon or lime juice

½ teaspoon roasted cumin powder (page 25)

¼ teaspoon salt

¾ teaspoon chaat masala (page 24), or purchased

¼ cup Tamarind Chutney (page 184), optional

¼ teaspoon cayenne pepper, optional

1. Drain and rinse the chickpeas. Place in a small serving bowl.

2. Peel and chop boiled potato into ¼-inch pieces. Add to the chickpeas. Add cilantro and stir.

3. In a small bowl, mix lemon juice, cumin powder, salt, and chaat masala. Pour over the chickpea mixture and stir. Let stand for about 10 minutes.

4. Enjoy as is or before serving, on each individual serving, drizzle 1 tablespoon of Tamarind Chutney and cayenne pepper, to taste, if desired.

GF, LF

....

Orange-Ginger Sherbet

Santara Sherbet

PREP: 10 minutes
COOK: 10 minutes
MAKES: 12 servings
SERVING SIZE: ½ cup

Growing up in India, I drank lots of orange squash concentrate in the summer. It was nothing more than orange-flavored sugar syrup added to water to quench the afternoon thirst. Sherbets (also called squash) have lost their popularity since the advent of soft drinks. I use fresh oranges to prepare this drink, although you can make it with prepared orange juice.

½ cup sugar

3 tablespoons ginger, peeled and grated

2 tablespoons orange zest

1 tablespoon lemon zest

3½ cups water, divided

6 oranges (about 3 cups of orange juice)

1 lime or lemon (about 2 tablespoons juice)

Thin strips of orange and lime or lemon rinds, for garnish, optional

1. In a small skillet, combine sugar, ginger, orange zest, lemon zest, and 1 cup water. Bring to a boil over medium heat. Reduce heat and simmer for 10 minutes. Let cool completely. Strain the liquid and discard the pulp.

2. In the meantime, squeeze out the juice of oranges and lime. Strain the juices in a strainer. Using the back of a spoon, squeeze out all the juice from the pulp. Discard the pulp.

3. In a juice pitcher, combine the zest liquid and strained juices. Add the remaining 2½ cups of cold water. Stir and refrigerate until completely chilled.

4. Stir before serving. Garnish with orange and lime rinds, if desired.

GF, LF

....

Mango Lemonade

Aam Neembu Pani

PREP: 10 minutes
COOK: 0 minutes
MAKES: 4 servings
SERVING SIZE: 1 cup

With the availability of mango nectar these days, it's easy to enjoy this beverage any time.

2 cups cold water

⅓ cup lemon or lime juice

⅓ cup sugar or sugar substitute equivalent

1 cup mango nectar

Crushed ice

Mint leaves, for garnish, optional

1. In a medium pitcher, mix water, lemon juice, and sugar. Add the mango nectar.

2. Serve over crushed ice. Garnish with mint leaves, if desired.

Lemonade

Neembu Pani

PREP: 10 minutes

COOK: 0 minutes

MAKES: 4 servings

SERVING SIZE: 1 cup

This is an Indian version of lemonade. These days, the lemonade stands at the amusement park or the state fair take me back to the *neembu-pani* kiosks in India. When lemons are in abundance and it's scorching-hot outside, *neembu pani*— also known as *shikanji*—is a welcome treat after the afternoon siesta.

¼ cup lemon or lime juice

⅓ cup sugar or sugar substitute equivalent

4 cups cold water or club soda

¼ teaspoon black salt or salt

⅛ teaspoon white pepper or black pepper

Crushed ice

4 lemon slices, for garnish

1. In a medium pitcher, mix lemon juice, sugar, and water. Stir in salt and white pepper.

2. Pour over crushed ice and garnish with lemon slice.

NUTRITION INFORMATION PER SERVING:
Calories: 64; Total Fat: 0 g (Saturated Fat: 0 g); Carbohydrate: 17 g; Protein: 0 g; Fiber: 0 g; Sodium: 145 mg

Basil-Ginger Herbal Tea

Tulsi-Adrak Chai

PREP: 5 minutes

COOK: 5 minutes

MAKES: 2 servings

SERVING SIZE: 1 cup

Tulsi is holy basil. The *tulsi* plant is found in many Hindu homes in India, and it is worshiped. *Tulsi* is known for its medicinal properties and is used in tea during winter to prevent colds and flu. You can add *tulsi* to the brewing tea leaves or make an herbal tea with *tulsi* leaves on their own. Ginger complements this tea in flavor and medicinal properties. Use tender leaves of any organic basil as a substitute for holy basil.

2 cups water

2 teaspoons ginger, grated

¼ cup *tulsi*, or any small tender organic basil leaves
Sugar, optional

1. In a small saucepan, boil water. Add ginger and *tulsi*. Remove from heat and steep for 3 to 5 minutes.

2. Strain tea. Serve hot, and add sugar, if desired.

NUTRITION INFORMATION PER SERVING:
Calories: 0; Total Fat: 0 g (Saturated Fat: 0 g); Carbohydrate: 0 g; Protein: 0 g; Fiber: 0 g; Sodium: 0 mg

Pomegranate Tea

Anari Chai

PREP: 5 minutes
COOK: 5 minutes
MAKES: 4 servings
SERVING SIZE: 1 cup

Pomegranate is a powerhouse of nutrients. It is now on many superfoods lists; loaded with antioxidants, it's great for preventing disease. Pomegranate juice is now easily available in supermarkets and natural foods stores.

3 cups water

4 cardamom pods, crushed open

1 cinnamon stick

2 teabags or 2 teaspoons tea leaves

3 tablespoons sugar

1 cup pomegranate juice

1. In a small saucepan, boil water with cardamom pods and cinnamon stick. Add tea bags and sugar. Remove from heat and steep for 3 to 5 minutes.

2. Remove teabags and strain tea into a pitcher or teapot. Stir in pomegranate juice. Serve hot or cold over ice.

NUTRITION INFORMATION PER SERVING: Calories: 75; Total Fat: 0 g (Saturated Fat: 0 g); Carbohydrate: 19 g; Protein: 0 g; Fiber: 0 g; Sodium: 2 mg

Green Mango Drink

Panna

PREP: 5 minutes
COOK: 15 minutes
MAKES: 8 servings
SERVING SIZE: 1 cup

This is one of those drinks that went out of style with all the bottled soft drinks available in India now. When I was growing up, it was a popular summer drink. I remember being told it would protect us against sunstroke and dehydration. Later, I realized that because mangoes are high in potassium and because the drink contains salt and sugar, *panna* replenishes the electrolytes, similar to Gatorade-type drinks.

2 raw green mangoes (about 1 pound)

7 cups cold water, divided

2 teaspoons salt

½ cup sugar

1 teaspoon roasted cumin powder (page 25)

½ teaspoon black pepper

2–3 tablespoons lemon or lime juice

¼ cup mint leaves

Crushed ice

1. Peel and slice the mangoes into large pieces. Discard pits.

2. In a medium saucepan, boil the mango slices with 2 cups of water for 5 minutes. Cool for about 10 minutes.

3. In a blender, grind the boiled mangoes with the water. Strain and discard fibrous pulp, if any. Pour into a serving pitcher.

4. Add salt, sugar, cumin powder, black pepper, and lemon juice. Stir well until sugar is dissolved. Add the remaining 5 cups of water. (You may need to adjust the lemon juice based on the tartness of the mangoes and personal taste preference.)

5. Finely chop about 2 tablespoons of mint leaves and add to mixture. Refrigerate to cool completely.

6. Serve over crushed ice. Garnish with remaining mint leaves.

NUTRITION INFORMATION PER SERVING:
Calories: 82; Total Fat: 0 g (Saturated Fat: 0 g); Carbohydrate: 21 g; Protein: 0 g; Fiber: 1 g; Sodium: 582 mg

---

GF, LF

Spicy-Sour Drink

Jal-Jeera

PREP: 10 minutes
COOK: 0 minutes
MAKES: 10 servings
SERVING SIZE: ¾ cup

The thought of *jal-jeera* makes my mouth water. It awakens all your taste buds: sour, salty, spicy, and sweet. Traditionally, *jal-jeera* is a roadside drink, usually sold on a stand in a large earthen pot. It is also the filling for *pani-puri*, a chaat made with crispy, tiny, puffed breads. Drink it by itself or purchase *pani-puri* shells from an Indian grocery and fill them with *jal-jeera*. For best results, use fresh tamarind sauce instead of paste for this recipe.

½ cup mint leaves, loosely packed

½ cup tamarind sauce (page 25) or 1 tablespoon tamarind paste

1 teaspoon roasted cumin powder (page 25)

1 teaspoon black salt

2 teaspoons salt

1 teaspoon cayenne pepper

6 cups cold water

1 tablespoon sugar

¼ cup lemon or lime juice

Carrot or celery sticks (4 to 6 inches long), for garnish

¼ cup boondi, optional (see Tip, below)

1. In a small blender jar, place mint leaves, tamarind sauce, cumin powder, black salt, salt, and cayenne pepper. Blend until a paste-like consistency forms.

2. Add water to a serving pitcher. Add the mint paste. Add sugar and lemon juice. Mix well.

3. Refrigerate for 4 hours or more. Stir before serving. Serve in small glasses with a carrot stick for stirring. Add a little bit of boondi in each glass, if desired.

TIP: If available in an Indian store near you, use boondi for extra flavor and taste. Soak boondi in lukewarm water for 5 minutes. Strain and discard the soaking water. Add boondi to the prepared *jal-jeera*.

NUTRITION INFORMATION PER SERVING:
Calories: 5; Total Fat 0 g: (Saturated Fat: 0 g); Carbohydrate: 1 g; Protein: 0 g; Fiber: 0 g; Sodium: 695 mg

---

Breakfast, Light Meals, and Soups

SINCE INDIAN VEGETARIANS do not eat eggs, egg dishes were never a part of the breakfast meal. Breakfast meats (for nonvegetarians) such as bacon and sausages were traditionally not available in India and are still not popular, so there is no need for meat substitutes for breakfast. But milk and yogurt are often served for breakfast. Today most Indians (wherever they live) prefer to eat toast and cereal for breakfast, with a special Indian breakfast served on weekends, much like Westerners enjoy.

Indians also serve foods similar to pancakes, crepes, and porridge for breakfast with one major exception—the food is savory and spicy instead of sweet and syrupy. In north India, *Cheele* or *pude* (similar to pancakes), and *parathas* and *puri* are the most popular breakfast items. In south India, *idli* (page 85) and *dosas* (page 83) are more popular for breakfast, although in the north they are served for lunch or dinner. When I visited south India recently, I was surprised that *dosa* was available only at breakfast. That goes to show that what we perceive as breakfast food is very much a regional tradition. Sweets such as *halwa* and *jalebi* are served only on special occasions. Eat whatever you like for breakfast as long as it's satisfying and nutritious.

Light Meals and Soups

What is a light meal? What one terms a light meal can be considered heavy by another. A light meal is one that is untypical and is often a simple meal, such as sandwiches. It's an individual perception, rather than a nutritional fact. Along with breakfast/brunch items, I've also added sandwiches or burgers to this category. Sandwiches and soups are becoming increasing popular as part of international fusion cooking.

Soups once associated with intercontinental dishes in India are the new craze. I'm sharing a few soups that you'll enjoy adding to your soup collection. These soups have all the Indian flavors, are naturally low in fat, and are perfect for a light meal or as appetizers.

Tomato and corn soups have become very popular in India. *Rasam*, a hot and tangy soup of south India, will clear your sinuses and leave you wanting more. Enjoy Indian soups with any crusty whole grain loaf bread, a flatbread, croutons, or a scoop of rice.

> Typically, Indians do not use soup stock to cook soups but instead simply simmer the vegetables or beans in the water and then add seasonings. The simmering enhances the flavor of the soup, as stocks do.

Cracked Wheat Pilaf

Uppama

PREP: 10 minutes
COOK: 10 minutes
MAKES: 6 servings
SERVING SIZE: ½ cup

Think of *uppama* as a savory cream of wheat or a pilaf. The most popular *uppama* is made of cream of wheat and is a quick and easy breakfast dish. Cracked wheat makes a heartier and nuttier *uppama*.

1 cup cracked wheat (bulgur) or cream of wheat

2 tablespoons canola or vegetable oil

1 teaspoon brown mustard seeds

½ cup onion, thinly sliced

6–8 curry leaves

2 teaspoons (split, hulled) chana dal

½ cup green beans, cut into ¼-inch pieces

1 cup carrots, diced into ¼-inch pieces

½ teaspoon cayenne pepper, or to taste

¾ teaspoon salt

2 cups water

¼ cup roasted peanuts, coarsely chopped, optional

1. Dry-roast cracked wheat in a heavy fry pan on medium heat, stirring frequently for 4 to 5 minutes, until the cracked wheat turns light brown. Transfer to a plate and set aside.

2. Heat oil in the same fry pan over medium-high heat. Add mustard seeds, cover with a lid, and fry for a few seconds until mustard seeds stop popping. Add onion and fry 2 to 3 minutes until golden brown. Add curry leaves and chana dal. Cook for a few seconds until dal is light brown.

3. Add green beans, carrots, cayenne pepper, and salt. Stir for a few seconds. Add water and bring to a boil.

4. Add the roasted cracked wheat to boiling water. Stir well, breaking up any lumps, until the cracked wheat is well mixed with the water. Cover with a lid, reduce heat, and simmer for 10 to 12 minutes until most of the water is absorbed.

5. Let stand until ready to serve. Stir, and garnish with roasted peanuts, if desired, just before serving.

NUTRITION INFORMATION PER SERVING:
Calories: 171; Total Fat: 5 g (Saturated Fat: 0.5 g); Carbohydrate: 27 g; Protein: 4 g; Fiber: 2 g; Sodium: 313 mg

---

Veggie Noodles

Savai Uppama

PREP: 5 minutes
COOK: 15 minutes
MAKES: 6 servings
SERVING SIZE: ¾ cup

Children and adults alike love this newfangled dish. *Savai* (noodles) used to be made by hand and were primarily used to make a pudding dessert on special occasions. With the arrival of commercially prepared noodles in India in the late 1980s, people became creative and started making all kinds of dishes with *savai*. Children loved it, and mothers could whip up some *savai* to feed a hungry crew any time. It's become one of the standard breakfast or lunch items in our house.

 1 cup savai (thin semolina noodles)
 1½ tablespoons canola or vegetable oil
 ½ teaspoon brown mustard seeds
 ½ cup onion, finely chopped

 1 to 2 teaspoons green chiles, finely chopped, optional
 ½ cup frozen peas★
 ½ cup carrots, diced into ¼-inch pieces★
 2 cups water, divided
 ½ teaspoon salt

1. Heat a medium nonstick fry pan on medium heat. Add the savai, and dry-roast until light brown, about 3 minutes. Remove from pan and set aside.

2. In the same fry pan, heat oil on medium-high heat. Add the mustard seeds, cover with lid, and fry for a few seconds until the mustard seeds stop popping. Remove lid. Add the onion and fry until light brown. Stir in the green chiles, if using.

3. Add the peas and carrots and ½ cup water. Bring to a boil. Cover with lid, reduce heat, and simmer for 5 to 7 minutes until vegetables are tender.

4. Add the salt and remaining water. Bring to a boil.

5. Add the noodles and stir. Bring to a boil, reduce heat to low, cover with lid, and simmer for 5 to 7 minutes until noodles are cooked and the water is absorbed.

6. Let stand covered until ready to serve. Serve hot.

NUTRITION INFORMATION PER SERVING:
Calories: 89; Total Fat: 4 g (Saturated Fat: 0.5 g); Carbohydrate: 13 g; Protein: 2 g; Fiber: 1 g; Sodium: 216 mg

---

★Use 1 cup frozen peas and carrots instead of peas and fresh carrots.

·:

Stuffed Mung Bean Pancakes

Bharva Cheele

SOAK: 2 hours to overnight
PREP: 15 minutes
COOK: 30 minutes
MAKES: 6 servings
SERVING SIZE: 2 *cheele*

Cheele are like pancakes or crepes, depending on how they are made. For this recipe, aim for a thickness somewhere between the two. The first time I had these stuffed *cheele* was at a wedding, in India. A chef was making hot *cheele* on a large griddle, and stuffing them to order. I liked them so much that I now make them for breakfast, especially when I have guests—they make an impressive display.

1 cup (split, hulled) mung dal

¾ cup water

½ teaspoon salt

1 cup tomatoes, finely chopped

½ cup red onion, finely chopped

2 tablespoons ginger, peeled and chopped

1–2 tablespoons green chile, finely chopped, optional

¼ cup cilantro, finely chopped

2 tablespoons canola or vegetable oil

1. Wash mung dal in 3 to 4 changes of water. Soak for 2 hours or overnight. Rinse in 1 to 2 changes of water. Drain the water.

2. In a food processor, grind dal with ¾ cup water to a slightly coarse batter. Transfer to a mixing bowl. Mix in salt.

3. Place all the chopped vegetables in individual bowls or on a large plate, keeping them separate. This allows you to individualize the filling as needed. (For example, children may not like the ginger or green chiles.)

4. Heat a nonstick fry pan or a grill pan on medium-high heat or preheat an electric grill pan to 400°F.

5. Lightly coat the pan with oil. Wipe off excess oil. Pour about 3 tablespoons of batter on the heated pan, and immediately with the back of a large spoon spread the batter to about 4- to 5-inch-wide circles. Pour ½ teaspoon of oil around the edges and cook until the edges start lifting from the pan. Cook for 3 to 4 minutes until one side is light brown. Lift gently and flip it over. Cook for another minute.

6. Flip *cheele* back to the first side. Place a little bit of tomatoes, onions, ginger, green chiles, and cilantro on one half of the cheele. Fold over. Gently press the filling.

7. Serve hot with Cilantro Chutney (page 185).

NOTE: If desired, make all the plain *cheele* first. Reheat and fill the *cheele* just before serving.

Refrigerate the mung bean batter for up to 3 days, and make fresh *cheele*, as desired.

FREEZING DIRECTIONS: Leftover dough can be frozen for up to 6 months. Thaw in refrigerator overnight. If necessary, add 1 to 2 tablespoons of water for desired consistency before making *cheele*. You can also freeze the prepared plain *cheele* for up to 1 month. Thaw at room temperature, reheat in a preheated pan, and fill as above.

NUTRITION INFORMATION PER SERVING:
Calories: 172; Total Fat: 5 g (Saturated Fat: 0.5 g); Carbohydrate: 24 g; Protein: 9 g; Fiber: 2 g
Sodium: 201 mg

VARIATION: If desired, add grated firm tofu in the filling.

···

Buckwheat-Zucchini Pancakes

Kuttu Cheele

PREP: **5 minutes**
COOK: **15 minutes**
MAKES: **6 servings**
SERVING SIZE: **2 *cheele***

Indian cooks use buckwheat primarily when they want to avoid grains (such as during fasts); buckwheat dishes are typically wheat-free and gluten-free. These *cheele* are soft and taste best when eaten fresh. Serve them with a sweet chutney, like tamarind or mango chutney, or pour some maple syrup over them, if desired.

> 1 cup buckwheat flour (kuttu atta)
> ⅞ cup water
> ¾ teaspoon salt
> ½ teaspoon ajwain, optional
> 2 teaspoons sugar
> ½ teaspoon cayenne pepper, or to taste
> ½ cup boiled potatoes, finely mashed
> 1 cup grated zucchini
> 2 tablespoons canola or vegetable oil

1. In a medium bowl, mix buckwheat, water, salt, ajwain, sugar, and cayenne pepper. Stir in mashed potatoes and grated zucchini. Let stand for 5 to 10 minutes.

2. Heat iron griddle on medium-high heat or use an electric griddle heated to 400°F. Lightly oil the griddle and wipe off the oil. Pour ¼ cup of batter onto the hot griddle and spread to a 3-inch circle. Add small amounts of oil on all sides and on top of the *cheele*. (You can cook several *cheele* at a time, based on the size of your griddle.)

3. Cook for 3 to 4 minutes until edges appear brown and the *cheele* comes off easily. Turn them over and cook for 1 minute.

4. Serve hot with chutney of choice.

NUTRITION INFORMATION PER SERVING:
Calories: 122; Total Fat: 5 g (Saturated Fat: 0.5 g); Carbohydrate: 17 g; Protein: 3 g; Fiber: 2 g; Sodium: 326 mg

---

···

Bean Burgers

Dal-Vada Burgers

PREP: **10 minutes**
COOK: **15 minutes**
MAKES: **4 servings**
SERVING SIZE: **1 sandwich**

Sandwiches are an easy way to enjoy a meal without a plate. Although not traditional Indian food, sandwiches are enjoyed by everyone today. If you like veggie burgers made with beans, you'll love these. This is my version of a bean burger that is easy to make and fun to eat.

> 1 (16-ounce) can chickpeas
> ¼ cup scallions (white and green parts), finely chopped
> ½ cup carrots, peeled and grated
> 2 teaspoons ginger, peeled and grated
> ½ teaspoon ground cumin
> ½ teaspoon salt
> 2 teaspoons green chiles, finely chopped, or to taste
> ½ teaspoon cayenne pepper, or to taste
> 1 tablespoon lemon or lime juice
> 2 tablespoons cilantro, finely chopped
> 2 tablespoons bread crumbs
> 2 tablespoons canola or vegetable oil
> 4 whole wheat hamburger buns
> 4 tomato slices, garnish
> 4 onion slices, garnish
> Cilantro Chutney (page 185), optional
> Tomato ketchup, optional

1. Drain and rinse the canned chickpeas. In a food processor, grind the beans until smooth.

2. In a medium mixing bowl, combine ground beans, scallions, carrots, ginger, cumin, salt, green chiles, cayenne pepper, lemon juice, cilantro, and bread crumbs. Mix well.

3. Oil your palms and make 4 patties. Set aside.

4. Heat 2 tablespoons oil on medium-high heat in a large skillet. Add patties and grill for 5 to 7 minutes on each side until golden brown. (If needed, add a little more oil to help brown the patties.)

5. In the meantime, lightly oil the buns and grill in a fry pan or a griddle until light brown.

6. Place a patty on the bottom half of bun, top with tomatoes, onions, cilantro chutney, and tomato ketchup, as desired.

NOTE: You can make the patties up to 1 day ahead and grill them when ready to eat. For a grilling party, fully prepare the patties and reheat on grill on aluminum foil.

NUTRITION INFORMATION PER SERVING:
Calories: 311; Total Fat: 11 g (Saturated Fat: 1 g); Carbohydrate: 45 g; Protein: 11 g; Fiber: 10 g; Sodium: 679 mg

---

Veggie Sloppy Joe Sandwiches

Pav-Bhaji

PREP: **15 minutes**
COOK: **40 minutes**
MAKES: **12 servings**
SERVING SIZE: **1 sandwich**

*P*av means "buns" and *bhaji* translates to "vegetables," so *pav-bhaji* is "vegetables on a bun." When I first saw sloppy joe sandwiches (ground loose meat on a bun), they reminded me of *pav-bhaji*. Although now available everywhere and a popular quick meal made at home, *pav-bhaji* is very much a Mumbai treasure. The Juhu beach in Mumbai is lined with street vendors selling their famous *pav-bhaji*. A large, shallow pan sits on a stove in the middle of the cart piled with prepared *bhaji*. Each order is individualized, but you have to speak up—quickly. Once you have ordered, the vendor scoops a heaping spoonful of *bhaji* on a hot griddle, adds a scoop of butter, and cooks until bubbling hot, grills the buns, piles on the *bhaji*, and spices it up with onions, chopped cilantro, and chutney. The traditional *pav-bhaji* is loaded with butter and will just melt in your mouth. I love the flavor of all the vegetables slow-cooked to perfection in this recipe, which is made with very little fat.

3 medium potatoes (about 3 cups), boiled

4 tablespoons canola or vegetable oil, divided

1½ cups onions, finely chopped

3 cups cauliflower florets, cut into ½-inch pieces

½ cup green peppers, cut into ¼-inch pieces

1 cup frozen peas

½ cup carrots, diced into ¼-inch pieces

2½ cups water, divided

½ teaspoon turmeric

1 teaspoon salt

2½ cups tomatoes, finely chopped

1½ tablespoons *pav-bhaji* masala, purchased*

12 small wheat or white buns

1 tablespoon lemon or lime juice

¼ cup red onion, finely chopped, for garnish

¼ cup cilantro, finely chopped, for garnish

Cilantro Chutney (page 185), optional

1. Peel boiled potatoes. Coarsely break up the potatoes with your fingers or chop them into about ½-inch pieces. Set aside.

2. Heat 3 tablespoons of oil in a medium skillet on medium-high heat. Add onion and fry 1 to 2 minutes until transparent. Add cauliflower, green peppers, peas, and carrots. Stir in 1 cup water, turmeric, and salt. Bring to a boil, reduce heat, cover, and simmer for about 12 minutes.

3. Add tomatoes and *pav-bhaji* masala and ½ cup water. Cook for another 5 to 7 minutes. Stir the vegetables, mashing and blending any large pieces.

4. Add the mashed potatoes and the remaining 1 cup water. Bring to a boil, reduce heat, and simmer for 12 to 15 minutes. Adjust the salt and cayenne pepper, to taste.

5. While the vegetables are cooking, lightly oil the bun halves with the remaining oil. Grill the buns in a fry pan or a griddle, oil-side down, until light brown.

6. To assemble sandwiches, place about ½ cup vegetables on a bun, garnish with chopped onions, cilantro, and cilantro chutney, as desired, and cover with top of bun. Or, serve as an open-faced sandwich.

*Pav-Bhaji Masala: Most Indian grocery stores now carry prepared *pav-bhaji* masala. If desired, substitute 1 tablespoon ground coriander, ¼–½ teaspoon cayenne pepper, 1 teaspoon amchur, and 1½ teaspoons garam masala for the *pav-bhaji* masala.

NUTRITION INFORMATION PER SERVING:
Calories: 212; Total Fat: 7 g (Saturated Fat: 0.5 g); Carbohydrate: 35 g; Protein: 6 g; Fiber: 6 g; Sodium: 369 mg

GF, LF

··

Mung Bean Crepes
Passhirattu Dosa

SOAK: **4 hours or overnight**
PREP: **15 minutes**
COOK: **60 minutes**
MAKES: **12 servings**
SERVING SIZE: **1 *dosa***

These *dosa* are thin like crepes, but do not compare them to French crepes in taste or texture. This *dosa* is easy to make and has a very different taste than the traditional white *dosa* you may be familiar with. It is not fermented and thus requires less planning. I soak the mung beans and rice in the evening and make the *dosa* the next morning. Enjoy them plain or with a potato filling. Serve them with a coconut-based chutney of choice.

1 cup whole mung beans

¼ cup long-grain rice

1 tablespoon ginger, peeled and chopped

1 tablespoon green chile, chopped, or to taste

1½ cups water, divided

2 teaspoons salt, or to taste

2 tablespoons cilantro, finely chopped

2 to 3 tablespoons canola or vegetable oil

2 cups Madras Potatoes (page 99), optional

1. Combine whole mung and rice in mixing bowl. Wash in 3 to 4 changes of water. Soak for 4 hours or overnight. Drain the water.

2. Combine dal mixture, ginger, green chiles, and 1 cup water. Grind half of the mixture at a time in a blender. Transfer ground mixture to a large bowl.

3. Mix in salt and cilantro. Add up to ½ cup water, to achieve a batter consistency. You may need to add 2 to 4 more tablespoons of water as you make the *dosas*, if the batter is too thick to spread.

4. Heat a nonstick fry pan or grill pan on medium-high heat or make the *dosas* on an electric grill pan heated to 400°F.

5. Lightly coat the pan with oil. Pour ¼ cup of batter in the center of the heated pan. With the back of a large spoon, immediately spread the batter into an 8-inch-wide circle, about the thinness of a crepe. Pour 1 teaspoon oil around the edges and cook until the edges start lifting from the pan. Cook for 3 to 4 minutes until one side is light brown. Gently lift *dosa*, flip over, and cook for 1 minute.

6. Serve *dosas* plain or stuff with potato filling (see Stuffed Dosa, below). Serve them with Tomato-Coconut Chutney (page 186) or Coconut Chutney (page 185).

> STUFFED DOSA: Use potato filling, Madras Potatoes (page 99). Cook *dosa* as above until step 5 and then flip the *dosa* to original side. Place about 2 tablespoons of potato filling in the center. Flip each side of the *dosa* over the filling, making a stuffed roll.

> NOTE: These are best served fresh cooked and hot. Refrigerate the leftover batter for up to 3 days and make fresh *dosa* when ready to eat.

NUTRITION INFORMATION PER SERVING: Calories: 95; Total Fat: 3 g (Saturated Fat: 0.5 g); Carbohydrate: 14 g; Protein: 4 g; Fiber: 3 g; Sodium: 197 mg

---

GF, LF

Bean-Rice Pancakes
Adai

SOAK: **4 hours to overnight**
PREP: **15 minutes**
COOK: **60 minutes**
MAKES: **12 servings**
SERVING SIZE: **1 *adai***

These pancake-like cakes are usually served for breakfast in southern India. I'm more likely to make them for dinner for a variation from my traditional dal *adai* and rice meal.

1 cup uncooked long-grain rice
½ cup (split, hulled) chana dal
¼ cup (split, hulled) urad dal
¼ cup (split, hulled) mung dal
1 tablespoon ginger, peeled and chopped
1 tablespoon green chile, finely chopped, or to taste
1 cup water
1 teaspoon salt
2 tablespoons cilantro, finely chopped
2–3 tablespoons canola or vegetable oil
½ onion, finely chopped

1. Combine rice and chana, urad, and mung dals in a mixing bowl. Wash in 3 to 4 changes of water. Soak for 4 hours or overnight. Rinse in 1 to 2 changes of water. Drain the water.

2. In a blender, grind the dal mixture with the ginger, green chile, and water. The mixture should be slightly coarse or grainy. Transfer to a large bowl.

3. Mix in salt and cilantro.

4. Heat a nonstick fry pan or grill pan on medium-high heat or make the *adai* on an electric grill pan heated to 400°F.

5. Lightly coat the pan with oil. Pour about ¼ cup of batter in the center of the heated pan and spread with the back of a large spoon to a 6-inch-wide circle. Pour 1 teaspoon oil around the edges and cook until the edges start lifting from the pan. Cook for 3 to 4 minutes until one side is light brown. Lift gently and flip it over. Cook for 1 minute. Repeat with remaining batter.

6. Flip *adai* back over and sprinkle each with 1 tablespoon of onions. Serve hot with Tomato-Coconut Chutney (page 186) or Coconut Chutney (page 185).

NOTE: These are best served fresh cooked and hot. Refrigerate the leftover batter for up to 3 days and make fresh *adai* when ready to eat.

NUTRITION INFORMATION PER SERVING: Calories: 139; Total Fat: 3 g (Saturated Fat: 0.5 g); Carbohydrate: 23 g; Protein: 5 g; Fiber: 1 g; Sodium: 200 mg

---

GF, LF

·.·

Quick Rice Dumplings
Quick Idli

SOAK TIME: **2 hours**
PREP: **20 minutes**
COOK: **10 minutes**
MAKES: **8 servings**
SERVING SIZE: **2 *idli***

*I*dli are steamed rice-and-bean dumplings. A southern Indian specialty, these are great anytime, although in the south you will only find them at breakfast. Making *idli* is a long process, as the batter has to be fermented overnight or longer. This quick and easy variation yields light and fluffy results every time. (For a traditional *idli* recipe, see my previous book, *New Indian Home Cooking*.) Serve *idli* with sambhar and coconut chutney.

⅓ cup (split, hulled) urad dal

¾ cup water, divided

⅞ cup cream of rice

¼ teaspoon salt

1 tablespoon lemon or lime juice

1 teaspoon ENO or baking powder

1. Wash urad dal in 3 to 4 changes of water until water is relatively clear. Soak for 2 hours or overnight. Drain dal in a strainer.

2. Place dal and ½ cup water into a blender jar. Grind to a fine paste.

3. In a small bowl, add cream of rice and ¼ cup of cold water. Mix well. Add the dal paste, salt, and lemon juice, and stir thoroughly. Let stand for 10 minutes.

4. Prepare the *idli* container★ and the steaming pot. Lightly brush or spray each *idli* indentation with oil. Place 1 cup water in the steaming pot and heat on medium-high heat.

5. Add ENO to batter just before ready to steam, and stir gently in circular motion. The mixture will start to bubble.

6. Fill *idli* container with rice mixture to the top line of the indentation, about ¼ cup each. Once the water is boiling, carefully place the filled *idli* container and cover with a lid. Once the steam is fully developed, reduce heat to medium and steam for 10 minutes. Remove the *idli* container and cool slightly. Using a butter knife, remove *idlies* and place in a container lined with a towel. Wrap with towel.

★An *idli* container is a gadget especially made for *idlies*. It comes in a stack of 3 to 4 trays with 4 concave dips in each tray, making 12 to 16 *idlies* at a time. The container has several holes to allow steam to pass through, which evenly steams the *idlies*. It may or may not come with its steaming pot. Find a large pot with lid that will comfortably hold the *idli* container with about 1 inch extra room above the top knob.

7. Serve warm with sambhar and Coconut Chutney (page 185).

> NOTE: If you do not have an *idli* container, use a 9-inch cake pan. Find a pot with a lid that is ½ inch larger than the cake pan, allowing the cake pan to easily slide in and out of the pot. Place a steamer rack or 1-inch-high ring at the bottom of the pot, and add water, covering the steam rack. The filled cake pan will rest on the rack to steam the *idli* dough. Follow the recipe above and place the dough in the oiled cake pan and steam as in step 6. Once steamed, using a butter knife, pass the knife around the edges, remove the *idli* from the container, and cut into 16 squares.

NUTRITION INFORMATION PER SERVING:
Calories: 104; Total Fat: 0 g (Saturated Fat: 0 g); Carbohydrate: 22 g; Protein: 3 g; Fiber: 1 g; Sodium: 138 mg

---

GF, LF

Lemon-Pepper Soup
Neembu Rasam

> PREP: 5 minutes
> COOK: 30 minutes
> MAKES: 8 servings
> SERVING SIZE: 1 cup

*R*asam is a southern Indian dish. It is a broth-like soup that is typically made with pigeon peas/toor dal as a base. There are numerous variations, but *rasams* are always flavorful and often quite spicy. I fell in love with this version the first time I tried it at my friend Simi's house. It was winter and I had a cold. The *rasam* was piping-hot and spicy, and it hit the spot as well as cleared my sinuses. Adjust the black pepper to your taste and enjoy this delicious soup by the cupful.

½ cup (split, hulled) toor dal

5 cups water, divided

¾ teaspoon salt

¼ teaspoon turmeric

½ teaspoon black pepper, or to taste

1 to 2 teaspoons green chiles, finely chopped, or to taste

4 tablespoons lemon or lime juice

1 tablespoon cilantro, chopped

SEASONING (*CHOUNK*)

1½ tablespoons canola or vegetable oil

½ teaspoon brown mustard seeds

½ teaspoon cumin seeds

¼ teaspoon asafetida powder

1–2 dried red chiles

6–8 curry leaves

1. Wash toor dal in 3 to 4 changes of water and drain.

2. (Cook toor dal in a pressure cooker or in a pan. To cook in pan, see Note below.) In a medium pressure cooker, add washed toor dal, 2 cups water, salt, and turmeric. Cover with the lid and put the pressure weight in place. Once pressure develops, reduce heat and cook under pressure for 5 minutes. Cool the cooker until the pressure is removed. Open the lid carefully. Using a wire whisk, blend the dal mixture until smooth.

3. Add the remaining 3 cups water, black pepper, and green chiles. Bring to a boil. Reduce heat and simmer for 10 minutes.

4. *Prepare seasoning:* In a small fry pan, heat the oil on medium-high heat. Add the mustard seeds, cover with lid, cook for a few seconds, until mustard seeds stop popping. Add cumin seeds, asafetida, and whole dried red chile. Cook for a few seconds, until cumin seeds turn brown. Remove from heat, add curry leaves, and cook for a few seconds.

5. Add seasoning to the *rasam*. Remove from heat.

6. Add lemon juice and chopped cilantro. Serve rasam hot in a soup bowl or cup.

> NOTE: *To cook in a skillet:* Soak the dal after washing it as in step 1 above. Soak the dal for 2 hours or longer. Combine drained dal, 4 cups of water, salt, and turmeric. Bring dal to a boil, reduce heat, and simmer for 25 to 30 minutes, until mixture is very soft. Follow steps 3 and 4 to finish the rasam. (You will need up to 6 or 7 cups of water when preparing in a pan, as it takes longer to cook and more water evaporates.)

NUTRITION INFORMATION PER SERVING:
Calories: 67; Total Fat: 3 g (Saturated Fat: 0 g); Carbohydrate: 8 g; Protein: 3 g; Fiber: 2 g; Sodium: 220 mg

GF, LF

·:·

Spicy Tomato Soup
Tamatar Rasam

PREP: 10 minutes
COOK: 30 minutes
MAKES: 8 servings
SERVING SIZE: 1 cup

This soup is like a tomato consommé on steroids. It's so flavorful, spicy, and delicious that you'll want to make it again and again.

½ cup (split, hulled) toor dal

8 cups water, divided

¾ teaspoon salt, divided

1 tablespoon ginger, peeled and grated

½ teaspoon turmeric

4 large tomatoes (about 1¼ pounds), coarsely chopped, or 1 cup tomato sauce

2 tablespoons rasam powder (page 25), or purchased

2 tablespoons lemon or lime juice

SEASONING (*CHOUNK*)

1 tablespoon canola or vegetable oil

½ teaspoon mustard seeds

⅛ teaspoon asafetida powder

½ teaspoon cumin seeds

2–3 dried red chiles

6–8 curry leaves

1. Wash toor dal in 3 to 4 changes of water and drain.

2. (Cook toor dal in a pressure cooker or in a pan. To cook in pan, see Note below.) In a pressure cooker, add washed toor dal, 2 cups water, ½ teaspoon salt, and turmeric. Cover with the lid and put the pressure weight in place. Once pressure develops, reduce heat and cook under pressure for 5 minutes. Cool the cooker until the pressure is removed. Open the lid carefully. Using a wire whisk, blend the dal mixture until totally smooth. (If necessary, strain the dal for a smooth consistency.)

3. In a separate 3- to 4-quart saucepan, add tomatoes, 2 cups water, and ¼ teaspoon salt. Boil for 10 minutes. Cool slightly. Using a hand mixer or blender, blend the tomato mixture until smooth. Strain the tomatoes and return to the saucepan.

4. Add dal to the tomatoes. Add 4 cups water and rasam powder. Bring to a boil. Reduce heat and simmer for 10 minutes. Remove from heat.

5. Add lemon juice, salt, and black pepper, and adjust seasonings to taste.

6. *Prepare seasoning:* In a small fry pan, heat the oil on medium–high heat. Add the mustard seeds, cover with lid, and cook for a few seconds, until mustard seeds stop popping. Add cumin seeds, asafetida, and whole dried red chile and cook for a few seconds, until cumin seeds turn brown. Remove from heat, add curry leaves, and cook for a few seconds.

7. Add seasoning to the rasam. Serve rasam hot in a soup bowl or a cup.

> NOTE: *To cook in a skillet:* Soak the dal after washing it as in step 1 above. Soak the dal for 2 hours or longer. Combine drained dal, 4 cups of water, salt, and turmeric. Bring dal to a boil, reduce heat, and simmer for 25 to 30 minutes, until the dal is very soft. Follow steps 3 and 4 to finish the rasam. (You will need up to 6 or 7 cups of water when preparing in a pan, as it takes longer to cook and more water evaporates.)

NUTRITION INFORMATION PER SERVING:
Calories: 76; Total Fat: 2 g (Saturated Fat: 0 g); Carbohydrate: 12 g; Protein: 4 g; Fiber: 3 g; Sodium: 225 mg

Curried Potato Soup
Aloo-Tamatar Soup

PREP: **10 minutes**
COOK: **20 minutes**
MAKES: **6 servings**
SERVING SIZE: **1 cup**

This is not your typical creamy potato soup. It is very low in fat and full of flavor. I grew up eating potato curry that was very watered down, for my dad loved to drink just the broth. Now, I just make it like a soup. I love to pack this for lunch, to accompany a sandwich.

2 medium potatoes (about 2 cups)
1 tablespoon canola or vegetable oil
2 tablespoons tomato sauce
½ teaspoon ground cumin
¼ teaspoon turmeric
1 teaspoon ginger, peeled and grated
2 teaspoons ground coriander
¼ teaspoon black pepper
4 cups water
¾ teaspoon salt
½ teaspoon garam masala (page 24)
1 tablespoon lemon or lime juice
1 tablespoon cilantro, chopped

1. Peel and wash potatoes. Cut into 1-inch pieces. Set aside.

2. Heat oil in a heavy saucepan over medium–high heat. Add potatoes, tomato sauce, cumin, turmeric, ginger, coriander, and black pepper. Stir for 2 to 3 minutes, coating the potatoes with spices.

3. Add water and salt. Bring to a boil. Reduce heat, cover with a lid, and simmer for 10 to 15 minutes. The potatoes should be tender and easily fall apart. Using the back of a spoon, break up some of the potato pieces. This will help the soup thicken.

4. Add the 2 remaining cups of water. Bring to a boil. Simmer for an additional 5 minutes. Stir in the garam masala and lemon juice.

5. Serve hot. Garnish with cilantro.

NUTRITION INFORMATION PER SERVING:
Calories: 77; Total Fat: 2 g (Saturated Fat: 0 g); Carbohydrate: 13 g; Protein: 2 g; Fiber: 2 g; Sodium: 323 mg

---

GF, LF

Mango Soup

Aam Soup

PREP: **10 minutes**
COOK: **15 minutes**
MAKES: **6 servings**
SERVING SIZE: **¾ cup**

In the summer, when mangoes are at their peak of flavor, my mom made this mango dish with *paratha*. Soft, plain *parathas* dipped in sweet-and-sour mango curry are heavenly. With the increased availability of mangoes, it's now possible to make this dish year-round.

½ pound (2–3) ripe mangoes

4 cups water, divided

1 tablespoon canola or vegetable oil

1 teaspoon cumin seeds

½ teaspoon turmeric

½ teaspoon salt

½ tablespoon ground coriander

¼–½ teaspoon cayenne pepper

1 teaspoon lemon or lime juice

1 tablespoon sugar

½ teaspoon garam masala (page 24)

2 tablespoons cilantro, chopped

1. Peel and chop half of 1 mango into ¼-inch pieces (about ½ cup) for garnish. Set aside.

2. Peel and slice the remaining mangoes, removing all the pulp from the pit. Discard the mango pits.

3. Add the mango slices and 2 cups of water in a blender jar and blend thoroughly. Strain the juice and discard the fibrous pulp, if any.

4. In a medium skillet, heat oil on medium-high heat. Add the cumin seeds and fry for a few seconds until golden brown. Add the mango juice and remaining 2 cups of water.

5. Add turmeric, salt, coriander, and cayenne pepper. Bring to a boil, reduce heat, and simmer for 7 to 8 minutes.

6. Add the lemon juice, sugar, and garam masala.

7. Serve hot. Garnish with cilantro and chopped mango.

NUTRITION INFORMATION PER SERVING:
Calories: 53; Total Fat: 2 g (Saturated Fat: 0 g); Carbohydrate: 9 g; Protein: 0 g; Fiber: 1 g; Sodium: 195 mg

---

Lentil-Vegetable Soup

Masoor-Subji Soup

PREP: 10 minutes
COOK: 30 minutes
MAKES: 8 servings
SERVING SIZE: ¾ cup

The mild seasoning of basil and pepper brings out the flavor of lentils. Use canned lentils for a quick and hearty soup. Serve with crusty bread or a rice pilaf.

2 tablespoons olive oil

1 cup onion, chopped into ½-inch pieces

1 teaspoon ginger, peeled and grated

1 teaspoon garlic, finely chopped

2 cups tomatoes, chopped

4 cups water

2 (16-ounce) cans lentils, drained, or 3 cups cooked lentils

1 cup carrots, diced into ½-inch pieces

2 cups cabbage, finely chopped

1 teaspoon salt

¼–½ teaspoon black pepper, to taste

2 tablespoons fresh basil (or holy basil, *tulsi*), chopped, or 1 teaspoon dried basil

½ teaspoon lemon zest

2 teaspoons lemon or lime juice

1. Heat oil in a large skillet on medium-high heat. Add onion and fry 1 to 2 minutes until transparent. Add ginger and garlic, cook for a few seconds. Stir in tomatoes. Cover and cook for 2 minutes. Mash the tomatoes with the back of a spoon or a potato masher.

2. Add water, lentils, carrots, cabbage, salt, black pepper, basil, and lemon zest. Bring to a boil. Reduce heat and simmer for 20 minutes.

3. Add lemon juice and serve hot.

NUTRITION INFORMATION PER SERVING:
Calories: 142; Total Fat: 4 g (Saturated Fat: 1 g); Carbohydrate: 21 g; Protein: 8 g; Fiber: 8 g; Sodium: 313 mg

Vegetables

VEGETABLES TAKE CENTER stage in an Indian meal. Indian vegetable dishes are unique in their preparation and are anything but boring. Although some raw vegetables are eaten as a relish (see Salads and Chutneys, page 183), it's the cooked vegetables that define the meal. Vegetables rarely, if ever, are just boiled and salted. Whether a simple dish or a lavish gourmet meal, cooks take pride in creating their special vegetable dishes. Even the plainest vegetable dish is seasoned with at least three spices, and the exquisite specialties may have up to eleven spices. Indian cooks are never bothered by the number of spices that go into a dish. They instinctively know that reducing the number of ingredients does not save time but can compromise the flavor, and they are never willing to do that. A sprinkle of this and that spice can totally change the flavor of the dish. That's a good thing, for if you're going to eat vegetables every day and at every meal, a variation in flavor yields a new dish.

Most of the vegetables in the Indian diet are now readily available in your local supermarket. I rarely have to go to an Indian or Chinese grocery store to buy vegetables. Even the local farmers market caters to the ethnic population and you can buy fresh vegetables like bitter melon and bottle gourds.

Methods of Preparation

The taste, appearance, and texture of the dish are determined by the seasonings and the cooking process. There are two primary ways of preparing vegetables (*subji*): either cooked dry (*sukhi subji*) or in a sauce (*tari subji*).

Braised (Dry) Vegetables (*Sukhi Subji*)

Calling the vegetable "dry" creates a misleading connotation but is the best translation of this type of vegetable dish. It is basically cooked with a minimum amount of water and does not have any gravy or curry-like sauce. The vegetables are seasoned with oil and spices and simmered in their own juices. The *sukhi subji* is often served with a meal that also has a dal or a yogurt dish, to add liquid. The notion of a completely dry meal—that is, a *sukhi subji* and a flatbread—is quite unpalatable to Indians. Something saucy is almost always served as an accompaniment. My parents were notoriously particular about this phenomenon. If for any reason we had just *parathas* (pan-fried flatbread) and a *sukhi subji* and we were out of yogurt, we would be served a glass of milk or tea to wash it down.

Most vegetables can be cooked dry or in a sauce. Some are better dry and some better in a sauce; there is no hard and fast rule. Personally, I find cauliflower, okra, and eggplant are best cooked dry, although small amounts of these vegetables can be a part of a saucy dish.

Vegetables in a Curry Sauce (*Tari Subji*)

The vegetables are seasoned with oil and spices and simmered in a fair amount of water until the spices and vegetables create a unique sauce. The consistency of the sauce can be different based on the vegetable and your personal preference. Onions, garlic, and ginger are used to thicken and flavor the sauces. Yogurt or cream (neither is used in these recipes) and/or nuts make the sauces richer. Thickeners such as cornstarch are rarely, if ever, used. The food is cooked down until the desired consistency is achieved.

There is another consistency that falls between the two methods of preparations; we call it *leeputwan*, meaning a sauce that clings to the vegetables. The consistency is similar to a thick stew. I will guide you to the best consistency for each vegetable dish on the following pages.

The Best Pan

I find that for cooking braised vegetables, a wide nonstick fry pan works best. A heavy skillet or a saucepan works well for curry sauce. Make sure the pan you use has a tight-fitting lid. You will often need to cover and simmer the vegetables. Occasionally, I use a pressure cooker to cook vegetables, but this requires extreme care, as the vegetables can easily be overcooked.

Fresh, Frozen, or Canned?

Whenever possible, I use fresh vegetables. The taste of fresh vegetables is unmatched—the best-tasting vegetables come from your own garden. But that said, I am more practical than a purist. I rarely use canned vegetables except beans and tomato products. I keep a good supply of tomato sauce and chopped and whole tomatoes. I always have a standing supply of frozen peas, spinach, green beans, and mixed vegetables. When I'm in a hurry, instead of forgoing vegetables I will reach for frozen ones. The type and the quality of frozen vegetables have improved significantly over the years. Some frozen vegetables actually taste better than the fresh ones available in the supermarket—for example, peas—and may even have more nutrients than fresh ones. Many "fresh" vegetables in grocery stores often don't arrive in the store until two weeks after being harvested and then they sit in our refrigerator.

Most of the vegetables used in this book are readily available in your local grocery store. You will find recipes from potatoes, carrots, and green beans to more unusual vegetables such as kohlrabi, eggplant, and okra. I have also included some recipes that use less familiar vegetables, such as bottle gourd and bitter melons. These are an acquired taste—but they deserve a try.

GF

Cauliflower and Peppers

Gobhi-Mirch Subji

PREP: **10 minutes**
COOK: **15 minutes**
MAKES: **6 servings**
SERVING SIZE: **½ cup**

Cauliflower is a much-desired vegetable among Indians. It is cooked by itself as well as mixed with other vegetables. The colored peppers with white cauliflower make this dish as pleasing to the eye as it is to the palate.

3 cups cauliflower, divided into 1-inch florets

3 cups green, yellow, and red peppers, cut into 1-inch squares

2 tablespoons canola or vegetable oil

¼ teaspoon asafetida powder

1 teaspoon cumin seeds

1 cup onion, ¼-inch thick slices

1 tablespoon ginger, peeled and grated

½ teaspoon turmeric

¾ teaspoon salt

2 teaspoons ground coriander

½ teaspoon cayenne pepper, or to taste

½ teaspoon amchur, or 2 teaspoons lemon juice

1. In a bowl, mix cauliflower and peppers. Set aside.

2. Heat oil in a heavy nonstick skillet over medium-high heat. Add asafetida and cumin seeds, and cook for a few seconds until seeds are golden brown. Add onion and fry 1 to 2 minutes until transparent. Stir in ginger.

3. Add vegetables and stir. Sprinkle with turmeric, salt, coriander, and cayenne pepper. Stir in a lifting and turning motion for 2 to 3 minutes, coating the vegetables with the spices.

4. Cover with the lid and reduce heat. Cook for 10 to 12 minutes, until cauliflower is tender. Stir the vegetables a couple of times. (The vegetables will cook in their own juices. If the vegetables tend to stick to the bottom, add 1 to 2 tablespoons of water.)

5. Sprinkle with amchur. Stir carefully in a lifting and turning fashion. Transfer to a serving platter. Do not cover the vegetables; otherwise they will continue to cook and become too soft.

NUTRITION INFORMATION PER SERVING:
Calories: 84; Total Fat: 5 g (Saturated Fat: 0.5 g); Carbohydrate: 9 g; Protein: 2 g; Fiber: 3 g; Sodium: 309 mg

---

Stuffed Cauliflower

Bharva Gobhi

PREP: **15 minutes**
COOK: **50 minutes**
MAKES: **8 servings**
SERVING SIZE: **½ cup**

This is an elaborate, special-occasion dish that is fun to make and serve. It never fails to arouse curious glances from guests—is it vegetarian?

1 medium head cauliflower (about 2 pounds)

1½ teaspoons salt, divided

1 cup water, divided

1 potato, boiled

2 medium raw potatoes (about 1 pound)

¼ cup canola or vegetable oil, divided

½ cup tomato sauce, or 1 medium tomato

1 cup onion, coarsely chopped

2 tablespoons ginger, peeled, and coarsely chopped

2 teaspoons garlic, coarsely chopped

1 teaspoon cumin seeds

1 green chile, chopped, or to taste

½ teaspoon turmeric

1 tablespoon ground coriander

½ teaspoon cayenne pepper, or to taste

½ teaspoon amchur, or 1 teaspoon lemon juice

½ teaspoon garam masala (page 24)

1. Remove the leaves and cut the stem at the base of the cauliflower, leaving the whole head intact. Wash the cauliflower, sprinkle with ½ teaspoon salt on all sides, and set aside.

2. Heat ½ cup water in a large skillet that can fit the whole cauliflower. Place a steamer rack in the pan. Place cauliflower on the steamer rack, cover with lid, and steam for 5 to 7 minutes, until the cauliflower is partially cooked. Carefully remove cauliflower and place in a baking dish or tray. Set aside.

3. Grate the boiled potato and set aside.

4. Preheat oven to 400°F.

5. Peel, wash, and slice the raw potatoes into ½-inch-thick circles. Place the sliced potatoes in a bowl and drizzle with 1 tablespoon of oil and ½ teaspoon salt. Stir to coat with oil. Place in a single layer on a baking tray. Set aside.

6. In a blender jar, combine tomato sauce, onion, ginger, garlic, cumin seeds, and green chiles. Grind to a paste. Set aside. (If needed, add 1 to 2 tablespoons of water to help grind the onions.)

7. Heat the remaining 2 tablespoons of oil in a nonstick fry pan on medium-high heat. Add the onion paste, cook until all the water evaporates and onion starts to come together in a dense mass, stirring frequently. Reduce heat to medium.

8. Add turmeric, coriander, cayenne pepper, amchur, and garam masala. Stir well, cook for about 2 minutes. Add ½ cup of water and stir well. Remove from heat.

9. Add the grated potatoes and ½ teaspoon of salt. Mix well to blend the spices.

10. Turn the cauliflower over, bottom side up, and carefully push about ⅓ of the onion masala into the holes. Turn the cauliflower over and layer the remaining onion masala on top of the cauliflower, completely covering the cauliflower.

11. Place the cauliflower and the potatoes (in separate trays) in preheated oven and bake for 20 to 25 minutes. Turn the potatoes once during cooking. Potatoes should be medium brown, cooked, and crispy. The cauliflower top should be brown and set.

12. To serve, place the cauliflower in the center of the serving tray and garnish with sliced baked potatoes. At the table, cut the cauliflower in thin wedges, and serve with 1 or 2 potato slices.

NUTRITION INFORMATION PER SERVING:
Calories: 121; Total Fat: 7 g (Saturated Fat: 0.5 g); Carbohydrate: 13 g; Protein: 3 g; Fiber: 4 g; Sodium: 553 mg

---

GF

·:·

Stuffed Banana Peppers

Besan Bhari Mirch

PREP: **15 minutes**
COOK: **15 minutes**
MAKES: **8 servings**
SERVING SIZE: **1 pepper**

Long, mild banana peppers are perfect for stuffing. The spiced *besan* (chickpea flour) paste fills the banana peppers as it cooks and expands. Serve this as a side dish with any meal.

8 banana peppers (about 1 pound)

⅔ cup besan

⅓ cup dry-roasted unsalted peanuts, coarsely ground

⅛ teaspoon asafetida powder

1 teaspoon cumin seeds

½ teaspoon turmeric

1 teaspoon salt

2 teaspoons ground coriander

½ teaspoon cayenne pepper, or to taste

1 teaspoon amchur, or 2 teaspoons lemon juice

2 tablespoons canola or vegetable oil

⅓ cup water

1. Wash and dry the peppers. Make a slit on one side from the stem end to the tip of the peppers, making an opening. Do not cut through the peppers. Set aside.

2. In a small bowl, mix together besan and ground peanuts. Add asafetida, cumin seeds, turmeric, salt, coriander, cayenne pepper, and amchur. Mix well. Add 1 tablespoon of oil and mix into the mixture, making it crumbly. Add the water and mix well. The mix will be thick and sticky.

3. Fill the peppers with batter. Using your thumbs to pry them open, add the batter, and with a finger spread the batter evenly into the opening. Fill the peppers about half full with batter. (Besan batter is very sticky and hard to work with. Some of the batter might stick to the outside of the peppers.)

4. Heat the remaining 1 tablespoon of oil in a large nonstick fry pan on medium-high heat. Add the stuffed banana peppers in a single layer, filled side up. Cover with lid and cook for 5 to 6 minutes until the peppers are tender (they change color and appear transparent. The besan stuffing will harden and fill the peppers). Turn the peppers occasionally using tongs, making sure to evenly brown all sides. Remove the lid and cook for another 2 minutes, turning occasionally.

5. Using tongs, transfer peppers to a serving dish. Discard any remaining oil.

NUTRITION INFORMATION PER SERVING:
Calories: 108; Total Fat: 7 g (Saturated Fat: 0.5 g); Carbohydrate: 8 g; Protein: 4 g; Fiber: 3 g; Sodium: 302 mg

---

Green Pepper Crumble

Besan Wali Shimla Mirch

PREP: 5 minutes
COOK: 15 minutes
MAKES: 6 to 8 servings
SERVING SIZE: ¼ cup

Besan (chickpea flour) adds a nutty taste and texture to these peppers. Cut the peppers into small pieces and cook them until just tender. The *besan* creates a light coating, making the mixture appear crumbly.

3 tablespoons canola or vegetable oil

½ teaspoon cumin seeds

½ cup besan

2 cups green peppers, chopped into ¼-inch pieces

¼ teaspoon turmeric

1 teaspoon ground coriander

¼ teaspoon cayenne pepper, or to taste

1 teaspoon salt

½ teaspoon amchur, or 1 teaspoon lemon juice

1. Heat oil in a heavy skillet on medium heat. Add cumin seeds and cook for a few seconds until golden brown. Add besan and mix well with the back of a spoon, breaking up any lumps. Cook for 2 to 3 minutes, until besan becomes bubbly.

2. Stir in the peppers. Add turmeric, coriander, cayenne pepper, and salt. Stir well. Reduce heat, cover, and cook for 6 to 8 minutes until peppers are slightly tender but still crunchy. Stir in amchur.

3. Immediately transfer to a serving bowl and leave open to avoid further cooking of the peppers.

NUTRITION INFORMATION PER SERVING:
Calories: 87; Total Fat: 7 g (Saturated Fat: 0.5 g); Carbohydrate: 6 g; Protein: 2 g; Fiber: 1 g; Sodium: 338 mg

Stuffed Baby Eggplant

Bharva Chote Baingun

PREP: 30 minutes
COOK: 30 minutes
MAKES: 6 servings
SERVING SIZE: ½ eggplant

This is an elegant as well as a delicious way to serve eggplants. Use small round eggplants (3 to 4 inches each). If you cannot find the little eggplants, use a large eggplant and cut it into pieces just before serving.

½ cup carrots, ¼-inch diced

½ cup potatoes, ¼-inch diced

½ cup frozen peas, thawed

3–4 small round eggplants (about 1½ pounds)

¾ teaspoon salt, plus extra for salting eggplants

3 tablespoons canola or vegetable oil, divided

½ cup onion, finely chopped

2 teaspoons green chile, finely chopped, or to taste

1 cup tomatoes, chopped

1 teaspoon ground cumin

½ teaspoon turmeric

2 teaspoons ground coriander

½ teaspoon fennel seeds, coarsely ground

½ cup water

1 teaspoon amchur, or 2 teaspoons lemon juice

1. Chop carrots and potatoes into ¼-inch pieces. In a small bowl, combine frozen peas, carrots, and potatoes. Set aside.

2. Cut the eggplants in half vertically from the stem down, leaving the stem on. Using a sharp knife, score the pulp about ½ inch from the skin. Scoop out the pulp with a spoon, making an eggplant shell. In a large bowl, mix cold water and 1 teaspoon salt and soak the eggplant. (This will help prevent the eggplants from browning.) Set aside.

3. Chop the eggplant pulp into small pieces and set aside.

4. In a large nonstick fry pan, heat 1 tablespoon oil on medium-high heat. Add onion and fry 2 to 3 minutes until golden brown. Add green chile and tomatoes. Stir, cover with lid, and cook for about 1 minute. Add cumin, turmeric, coriander, fennel seed powder, and salt and stir to mix. Add the eggplant pulp, peas, carrots, and potatoes. Stir in ½ cup water. Cover with lid, reduce heat, and simmer for 7 to 9 minutes, until the potatoes are fork-tender, stirring occasionally. Uncover and stir in amchur. Let cool for about 5 minutes.

5. Remove eggplant halves and pat dry inside and outside of the shells. Fill the eggplant shells with the stuffing.

6. Heat the remaining 2 tablespoons of oil on medium-high heat in a nonstick fry pan large enough to hold all the eggplant halves in a single layer. Add the stuffed eggplants with filled side up in a single layer. Cover with lid and cook for 5 to 7 minutes, until the eggplant shells are tender. (The bottom of the eggplants will be slightly burned.) Remove lid and cook for another 2 minutes.

7. Using tongs, transfer eggplants to a serving dish. Serve hot over bed of rice or with flatbread.

NUTRITION INFORMATION PER SERVING:
Calories: 123; Total Fat: 7 g (Saturated Fat: 0.5 g); Carbohydrate: 14 g; Protein: 2 g; Fiber: 5 g; Sodium: 413 mg

GF

Mashed Eggplant
Baingan Bharta

PREP: 10 minutes
COOK: 60 minutes
MAKES: 4 servings
SERVING SIZE: ¼ cup

*B*harta is usually made by grilling the eggplant until the skin is burned, giving the eggplant a smoky flavor. The charcoaled skin is removed and the tender inside pulp of the eggplant is spiced to perfection.

1 medium eggplant (about 1 pound)
2 tablespoons canola or vegetable oil
½ teaspoon cumin seeds
¾ cup onion, finely chopped
1 cup tomatoes, finely chopped
2 teaspoons green chiles, finely chopped, or ½ teaspoon cayenne pepper, to taste
2 teaspoons ground coriander
1 teaspoon fennel seeds, ground
½ teaspoon salt

1. (The eggplant can be grilled or baked in the oven.) Preheat grill.

2. Grill the eggplant on high heat for 20 to 30 minutes, turning periodically. (Or preheat the oven to 450°F. Lightly oil the eggplant, place in an oven-safe tray, and bake for 30 to 40 minutes, turning once or twice.) The skin of the eggplant will become dark brown to almost burned. Place in a bowl and cover with lid for 10 to 15 minutes.

Once the eggplant is cool enough to handle, slowly remove the skin, scraping all eggplant pulp from the skin. Keep all the juices that come out of the eggplant. Discard the skin. Mash the pulp with a fork and set aside. (You'll have about 1 cup pulp.)

3. Heat oil in a nonstick skillet over medium-high heat. Add cumin seeds and cook for a few seconds until golden brown. Add onion and fry 2 to 3 minutes until golden brown. Add tomatoes and green chiles. Cover and cook for 2 to 3 minutes. Mash the tomatoes with the back of a spoon or a potato masher, making a sauce-like consistency. Stir in coriander, fennel seed powder, and salt.

4. Stirring in a folding motion, add the mashed eggplant. Reduce heat and cook for 5 to 7 minutes, stirring occasionally, until the eggplant becomes shiny as the oil rises to the top. Transfer to a serving container and serve hot with flatbread and dal.

NOTE: If desired, especially in summer (eggplant season), grill or bake several eggplants at a time, remove the skin, and make pulp. Divide the eggplant into 1-cup portions and freeze up to 6 months. Thaw and follow steps 2 to 4.

NUTRITION INFORMATION PER SERVING:
Calories: 108; Total Fat: 7 g (Saturated Fat: 1 g); Carbohydrate: 11 g; Protein: 2 g; Fiber: 5 g; Sodium: 296 mg

---

Potato Stew
Lipte Aloo

PREP: **10 minutes**
COOK: **30 minutes**
MAKES: **6 servings**
SERVING SIZE: **½ cup**

Potato curry goes with anything. It is a favorite of children and adults alike. The curry or the sauce can be runny or fairly thick, depending on what you are in the mood for or what else you're serving. I use canned tomato sauce for convenience. Serve with *Puri* (page 166) and turn any meal into a festive one.

3 medium potatoes (about 3 cups), peeled and diced

½ teaspoon whole coriander seeds

¼ teaspoon fennel seeds

⅛ teaspoon asafetida powder

½ teaspoon cumin seeds

¼ teaspoon fenugreek seeds

3–4 whole red chiles

1 tablespoon canola or vegetable oil

¼ cup tomato sauce, or 1 medium tomato, crushed

½ teaspoon turmeric

2 teaspoons ground coriander

¼ teaspoon cayenne pepper, or to taste

¾ teaspoon salt

2½ cups water

½ teaspoon amchur, or 2 teaspoons lemon juice

½ teaspoon garam masala (page 24)

2 tablespoons chopped cilantro

1. Peel and wash potatoes. Cut into 1-inch pieces. Set aside.

2. Lightly crush whole coriander seeds and fennel seeds with a mortar and pestle or with a rolling pin. In a small bowl, place crushed seeds, asafetida, cumin seeds, fenugreek seeds, and whole red chiles. Set aside.

3. Heat oil in a heavy saucepan over medium heat. Add spice mixture and cook for a few seconds until the cumin seeds are golden brown.

4. Add the potatoes and tomato sauce. Stir. Add turmeric, coriander, and cayenne pepper. Stir to coat potatoes with the spices.

5. Add salt and water. Bring to a boil. Reduce heat to a low boil, cover with a lid, and simmer for 20 to 25 minutes. The potatoes should be tender, slightly falling apart. The curry sauce should be thick and coating the potatoes like a stew.

6. Stir in amchur and garam masala. Transfer to a serving dish and garnish with cilantro.

NUTRITION INFORMATION PER SERVING:
Calories: 105; Total Fat: 2 g (Saturated Fat: 0 g); Carbohydrate: 19 g; Protein: 2 g; Fiber: 2 g; Sodium: 350 mg

---

GF
···

Madras Potatoes

Madrasi Aloo

PREP: **10 minutes**
COOK: **10 minutes**
MAKES: **4–6 servings**
SERVING SIZE: **½ cup**

Mustard seeds and chana dal give this potato dish a very unique flavor—typical of south India. These potatoes make a great dosa stuffing (see Mung Bean Crepes, page 83), or enjoy them as a side dish.

2 medium potatoes (about 2 cups), boiled
2 tablespoons canola or vegetable oil

1 cup onion, thinly sliced
½ teaspoon brown mustard seeds
7–8 curry leaves
1 teaspoon (split, hulled) chana dal
⅛ teaspoon turmeric
1 teaspoon ground coriander
½ teaspoon cayenne pepper, or to taste
½ teaspoon salt
¾ cup water, divided
2 teaspoons lemon or lime juice

1. Peel and dice potatoes into ¼-inch pieces. Set aside.

2. Heat oil in a nonstick fry pan on medium high heat. Add the mustard seeds and cook for a few seconds, until mustard seeds stop popping (use a lid to prevent seeds from popping out). Add curry leaves and chana dal, and cook for a few seconds. Add the potatoes, turmeric, coriander, cayenne pepper, and salt. Stir using a lifting motion. Stir in water. Bring to a boil. Reduce heat, cover with lid, and cook for about 5 minutes.

3. Squeeze in lemon juice and stir. Any remaining water will be absorbed as the potatoes cool.

NUTRITION INFORMATION PER SERVING:
Calories: 127; Total Fat: 6 g (Saturated Fat: 0.5 g); Carbohydrate: 18 g; Protein: 2 g; Fiber: 2 g; Sodium: 239 mg

Curried Potatoes

Sukhe Aloo

PREP: **5 minutes**

COOK: **10 minutes**

MAKES: **6 servings**

SERVING SIZE: **½ cup**

Children and adults alike will devour this dish, which is one of the most popular ways to prepare potatoes in India. These can be served either hot or cold with any meal. They are great for traveling and picnics too.

> 4 medium (about 1 ½ pounds) potatoes, boiled
>
> 3 tablespoons canola or vegetable oil
>
> 1 teaspoon cumin seeds
>
> 2 teaspoons ginger, peeled and grated
>
> ½ teaspoon turmeric
>
> ½ teaspoon cayenne pepper, or to taste
>
> 1 tablespoon ground coriander
>
> ¾ teaspoon salt
>
> 1 teaspoon garam masala (page 24)
>
> 1 teaspoon amchur or 2 teaspoons lemon juice

1. Peel and cube boiled potatoes into ¾-inch pieces. Set aside.

2. Heat oil in a nonstick skillet over medium-high heat. Add cumin seeds. Fry for a few seconds until roasted.

3. Add ginger and stir for a few seconds. Add potatoes. Sprinkle with turmeric, cayenne pepper, coriander, salt, garam masala, and amchur. Using a wide spatula, stir in a lifting and turning motion to coat potatoes with the spices. Avoid breaking the potatoes.

4. Stir-fry for 3 to 5 minutes until the potatoes are lightly roasted. Transfer to a serving dish.

NUTRITION INFORMATION PER SERVING:
Calories: 171; Total Fat: 7 g (Saturated Fat: 0.5 g); Carbohydrate: 25 g; Protein: 3 g; Fiber: 3 g; Sodium: 299 mg

Grilled Vegetables

Bhuni Subji

PREP: **20 minutes**

COOK: **10–15 minutes**

MAKES: **6 servings**

SERVING SIZE: **½ cup**

I usually make these vegetables for a summer backyard party. I put some toothpicks out, and people love picking at the vegetables throughout the evening. For a grilling party with an Indian twist, serve with Bean Burgers (page 81) and Grilled Corn (page 101).

> 2 cups zucchini, cut into ¼-inch slices
>
> 1 cup onion, cut into ¼-inch wedges
>
> 2 cups green and red peppers, cut into ½-inch wedges
>
> 1 cup carrot, cut into ¼-inch slices
>
> 2 tablespoons olive oil
>
> 1 tablespoon vinegar or lemon juice
>
> ½ teaspoon ground cumin
>
> ½ teaspoon chili flakes
>
> ¼ teaspoon black pepper
>
> ½ teaspoon salt

1. In a bowl, mix together zucchini, onion, peppers, and carrots.

2. Add oil, vinegar, cumin, chili flakes, and black pepper. Toss well to coat the vegetables. Marinate for 10 to 30 minutes (the longer you marinate, the stronger the flavor will be). Just before grilling, stir in the salt.

3. Preheat the grill. Spread the grill with thick aluminum foil. Spread the vegetables in a single layer. Grill until the vegetables are light brown on both sides, turning frequently, about 5 minutes. Transfer to a serving platter. Serve hot.

NOTE: If desired, bake the vegetables in a 400°F preheated oven. Follow steps 1 and 2 as above. Place the vegetables in an oven-safe tray in a single layer and bake for about 10 minutes until vegetables are just tender. Move the tray to the top shelf and broil for 2 to 3 minutes, until the vegetables are slightly charred.

NUTRITION INFORMATION PER SERVING:
Calories: 62; Total Fat: 3 g (Saturated Fat: 0.5 g); Carbohydrate: 7 g; Protein: 1 g; Fiber: 2 g; Sodium: 218 mg

GF, LF

Grilled Corn

Bhutta

PREP: **5 minutes**
COOK: **15 minutes**
MAKES: **6 servings**
SERVING SIZE: **1 ear of corn**

Bhutta, or grilled corn on the cob, is very dear to my heart. Once you taste these, you'll want to grill corn all the time. During corn season in northern India, hawkers sell fresh-grilled *bhutta* by the roadside. Choose firm, large-kernel corn—mature corn for grilling. Soft, tender corn contains too much water and does not grill well. At least once during the corn season, I have a *bhutta* party where grilled corn takes center stage. I like to make sure there are two ears for each person, for it's hard to eat just one.

6 ears fresh corn, husks on

1 teaspoon salt

¼ teaspoon black pepper

¼ teaspoon cayenne pepper, or to taste

1 lime or lemon, halved

1. Move the grill rack close to the coal. Light the grill and preheat until the coal is bright red. If using a gas grill, preheat the grill on high.

2. Remove the corn husks and the threads. Leave about 1 inch of the stem on the corn. Set aside.

3. Mix together salt, black pepper, and cayenne pepper on a plate, and set aside. Cut the lime in half. Set aside.

4. Grill corn on the cob, turning occasionally until the corn kernels are golden brown to lightly charred on all sides.

5. Dip the lime half in salt mixture and lightly squeeze over the corn. Based on individual preference, squeeze the lime with salt masala to taste. Enjoy on the *bhutta*. (Some of the salt mixture will be left over.)

NUTRITION INFORMATION PER SERVING:
Calories: 77; Total Fat: 1 g (Saturated Fat: 0 g); Carbohydrate: 17 g; Protein: 3 g; Fiber: 2 g; Sodium: 207 mg

••

Coconut Curry

Nariyal Subji

PREP: **15 minutes**
COOK: **15 minutes**
MAKES: **8 servings**
SERVING SIZE: **½ cup**

This quick-and-easy creamy, coconut-flavored curry is a crowd pleaser. Canned coconut milk makes it simple to prepare. I like to serve this over plain jasmine or basmati rice.

1 tablespoon canola or vegetable oil, divided

4 green cardamom pods

4 cloves

1-inch cinnamon stick

1–2 green chiles, split lengthwise

1 cup onion, chopped into 1-inch pieces

1 cup green beans, cut into 1-inch pieces

2 cups cauliflower, cut into 1-inch florets

1 cup carrot, diced into ½-inch pieces

1 cup potatoes, cut into 1-inch slices

½ cup water

1 teaspoon salt

1 teaspoon cornstarch

1 (14-ounce) can coconut milk

1. Heat oil in a medium skillet on medium-high heat. Add cardamom pods (open the pods with your hands, just enough to create a slit), cloves, cinnamon stick, and green chiles and cook for a few seconds until the spices puff. Add onion and fry 1 to 2 minutes until onions are transparent.

2. Add green beans, cauliflower, carrot, and potatoes. Add water and salt. Cover and simmer for 5 to 7 minutes, until the potatoes are tender.

3. Mix cornstarch with 2 tablespoons of coconut milk until well blended. Set aside.

4. Add coconut milk. Stir and bring to a boil. Add the cornstarch mixture and stir until thickened, 1 to 2 minutes. Transfer to a serving dish. Serve over rice.

NUTRITION INFORMATION PER SERVING:
Calories: 154; Total Fat: 12 g (Saturated Fat: 9 g); Carbohydrate: 11 g; Protein: 3 g; Fiber: 2 g; Sodium: 318 mg

••

Creamy Vegetable Stew

Subji Korma

PREP: **15 minutes**
COOK: **15 minutes**
MAKES: **6 servings**
SERVING SIZE: **½ cup**

A dish that is very popular in restaurants, *korma* is mildly sweet and creamy, typically made with heavy cream. For this vegan recipe, cashews give the *korma* a creamy taste and texture. Don't let the number of ingredients intimidate you. Once you gather all the ingredients, the dish is prepared fairly quickly—besides, it'll totally be worth your effort.

3 tablespoons canola or vegetable oil, divided

1 cup onion, sliced

1 teaspoon ginger, peeled and chopped

1 teaspoon garlic, chopped

1–2 teaspoons green chile, chopped

¼ cup raw cashews, coarsely chopped

1½ cups water, divided

½ cup onion, cut into ½-inch pieces

½ cup green beans, cut into ½-inch pieces

2 cups cauliflower, cut into ½-inch florets

½ cup carrot, diced into ¼-inch pieces

½ cup frozen peas

1 cup yellow pepper, cut into ½-inch pieces

1 teaspoon salt

½ teaspoon cayenne pepper, or to taste

2 tablespoons slivered almonds

1 tablespoon golden raisins

½ cup coconut milk

1 tablespoon lemon or lime juice

2 tablespoons cilantro, chopped

1. In a large nonstick fry pan, heat 2 tablespoons of oil on medium-high heat. Add onion and fry 1 to 2 minutes until transparent. Add ginger, garlic, green chile, and cashews. Stir and fry for 1 minute. Remove from heat. Transfer the onion mixture to a bowl and cool slightly.

2. In a blender, grind the onion mixture with ½ cup water to a smooth paste. Set aside.

3. In the same fry pan, add the remaining 1 tablespoon oil. Heat on medium-high heat. Add chopped onion and fry 1 to 2 minutes until transparent. Add green beans, cauliflower, carrot, peas, pepper, salt, cayenne pepper, and 1 cup water. Stir to mix. Cover and simmer for 5 to 7 minutes, until the vegetables are crisp-tender.

4. Add the onion paste. Stir and cook for about 5 minutes.

5. Add the almonds, raisins, and coconut milk. Stir and simmer for another 5 minutes. Stir in the lemon juice. Transfer to a serving dish, garnish with cilantro, and serve hot.

NUTRITION INFORMATION PER SERVING:
Calories: 202; Total Fat: 16 g (Saturated Fat: 5 g); Carbohydrate: 15 g; Protein: 4 g; Fiber: 3 g; Sodium: 425 mg

---

GF

·.·

Creamy Mushroom Curry
Khumb Ki Subji

PREP: **10 minutes**
COOK: **15 minutes**
MAKES: **4 servings**
SERVING SIZE: **½ cup**

Mushrooms cook in a few minutes and turn any dish into a gourmet creation. This creamy mushroom curry is great over plain rice or scooped up with flatbread.

3 tablespoons canola or vegetable oil

1 cup onion, sliced

1 teaspoon ginger, peeled and chopped

1 teaspoon garlic, chopped

1 teaspoon green chile, chopped, or to taste

2 tablespoons sliced almonds

12 raw cashews, coarsely chopped

2 cups water, divided

6 cups (16 ounces) mushrooms, sliced

½ teaspoon turmeric

¾ teaspoon salt

¼ teaspoon cayenne pepper, or to taste

1. In a large nonstick fry pan, heat 2 tablespoons oil on medium-high heat. Add onions and fry for 2 to 3 minutes until golden brown. Add ginger, garlic, green chile, almonds, and cashews. Stir and fry for a minute. Remove from heat. With a slotted spoon, remove the onion mixture to a bowl and cool slightly, reserving the oil in the same pan.

2. In a blender, grind the onion mixture with ½ cup water to a smooth paste.

3. In the same fry pan, add the remaining tablespoon of oil to the existing oil. Heat on medium-high heat. Add mushrooms and fry for 2 to 3 minutes until the mushrooms are cooked. Add the onion mixture, turmeric, salt, and cayenne pepper. Stir and cook for 2 to 3 minutes, coating the mushrooms. Add remaining 1½ cups water, bring to a boil, cover with lid, and simmer for 5 minutes.

4. Transfer to a serving dish and serve hot.

NUTRITION INFORMATION PER SERVING:
Calories: 175; Total Fat: 15 g (Saturated Fat: 2 g); Carbohydrate: 8 g; Protein: 5 g; Fiber: 2 g; Sodium: 443 mg

---

GF

·'·

Curried Mushrooms and Peas
Khumb-Matar

PREP: **10 minutes**
COOK: **10 minutes**
MAKES: **4 servings**
SERVING SIZE: **½ cup**

Mushrooms and peas are a winning combination. Serve this easy-to-prepare dish alongside any meal. If desired, add slivered almonds for a nutty texture.

2 tablespoons canola or vegetable oil

½ teaspoon brown mustard seeds

1 cup red onion, thinly sliced

1 teaspoon ginger, peeled and finely grated

2 cups (12 ounces) mushrooms, sliced

1 cup frozen peas, thawed

½ teaspoon turmeric

½ teaspoon salt

1 teaspoon ground coriander

¼ teaspoon cayenne pepper, or to taste

½ cup water

¼ teaspoon garam masala (page 24)

2 tablespoons slivered almonds, lightly roasted, optional

1. Heat oil in a nonstick fry pan on medium-high heat. Add mustard seeds, cover with lid, and cook for a few seconds, until the seeds stop popping. Add onion and fry 1 to 2 minutes until transparent. Add ginger and stir.

2. Add mushrooms and stir-fry for 2 to 3 minutes. Add peas, turmeric, salt, coriander, and cayenne pepper. Add the water, bring to a boil, cover with lid, and cook for 5 to 7 minutes, or until the peas are cooked.

3. Sprinkle garam masala over mushroom mixture. Transfer to a serving dish and garnish with almonds, if desired.

NUTRITION INFORMATION PER SERVING:
Calories: 107; Total Fat: 7 g (Saturated Fat: 0.5 g); Carbohydrate: 8 g; Protein: 3 g; Fiber: 2 g; Sodium: 330 mg

---

GF, LF

·'·

Plantain Stew
Kele Ka Kootu

PREP: **10 minutes**
COOK: **40 minutes**
MAKES: **12 servings**
SERVING SIZE: **½ cup**

In southern India, banana trees and coconut trees are everywhere. Plantains (raw bananas) are used to make a variety of dishes. Before bananas ripen, they have a unique taste and texture, and are cooked as a vegetable. Once ripe, they become sweet and soft and are eaten as a fruit.

Kootu is a vegetable dish with a stew-like consistency and a coconut base. You can use fresh coconut, but for convenience I use the frozen grated coconut available in Indian grocery stores.

1 pound plantains

1 tablespoon canola or vegetable oil

½ teaspoon brown mustard seeds

⅛ teaspoon asafetida powder

8–10 curry leaves

1 cup carrot, cut into 1-inch strips

1 cup green beans, cut into 1-inch pieces

½ teaspoon turmeric

1½ teaspoons salt

2 cups water

KOOTU MASALA

1 teaspoon canola or vegetable oil

2–3 dried red chiles, or to taste

2 teaspoons cumin seeds

1 tablespoon coriander seeds

½ teaspoon black peppercorns

1 cup fresh or frozen grated coconut

1 cup warm water

1 teaspoon brown sugar

2 teaspoons tamarind paste or 2 tablespoons lemon juice

1. Peel plantains with a peeler, removing just the thin green outer layer. In a medium bowl, add some water. Cut plantain into ½-by-1-inch-long strips and soak in water. (Water prevents plantains from turning brown.) Set aside. Drain the water just before cooking.

2. In a medium saucepan, heat oil on medium-high heat. Add the mustard seeds, cover with lid, and cook for a few seconds, until mustard seeds stop popping. Add asafetida and curry leaves and cook for a few seconds. Add the drained plantains, carrots, and green beans. Stir to mix. Add turmeric, salt, and water. Bring to a boil. Reduce heat, cover with lid, and cook for 10 to 12 minutes, until the vegetables are tender.

3. *In the meantime, prepare kootu masala:* In a small fry pan, heat oil on medium heat. Add cumin

seeds, red chiles, coriander seeds, and peppercorns. Roast all ingredients until golden brown. In a small blender jar, add grated coconut, roasted spices, and warm water. Grind until smooth.

4. Once the plaintains are tender, add the kootu masala. Bring to a boil, reduce heat, and simmer for 15 to 20 minutes, until mixture is a stew-like consistency. Add brown sugar and tamarind paste. Transfer to a serving bowl. Serve warm with rice.

NUTRITION INFORMATION PER SERVING:
Calories: 91; Total Fat: 4 g (Saturated Fat: 2 g); Carbohydrate: 15 g; Protein: 1 g; Fiber: 2 g; Sodium: 304 mg

---

GF

Coconut Green Beans
Sem-Nariyal

PREP: **10 minutes**
COOK: **10 minutes**
MAKES: **6 servings**
SERVING SIZE: **½ cup**

Mustard seeds and coconut add a nutty taste to these finely chopped green beans. Enjoy them as a side dish or salad. For best result, use fresh green beans, although frozen can be substituted in a pinch.

3 cups (1 pound) green beans, cut into ¼-inch pieces

1 tablespoon canola or vegetable oil

1 teaspoon brown mustard seeds

2–3 dried red chiles

6–8 curry leaves

½ teaspoon salt

2 tablespoons water

¼ cup frozen or fresh coconut, finely grated

1. Heat oil in a nonstick fry pan on medium-high heat. Add the mustard seeds, cover with lid, and cook for a few seconds, until the mustard seeds stop popping. Add red chiles and curry leaves, and cook for a few seconds. Cover loosely with lid to contain the popping seeds.

2. Add the green beans, salt, and water. Stir to mix. Cover with lid, reduce heat, and simmer for 5 to 7 minutes, until the green beans are cooked.

3. Transfer to a serving container and add the grated coconut. Toss lightly.

NUTRITION INFORMATION PER SERVING:
Calories: 50; Total Fat: 4 g (Saturated Fat: 1 g); Carbohydrate: 4 g; Protein: 1 g; Fiber: 2 g; Sodium: 198 mg

GF, LF

Green Beans and Potatoes
Sem-Aloo

PREP: **5 minutes**
COOK: **10 minutes**
MAKES: **4 servings**
SERVING SIZE: **½ cup**

For this dish, I typically use frozen green beans for convenience, except in the summer when fresh beans are plentiful. It's a quick and easy favorite that goes with any dal.

2 teaspoons canola or vegetable oil

½ teaspoon cumin seeds

2 cups (8 ounces) fresh or frozen green beans

½ cup potatoes, peeled and cut into thin 1-inch pieces

½ teaspoon turmeric

½ teaspoon salt

2 teaspoons ground coriander

¼ teaspoon cayenne pepper, or to taste

2 tablespoons water

1. Heat oil in a nonstick fry pan on medium-high heat. Add cumin seeds and cook for a few seconds until golden brown. Add green beans and potatoes and stir.

2. Sprinkle with turmeric, salt, coriander, and cayenne pepper. Stir well. Add water. Cover with lid and reduce heat to medium-low. Simmer for 8 to 10 minutes, or until potatoes are tender. Stir occasionally.

3. Transfer to a serving bowl.

NUTRITION INFORMATION PER SERVING:
Calories: 51; Total Fat: 2 g (Saturated Fat: 0 g); Carbohydrate: 7 g; Protein: 1 g; Fiber: 2 g; Sodium: 295 mg

GF, LF

Snow Peas
Matar-Chilke Ki Subji

PREP: **10 minutes**
COOK: **10 minutes**
MAKES: **4 servings**
SERVING SIZE: **½ cup**

Snow peas are tender and sweet and cook in no time at all. I like to just lightly season them, maintaining the sweetness of the pods. When peas are in abundance in India, we would often sit and remove the peas from the pods. We would sometimes also carefully skin the inside layer from the pod and then cook the pods too. Snow peas remind me of the same taste without the hassle.

1 pound fresh snow peas

1 tablespoon canola or vegetable oil

½ teaspoon cumin seeds

1 cup frozen peas, thawed

½ teaspoon turmeric

½ teaspoon salt

½ teaspoon cayenne pepper, or to taste

¼ cup water

1. Cut pointy tips from both ends of the snow peas. Cut the pods into ¾-inch pieces. Set aside.

2. Heat oil in a medium nonstick fry pan on medium-high heat. Add cumin seeds and cook for a few seconds until golden brown. Add the snow peas and peas and stir.

3. Add turmeric, salt, and cayenne pepper. Stir well. Stir in water. Cover with lid. Reduce heat and simmer for 5 to 7 minutes, or until snow peas are crisp-tender. Transfer to a serving platter.

NUTRITION INFORMATION PER SERVING:
Calories: 84; Total Fat: 3 g (Saturated Fat: 0.5 g); Carbohydrate: 11 g; Protein: 4 g; Fiber: 4 g; Sodium: 265 mg

GF

Kohlrabi
Ganth Gobhi

PREP: **10 minutes**
COOK: **30 minutes**
MAKES: **6 servings**
SERVING SIZE: **½ cup**

Kohlrabi is one of those vegetables that take a little getting used to. It is fairly common in northern India and tastes good with a good spicy sauce. It's from the cabbage family, but the texture is similar to a turnip. My daughter and son-in-law took an instant liking to this recipe. The surprise was in the unknown—it's not potatoes, but what is it? If you like kohlrabi, you'll love this recipe, and if you don't like kohlrabi or think you don't like it, you'll want to try it again.

1 pound fresh kohlrabi with green tops

2 tablespoons canola or vegetable oil

1 teaspoon cumin seeds

1 tablespoon ginger, peeled and grated

1 teaspoon garlic, finely chopped

2 teaspoons green chiles, finely chopped, or to taste

½ cup tomato sauce

1 teaspoon turmeric

½ teaspoon salt

½ teaspoon cayenne pepper, or to taste

½ cup water

½ teaspoon sugar

1 teaspoon garam masala (page 24)

1. Remove the greens from the kohlrabi. Discard any yellow or tough leaves. Wash and finely chop the tender leaves and stems into ¼-inch pieces. Place in a bowl. Peel the outer layer of kohlrabi. Remove the tough top and bottom (about ¼ inch) of kohlrabi and cut in half lengthwise. Place cut side down and slice into ¾-inch slices. Add to the greens. Set aside.

2. Heat oil in a nonstick fry pan on medium-high heat. Add cumin seeds and cook for a few seconds, until golden brown. Add ginger, garlic, and green chiles, and stir for a few seconds. Stir in the tomato sauce.

3. Add the kohlrabi and greens. Add turmeric, salt, and cayenne pepper. Stir for 2 to 3 minutes, coating the kohlrabi with the sauce.

4. Stir in water. Cover with lid. Reduce heat and simmer for 15 to 18 minutes, until kohlrabi is tender.

5. Stir in the sugar and garam masala. Transfer to a serving platter.

GF, LF

Cabbage Mixed Vegetables

Bund Gobhi Milli Subji

PREP: **10 minutes**
COOK: **10 minutes**
MAKES: **4 servings**
SERVING SIZE: **½ cup**

Cabbage is inexpensive and versatile. It cooks up quickly and is eaten in a variety of curry dishes. This mixed vegetable dish makes a great accompaniment to any meal. I like to roll the leftover vegetables in a flatbread and serve it like a wrap.

1 tablespoon canola or vegetable oil

½ teaspoon brown mustard seeds

¾ cup onion, cut into ½-inch pieces

2 teaspoons ginger, peeled and grated

2 cups cabbage, finely chopped

½ cup frozen peas

½ cup carrot, diced into ¼-inch pieces

½ cup potatoes, peeled and diced into ½-inch pieces

¼ teaspoon turmeric

½ teaspoon salt

1 teaspoon ground coriander

¼ teaspoon cayenne pepper, or to taste

2 tablespoons water

1 teaspoon lemon or lime juice

1. Heat oil in a medium nonstick pan on medium-high heat. Add mustard seeds, cover with lid, and cook for a few seconds, until they stop popping. Add onion and fry 1 to 2 minutes until onions are transparent. Add ginger and stir.

2. Add cabbage, peas, carrot, and potatoes. Stir well. Sprinkle turmeric, salt, coriander, and cayenne pepper over mixture. Stir well. Add water. Cover and simmer for 7 to 8 minutes, until potatoes are tender.

3. Stir in lemon juice. Transfer to a serving container. Serve hot.

GF

Curried Onions

Pyaj Ki Subji

PREP: **10 minutes**
COOK: **15 minutes**
MAKES: **6 servings**
SERVING SIZE: **⅓ cup**

This is one of my husband's favorite vegetable dishes. Every time I make it, he tells me the same story of his college days in India: "In my dorm cafeteria, the cook used to make this onion vegetable every Tuesday and I just loved it." It's easy, quick, and flavorful. I have used any onions on hand, but for a sweeter taste, use white or Vidalia onions.

3 to 4 (about 1½ pounds) large sweet onions

3 tablespoons canola or vegetable oil

½ teaspoon cumin seeds

1 tablespoon garlic, finely chopped

¼ teaspoon turmeric

½ teaspoon salt

1 teaspoon ground coriander

½ teaspoon cayenne pepper, or to taste

¾ cup water

¼ teaspoon garam masala (page 24)

2 teaspoons lemon or lime juice

2 tablespoons cilantro, chopped

1. Peel and slice onions into ¼-by-2-inch-long slices. Set aside.

2. Heat oil in a medium nonstick fry pan on medium-high heat. Add cumin seeds. Fry for a few seconds until seeds are golden brown. Add onions and garlic and stir. Fry for 1 to 2 minutes until onions are transparent.

3. Sprinkle turmeric, salt, coriander, and cayenne pepper over mixture. Stir well. Add water. Bring to a boil. Cover with lid and reduce heat to medium-low. Simmer for 3 to 5 minutes.

4. Stir in garam masala, lemon juice, and cilantro. Transfer to a serving bowl and serve hot.

NUTRITION INFORMATION PER SERVING:
Calories: 107; Total Fat: 7 g (Saturated
Fat: 0.5 g); Carbohydrate: 11 g; Protein: 1 g;
Fiber: 2 g; Sodium: 198 mg

GF, LF

··

Carrots and Turnips

Gajar-Shalgum

PREP: **10 minutes**
COOK: **10 minutes**
MAKES: **6 servings**
SERVING SIZE: **½ cup**

Turnips are great raw, either in a salad or just sliced and lightly sprinkled with salt, like cucumbers. But here's a great way to serve them cooked. Combined with carrots, they're a great side dish with any meal.

1 tablespoon canola or vegetable oil

½ teaspoon cumin seeds

2 cups carrots, peeled and cut into ¼-inch-thick slices

2 cups turnips, peeled and sliced into ¼-inch wedges

¼ teaspoon turmeric

½ teaspoon salt

1 teaspoon ground coriander

¼ teaspoon cayenne pepper, or to taste

2 tablespoons water

1 teaspoon sugar

¼ teaspoon garam masala (page 24)

1 teaspoon lemon or lime juice

1. Heat oil in a nonstick fry pan on medium-high heat. Add cumin seeds and cook for a few seconds, until seeds are golden brown. Add carrots and turnips, and stir to coat with oil.

2. Sprinkle with the turmeric, salt, coriander, and cayenne pepper. Stir well. Add water. Cover with lid and reduce heat to medium-low. Simmer for 5 to 7 minutes, until carrots are tender.

3. Stir in sugar, garam masala, and lemon juice. Transfer to a serving bowl.

NUTRITION INFORMATION PER SERVING:
Calories: 52; Total Fat: 2 g (Saturated Fat: 0 g);
Carbohydrate: 7 g; Protein: 1 g; Fiber: 2 g;
Sodium: 231 mg

···

Okra and Onions

Bhindi-Pyaj

> PREP: **10 minutes**
> COOK: **25 minutes**
> MAKES: **6 servings**
> SERVING SIZE: **¼ cup**

Okra (*bhindi*) is an exotic vegetable that is often thought of as difficult to prepare. Okra is well liked and cooked in a variety of ways in India, but it is rarely breaded and fried. It's important to use tender okra and wash and dry them before cutting. (Too much water will make the okra slimy.) This dish is delicious with rice or flatbread.

> ½ pound fresh okra, or 12 ounces frozen sliced okra
>
> 2 tablespoons canola or vegetable oil
>
> ½ teaspoon cumin seeds
>
> 1 medium onion, finely chopped
>
> ½ teaspoon turmeric
>
> ¾ teaspoon salt
>
> 2 teaspoons ground coriander
>
> ½ teaspoon cayenne pepper, or to taste
>
> 2 tablespoons water
>
> ½ teaspoon amchur, or 1 teaspoon lemon juice
>
> ½ teaspoon sugar

1. Wash and dry okra on a towel. Cut ends off and slice into ½-inch circles. Set aside. (If using frozen okra, thaw in microwave or at room temperature.)

2. In a medium skillet, heat oil on medium-high heat. Add cumin seeds and cook for a few seconds, until seeds turn golden brown. Add the onion and fry for 1 to 2 minutes until transparent.

3. Add okra and stir. Add turmeric, salt, coriander, and cayenne pepper. Stir in 2 tablespoons of water (do not add any water if using frozen okra). Reduce heat to medium. Cover with lid and cook for 10 minutes, stirring once or twice.

4. Stir in amchur and sugar. Transfer to a serving bowl.

NUTRITION INFORMATION PER SERVING:
Calories: 93; Total Fat: 7 g (Saturated Fat: 0.5 g); Carbohydrate: 7 g; Protein: 1 g; Fiber: 2 g; Sodium: 442 mg

---

···

Stuffed Okra

Bharva Bhindi

> PREP: **15 minutes**
> COOK: **20 minutes**
> MAKES: **6 servings**
> SERVING SIZE: **4–5 okras**

Use fresh, tender okra. The best way to pick okra is to snap the pointy end; if it snaps in two quickly, it is tender, but if it bends before breaking, it is too mature and will taste woody. Stuffing little okra takes time, but you'll love the results.

> ½ pound fresh okra
>
> ¾ teaspoon salt
>
> 1 tablespoon ground coriander
>
> 1 teaspoon fennel seed powder
>
> ½ teaspoon cayenne pepper, or to taste
>
> 1 teaspoon amchur, or 2 teaspoons lemon juice
>
> 2 tablespoons canola or vegetable oil

1. Wash and dry okra on a towel. Slit the okra from top to bottom about ¼ inch deep. Leave about ⅛ inch intact on both ends. Set aside.

2. In a small bowl, mix together salt, coriander, fennel seed powder, cayenne pepper, and amchur.

3. Fill 1 okra at a time with a little bit of the dry masala. Use your finger to slide the masala through the opening.

4. Heat oil in a fry pan on medium-high heat. Add the stuffed okra in a single layer. Stir slowly to cover with oil. Reduce heat to medium. Cover with lid and cook for about 5 minutes.

5. Open the lid, turn okra over, and cook, uncovered, for another 5 minutes, turning occasionally. Transfer to a serving bowl.

NUTRITION INFORMATION PER SERVING:
Calories: 53; Total Fat: 5 g (Saturated
Fat: 0.5 g); Carbohydrate: 3 g; Protein: 1 g;
Fiber: 1 g; Sodium: 294 mg

GF

Stuffed Bitter Melons
Bharva Karele

PREP: **2 to 4 hours**
COOK: **20 minutes**
MAKES: **6 servings**
SERVING SIZE: **½–1 piece**

Bitter melon, as the name implies, is bitter in taste. Indians either love or hate it. It has been in the news recently for its benefits in reducing blood glucose levels in people with type 2 diabetes, although more studies are needed to confirm the findings.

This is not an easy dish to prepare, but it is one of the best ways to serve bitter melons. Choose melons that are small and tender. The juices and the flesh can be intolerably bitter if not treated properly. Salt them to reduce the bitterness, as directed in the recipe.

½ pound small (3–4 inches long) bitter
melons (karele)

¾ teaspoon salt, plus more for salting

3 tablespoons canola or vegetable oil, divided

¾ cup onion, grated

½ teaspoon turmeric

1 tablespoon ground coriander

1 teaspoon fennel seeds, coarsely ground

½ teaspoon cayenne pepper, or to taste

1 tablespoon lemon juice

1. Peel the top ridges of the bitter melon. Slit the bitter melon from top to bottom about ¼ inch deep, leaving about ¼ inch intact on both ends. Liberally sprinkle salt on top and inside the melon. Let sit for 2 hours to overnight. Rinse the bitter melons and lightly squeeze to remove excess water.

2. Heat 1 tablespoon oil on medium-high heat in a nonstick pan. Add the grated onion, stir and cook for 1 to 2 minutes until onions are transparent. Transfer to a small bowl.

3. Add the turmeric, salt, coriander, fennel seed powder, cayenne pepper, and lemon juice. Stir well. Cool to room temperature.

4. Fill the bitter melons with onion masala.

5. Using a common sewing thread, wrap the bitter melons a few times with the thread. This keeps the stuffing from falling out.

6. Heat 2 tablespoons of oil in a nonstick fry pan. Add the bitter melons in a single layer. Cover with lid. Cook for 5 minutes. Turn over with tongs. Cover and cook for another 2 to 3 minutes. Open lid and continue to fry until the melons are golden brown (slightly blackened), about 10 minutes.

7. Using kitchen scissors or tweezers, remove the thread. Transfer to a serving platter.

NOTE: Prepared bitter melons will keep in refrigerator for up to 2 weeks. Or freeze for up to 3 months. Thaw and reheat before serving.

NUTRITION INFORMATION PER SERVING:
Calories: 79; Total Fat: 7 g (Saturated Fat: 0.5 g); Carbohydrate: 3 g; Protein: 1 g; Fiber: 1 g; Sodium: 384 mg

GF, LF

Mixed Greens

Punjabi Saag

PREP: **10 minutes**
COOK: **30 minutes**
MAKES: **10 servings**
SERVING SIZE: **½ cup**

Saag means any type of greens. When this dish is made with mixed greens, it is associated with the state of Punjab. It is made with two to four different greens, mixed together, slow cooked, blended to a smooth consistency, and served with fresh corn or wheat roti (flatbreads).

1 (16-ounce) package frozen chopped mustard greens, or fresh mustard greens

2 cups fresh spinach, finely chopped, or 1 cup frozen chopped spinach

2 cups collard greens, finely chopped, or 1 cup frozen chopped collard greens

1 cup onion, coarsely chopped

2 teaspoons ginger, peeled and chopped

½ teaspoon turmeric

1 teaspoon salt

3 cups water, divided

3 tablespoons besan or cornmeal

SEASONING (*CHOUNK*)

2 tablespoons canola or vegetable oil

1 teaspoon cumin seeds

3–4 dried red whole chiles

½ teaspoon cayenne pepper, or to taste

1. In a heavy skillet, add the chopped greens, onion, ginger, turmeric, salt, and 1 cup water. Bring to a boil on medium-high heat. Reduce heat and simmer for 10 minutes. Set aside to cool.

2. In a blender, grind half of the greens at a time. Grind the greens for just a few seconds, using the pulse button if available. You want the greens to blend together, but do not grind too fine. Add water as needed to grind easily.

3. Mix besan with ¼ cup water. Set aside.

4. Return pureed greens to the skillet. Add besan mixture and remaining 1¾ cups water. Cover and bring to a boil. Reduce heat and simmer for 20 minutes, stirring occasionally. (VERY IMPORTANT: Before stirring, remove the skillet from the heat and carefully remove the lid. The *saag* tends to splatter and can burn.) Remove from heat. Transfer to a serving dish.

5. *Prepare seasoning:* Heat oil in a small fry pan over medium heat. Add cumin seeds and red chiles. Cook for a few seconds until seeds turn golden brown. Remove from heat and add cayenne pepper. Drizzle seasoning over greens. Serve hot.

NUTRITION INFORMATION PER SERVING:
Calories: 51; Total Fat: 2 g (Saturated Fat: 0 g); Carbohydrate: 5 g; Protein: 2 g; Fiber: 2 g; Sodium: 254 mg

···

Seasoned Zucchini

Sukhi Lauki

PREP: 10 minutes
COOK: 10 minutes
MAKES: 4–6 servings
SERVING SIZE: ½ cup

Bottle gourd, or *lauki*, has a similar texture to zucchini and is a good substitute in this dish. I use zucchini (available year-round) most of the time and *lauki* when in season and readily available. It is a nice accompaniment to a simple dal and rice meal. Cook only until tender for a fresh taste.

2 pounds zucchini or bottle gourd (*lauki*)

1 tablespoon canola or vegetable oil

1 teaspoon cumin seeds

½ teaspoon turmeric

¾ teaspoon salt

¼ teaspoon cayenne pepper, or to taste

2 teaspoons ground coriander

¼ cup water

½ teaspoon garam masala (page 24)

1 teaspoon lemon or lime juice

2 tablespoons cilantro, chopped

1. Trim zucchini ends and slice in two lengthwise. Then cut into ½-inch thick pieces. If using bottle gourd, peel and cut into ½-inch thick 1-inch pieces. Set aside.

2. Heat oil in a nonstick fry pan on medium-high heat. Add cumin seeds and cook for a few seconds until golden brown. Add zucchini and stir.

3. Stir in turmeric, salt, cayenne pepper, and coriander.

4. Add water. Cover with lid. Reduce heat and simmer for 5 to 7 minutes, until zucchini is tender.

5. Sprinkle garam masala and lemon juice over mixture and stir. Transfer to a serving platter and garnish with chopped cilantro.

NUTRITION INFORMATION PER SERVING:
Calories: 54; Total Fat: 3 g (Saturated Fat: 0.5 g); Carbohydrate: 6 g; Protein: 2 g; Fiber: 2 g; Sodium: 367 mg

Beans, Legumes, and Pulses (Dal)

*D*AL IS THE generic name for all dried beans, peas, lentils, legumes, or pulses. The word *dal* is used interchangeably for both dry and cooked beans. Dals are a staple in Indian cuisine. The fact that beans are a nutrition powerhouse is just beginning to garner attention in the Western world, but in India they have been an essential part of the diet for centuries. Dals are very versatile. Most have a mild but distinct taste and texture. The plethora of dal dishes is so vast that you can have a different preparation every day for months without repetition. Dal dishes can be served for breakfast, dinner, or snacks. They are prepared as soups, stews, crepes, pancakes, chutneys, snacks, and desserts. Dals are gloriously celebrated and take a central place in the Indian diet.

The nutritional benefits of dal are well recognized; they are high in protein, B vitamins, iron, and fiber. The protein in the dals is considered to be incomplete, but when combined with grains, nuts, or milk products, it is complete. For centuries, Indians have combined dal with rice or roti (flatbread) for the main course. The latest research indicates that plant proteins do not have to be combined in the same meal, thus making it easier to obtain the necessary protein for a vegetarian diet. Dals are the core protein source for vegans and vegetarians and are often the "entrée" in an Indian meal. The meal is often planned around what goes best with the particular dal, similar to a nonvegetarian meal being planned around meat.

Dals are used as whole beans; split with husk; split and hulled; and washed and polished, commonly known as washed dal—*dhulli dal* (see Glossary of Dals, page 117). Some dals are also ground into flour, such as *gram* or *besan* (chickpea flour). Most of the dals are available in Indian grocery stores or those with large ethnic foods sections. Local supermarkets also have some dals (Indian specific) but usually only carry whole beans—for example, chickpeas, brown lentils, or kidney beans. Health foods stores and co-ops now carry more varieties of beans, even some of the split and hulled varieties such as pink lentils.

Cooking Dals

Preparing dals can take time, especially whole dals. Most Indians own and use pressure cookers for cooking dals, which saves a significant amount of cooking time as well as fuel. I have included both pressure cooker and saucepan directions under each recipe. If you will be cooking beans often—which as a vegan you should be, a pressure cooker is well worth the investment (see Using the Pressure Cooker Safely, page 9). Follow these simple rules and you can prepare any type of beans:

1. *Clean dal:* Most dals today, including those sold at Indian grocery stores, do not have any rocks or dirt. But dal should be washed before cooking. Wash in three to four changes of water, until the rinse water is relatively clear, rubbing the dal between your fingers and palm of one hand to help remove any dirt. Using a strainer or colander, drain the water. Use beans as directed in the recipe.

2. If recommended in the recipe, especially with whole beans, soak the dal after washing in two to three inches of water, to allow adequate room for beans to expand. Soaking cuts down on the cooking time and causes the beans to cook up more evenly. Using a strainer or colander, drain the water and rinse the beans again under running water.

3. Cook in a saucepan or a pressure cooker (see individual recipe). Make sure you add enough water for the cooking time—the longer you cook them, the more water you will need. Most dals need a minimum of two times the water-to-beans ratio. Without enough water, the dal will stick to the bottom and burn.

4. Cook dal to desired consistency. In most recipes, dal is cooked to a soup consistency. The grain will be very soft and blend well with the cooking liquid, creating its own flavor.

Digesting Beans

Indian seasonings and spices are added to the dals just as much for digestion as for the flavor and taste. If you are not used to eating beans, start with a small serving and increase it gradually as your tolerance increases (see Fiber, page 33).

GLOSSARY OF DALS

Dals used in this book are listed below in alphabetical order. All dals are available in Indian grocery stores or online (see page 29). In addition to dried varieties, more and more local grocers are also carrying canned, frozen, and vacuum-sealed dals as well.

DAL	DESCRIPTION	FORMS
Adzuki Beans *(Chori)*	Small, oval, and dark red beans with a white streak.	Dry whole beans Canned
Bengal Gram *(Chana)*	A generic name for chickpeas and black chana. See Chana and Chickpeas.	
Black Gram **Mungo Beans** *(Urad Dal)*	See Urad Dal	
Black-Eyed Peas **Cowpeas** *(Lobhia)*	As the name implies, these whole beans have a black spot on them.	Dry whole beans Canned Frozen
Chana Dal *(split and hulled Bengal Gram)* **Whole Black Bengal Gram** *(Kalla Chana)*	A smaller, black version of chickpeas. Although they fall in the same category as chickpeas, they have a different taste, texture, and flavor. They are occasionally cooked as whole beans. Most often the split, hulled, and polished version called chana dal is used. Chana dal looks similar in shape, color, and size to split yellow peas, with a nuttier taste and a firmer texture. (Make sure you label them properly, as they are easy to mix up!) This dal is one of the most versatile—it is used in seasonings, and to make dal, crepes, and pancakes.	(Sold in Indian stores) Dry, split, hulled (yellow in color) Dry, whole beans sold as Bengal Gram or Kalla Chana Besan (gram flour)
Chickpeas **Garbanzo Beans** **Ceci Beans** *(Kabuli Chana)*	Tan-colored beans that look like little acorns, with a robust flavor and nutty texture. For most recipes, I prefer to use the dried beans, as the cooking juices impart their own flavor. Canned chickpeas are convenient and are great in some recipes.	Dry whole beans Canned Chickpea flour (not the same as besan, but a good substitute)
Kidney Beans **Red Kidney Beans** **Dark Red Kidney Beans** *(Rajmah)*	Shiny red and dark red, kidney shaped. Used primarily as whole beans.	Dry whole beans Canned red and dark red
Lentils *(Masoor)* **Pink Lentils** *(Masoor Dal)*	These are probably the oldest and most popular beans available in the United States. (Indians sometimes call all dals "lentils," which can be confusing to non-Indians.) There are many varieties of these tiny, disk-shaped beans. They can be different shades of brown or green and from pinhead size to pea size.	Dry whole beans Dry pink lentils Canned whole beans Fresh, vacuum-packed whole lentils

DAL	DESCRIPTION	FORMS
	The split and hulled lentils are called pink or red lentils. They cook up quickly and have become very popular. Pink or red lentils can be found in natural foods stores.	
Mung Beans **Whole Mung Beans** *(Sabut Mung or Moong)* **Split Mung Beans with husk** *(Chilke-Wali Mung Dal)* **Mung Dal (Split and Hulled)** *(Mung Dal)*	These tiny, dull green, pellet-shaped beans have become readily available in natural foods stores. In Indian cooking, mung beans are used extensively in all their forms. Each has a different taste, so use the one the recipe calls for. The whole beans are soaked and sprouted as well as cooked in soups. The split with husk beans are used in porridge (*khichri*). It is the split and hulled variety called mung dal that is used ubiquitously. They are a shiny yellow color.	Dry whole beans Dry split with husk mung beans (sold in Indian stores) Mung dal: Dry split and hulled (sold in Indian stores) Mung bean flour (Rarely used; it does not keep well. Found in Indian stores.)
Pigeon Peas *(Toor Dal, Arhar Dal—split and hulled)*	Red pigeon peas are the most popular variety in India. Although whole beans are used occasionally, it is the split beans that are hulled, washed and polished (toor dal) that are used most often. They are orange-yellow in color, and slightly smaller than split peas. Label them, since it's easy to confuse them with other split yellow beans.	Dry whole red beans Dry split, washed and polished toor dal. (Available as oily and plain in Indian stores; use either one.)
Split Peas **Yellow Split Peas** **Green Split Peas**	These split and hulled peas are rarely used in Indian cooking. They are occasionally used in making bean cakes and crepes. Some people substitute the yellow split peas for chana dal, but they do not cook the same. The peas have a softer and mushier texture. Substitute only as a last option.	Dry yellow split peas Dry green split peas
Urad Dal *(Black Gram, Mungo Beans)* **Whole Urad Dal** *(Sabut Urad)* **Split Urad Dal with husk** *(Chilke-Wali Urad Dal)* **Urad Dal (Split and Hulled)** *(Urad Dal)*	These look similar to mung beans in shape and size, and are black with tiny white lines. They are very different in texture and taste, and should not be interchanged with mung beans. In English, they are called Black Gram, but to keep beans clearly identified, I refer to these as Urad Dal. Urad dal, in all its forms, is used extensively in Indian cooking, though the split and hulled variety is most often used. It is a dull off-white color. When ground, it is paste-like and used in a variety of dishes from snacks to desserts.	(Found in Indian stores) Dry whole beans Dry, split with husk urad dal Dry split, hulled urad dal (an off-white color) Urad dal flour (Rarely used, as it does not keep well. Refrigerate after opening.)

Pigeon Peas

Toor Dal

SOAK: 2 hours or longer (optional)
PREP: 10 minutes
COOK: 20 minutes
MAKES: 6 servings
SERVING SIZE: ½ cup

Toor dal is one of the most popular everyday dals enjoyed in Indian homes. It is easy to make and cooks up quickly in a pressure cooker. It can be lightly seasoned or spiced as desired. In northern India, it is typically served plain. In southern India, vegetables are added to the cooked dal and highly seasoned to make sambhar (page 24). I remember my baby sister once complaining after school to our mom, "It's always toor dal, toor dal, toor dal. Don't you know how to make anything else?" (I think she was really hungry and wanted something special.) Toor dal is the good old standby; it complements most vegetable side dishes and is great with roti and or rice.

¾ cup (split, hulled) toor dal

3 cups water

1 teaspoon ginger, peeled and grated

½ teaspoon turmeric

¾ teaspoon salt, or to taste

¼ teaspoon garam masala (page 24)

SEASONING (*CHOUNK*)

2 teaspoons canola or vegetable oil

⅛ teaspoon asafetida

½ teaspoon cumin seeds

1 teaspoon ground coriander

¼ teaspoon cayenne pepper, or to taste

3 tablespoons tomato sauce

2 tablespoons chopped cilantro, optional

1. Wash dal in 2 to 3 changes of water. Soak for 2 hours or longer. (Dal can be cooked without soaking if you don't have time and are using the pressure cooker. If cooking in a saucepan, you should soak the dal.) Drain the soaking water.

2. (Cook beans in a pressure cooker or a skillet. To cook in pan, see Note below.) In a pressure cooker, add dal, 3 cups water, ginger, turmeric, and salt. Cover with a pressure cooker lid and put the pressure weight in place. Once pressure develops, reduce heat to medium and cook under pressure for 5 minutes. Cool the cooker to remove pressure. Open the lid carefully. Return dal to stove, and simmer for 5 to 8 minutes, until the dal is of desired consistency.

3. *Prepare seasoning:* In a small fry pan, heat oil on medium-high heat. Add the asafetida and cumin seeds. Cook for a few seconds until cumin seeds are golden brown. Remove from heat, add coriander and cayenne pepper, and cook for a few seconds. Stir in tomato sauce. Add seasoning to the dal. Stir.

4. Transfer to a serving bowl and garnish with chopped cilantro if desired. Serve hot. Dal thickens as it cools.

NOTE: *To cook in a skillet:* Follow step 1 above to wash and soak dal. Combine drained dal, 5 cups of water, ginger, turmeric, and salt. Bring to a boil on medium-high heat. Reduce heat and simmer for 20 to 30 minutes, until the beans are very soft. Follow steps 3 and 4 to finish cooking.

NUTRITION INFORMATION PER SERVING:
Calories: 103; Total Fat: 2 g (Saturated Fat: 0 g); Carbohydrate: 17 g; Protein: 6 g; Fiber: 4 g; Sodium: 336 mg

Quick Kidney Beans

Rajmah

PREP: 10 minutes
COOK: 15 minutes
MAKES: 4 servings
SERVING SIZE: ½ cup

Traditional *rajmah*, made with dry beans that are soaked overnight and then cooked, takes a long time to prepare. Canned kidney beans are a good alternative for those rushed meals. They turn this into a quick and easy dish you'll want to make again and again.

1 (16-ounce) can red kidney beans, or 1½ cups cooked kidney beans

2 tablespoons canola or vegetable oil

⅛ teaspoon asafetida powder

½ teaspoon cumin seeds

1 cup onion, finely chopped

1 teaspoon garlic, finely chopped

1 teaspoon ginger, peeled and grated

2 tablespoons tomato sauce

¼ teaspoon turmeric

1 teaspoon ground coriander

¼ teaspoon cayenne pepper, or to taste

¼ teaspoon salt

1½ cups water

½ teaspoon garam masala

1 teaspoon lemon or lime juice

2 tablespoons cilantro, chopped

1. Drain and rinse kidney beans. Set aside.

2. Heat oil in medium fry pan on medium-high heat. Add asafetida and cumin seeds and cook for a few seconds until cumin seeds turn darker brown. Add onion and fry 2 to 3 minutes until golden brown. Add garlic and ginger, cook for a few seconds. Add tomato sauce, turmeric, coriander, and cayenne pepper and stir for a few seconds.

3. Add the drained kidney beans and stir to coat with the spices. Add salt and water. Bring to a boil, reduce heat to a low boil, and simmer for about 10 minutes. Using the back of spoon, mash a few kidney beans against the pan.

4. Add garam masala and lemon juice.

5. Transfer to a serving bowl and garnish with cilantro. Serve with rice or flatbread.

NUTRITION INFORMATION PER SERVING:
Calories: 170; Total Fat: 7 g (Saturated Fat: 0.5 g); Carbohydrate: 20 g; Protein: 7 g; Fiber: 6 g; Sodium: 355 mg

Blackened Spicy Chickpeas

Chole

SOAK: **6 hours or longer**
PREP: **10 minutes**
COOK: **40 to 70 minutes**
MAKES: **8 servings**
SERVING SIZE: **½ cup**

Chole is a Punjab specialty that is often found at Indian parties. For best results, start with dried beans. *Chole* goes with everything, including rice, flatbread, or toast—but for a special treat, serve it with Bhatura (page 167).

1½ cups dry chickpeas

5 cups water, divided

1¼ teaspoons salt

2 teabags or 2 teaspoons tea leaves (any type of black tea)

2 tablespoons canola or vegetable oil

1 teaspoon cumin seeds

¾ cup onion, finely chopped

2 teaspoons garlic, finely chopped

2 teaspoons ginger, peeled and grated

2 teaspoons green chiles, chopped, or ½ teaspoon cayenne pepper, or to taste

1½ teaspoons tamarind paste, or 3 tablespoons tamarind sauce (page 25)

1 tablespoon ground coriander

1½ teaspoons garam masala

2 tablespoons cilantro, chopped, for garnish

¼ cup red onion, sliced, for garnish

4 to 6 tomato slices, for garnish

1. Rinse chickpeas in 2 to 3 changes of water. Soak beans in at least 3 inches of water, for 6 hours or longer. Drain the soaking water.

2. (For best results, prepare in a pressure cooker. To cook in a skillet, see Note below.) In a pressure cooker, place chickpeas, 4 cups of water, and salt. Bring to a boil. After 3 to 4 minutes, skim off the foam with a large slotted spoon and discard. Cover with a pressure cooker lid and put the pressure weight in place. Cook on medium-high heat until the pressure develops. Reduce heat to medium and cook under pressure for about 17 minutes. Cool the cooker until all the pressure is removed. Open the lid carefully. Check beans for tenderness. The chickpeas should easily mash with a spoon against the side of the pan. As you stir the chickpeas, some of them will fall apart (that is how soft you want them).

3. In the meantime, in a separate pan or a microwave-safe bowl, bring 1 cup water to a boil. Add teabags and let steep for about 10 minutes. Squeeze and discard the tea bags. Set aside.

4. Heat oil in a nonstick fry pan over medium-high heat. Add cumin seeds and cook for a few seconds until golden brown. Add onion and fry 2 to 3 minutes until golden brown, stirring frequently. Stir in garlic, ginger, and green chiles, and cook for a few seconds.

5. Add the cooked chickpeas and stir. Add tea water, tamarind, coriander, and garam masala. Bring to a boil and reduce heat. Cover and simmer for about 20 minutes, stirring occasionally. If necessary, add more water, to avoid sticking to the bottom. The finished product should be like a thick stew. It will thicken as it cools.

6. Transfer to a serving platter. Garnish with chopped cilantro, sliced onions, and tomato rings.

NOTE: *To cook in a skillet:* **Combine soaked, drained chickpeas, 6 cups water, and salt. Add**

¼ teaspoon baking soda. Skim off the foam after 3 to 4 minutes with a large slotted spoon and discard. Reduce heat to a low boil and simmer for 40 to 50 minutes, until beans are very tender. The chickpeas should be slightly split and mash easily with a spoon against the side of the pan. As you stir the chickpeas, some of them will fall apart (that is how soft you want them). Continue to follow steps 3 to 6.

NUTRITION INFORMATION PER SERVING:
Calories: 173; Total Fat: 6 g (Saturated Fat: 0.5 g); Carbohydrate: 24 g; Protein: 7 g; Fiber: 7 g; Sodium: 373 mg

GF, LF

Quick Chickpea Curry
Kabuli Chane Ki Subji

PREP: **10 minutes**
COOK: **15 minutes**
MAKES: **8 servings**
SERVING SIZE: **¾ cup**

On those late days at the office, this is my standby last-minute bean dish. Everyone loves it, and it's easy to pull together in less than thirty minutes. Serve with plain rice and salad.

2 (16-ounce) cans chickpeas, or 3 cups cooked chickpeas

2 tablespoons canola or vegetable oil

⅛ teaspoon asafetida powder

1 teaspoon cumin seeds

1 cup onion, finely chopped

2 teaspoons ginger, peeled and grated

1½ cups tomatoes, chopped, or ½ cup canned chopped tomatoes

½ teaspoon turmeric

2 teaspoons ground coriander

½ teaspoon cayenne pepper, or to taste

½ teaspoon salt

3 cups water

½ teaspoon garam masala

2 teaspoons lemon or lime juice

2 tablespoons cilantro, chopped

1. Rinse canned beans in a strainer. Set aside.

2. Heat oil in medium skillet on medium-high heat. Add asafetida and cumin seeds, and cook for a few seconds until cumin seeds turn golden brown. Add onion and fry 2 to 3 minutes until golden brown. Add ginger and tomatoes. Cover and cook for about 2 minutes. Use a masher or the back of a spoon to mash the tomatoes until well blended.

3. Add turmeric, coriander, and cayenne pepper, and stir for a few seconds. Add the chickpeas and stir to coat with the spices. Add salt and water. Bring to a boil, reduce heat to a low boil, and simmer for about 10 minutes. Using the back of a spoon, mash a few chickpeas against the pan.

4. Add garam masala and lemon juice. Transfer to a serving bowl and garnish with cilantro.

NUTRITION INFORMATION PER SERVING:
Calories: 156; Total Fat: 5 g (Saturated Fat: 0.5 g); Carbohydrate: 22 g; Protein: 6 g; Fiber: 6 g: Sodium: 297 mg

••

Black Chickpea Curry

Kaale Chane

SOAK: **6 hours or longer**
PREP: **10 minutes**
COOK: **40 minutes (pressure cooker)**
MAKES: **8 servings**
SERVING SIZE: **½ cup**

Though they are similar in shape and size, black (*kaale*) chana taste very different from chickpeas. Black chana have a firmer texture and taste nuttier and heartier than chickpeas. Although you can substitute chickpeas, if desired, I would encourage you to try the black chana and experience the difference. These beans take a long time to cook; for best results, use a pressure cooker.

1 cup whole black chana (kalla chana)

4 cups water

1 teaspoon salt

1 teaspoon turmeric

PASTE

½ cup tomato sauce or 1 cup tomatoes, chopped

1 cup onion, chopped

2 teaspoons ginger, peeled and chopped

2 teaspoons garlic, chopped

1 teaspoon green chiles, chopped, or ½ teaspoon cayenne pepper, or to taste

¼ cup raw cashews or slivered almonds

1 teaspoon cumin seeds

2 teaspoons ground coriander

2 tablespoons canola or vegetable oil

½ teaspoon sugar

½ teaspoon garam masala

1 tablespoon lemon or lime juice

2 tablespoons chopped cilantro

1. Wash beans in 2 to 3 changes of water. Soak for 6 hours or overnight. Drain the water.

2. (For best results, cook in a pressure cooker. To cook in a skillet, see Note below.) In a pressure cooker, combine beans, 4 cups water, salt, and turmeric. Cover with a lid and put the pressure weight in place. Once pressure develops, reduce heat and cook under pressure for 20 minutes. Cool the cooker until the pressure is removed. Open the lid carefully. Check beans for tenderness. The beans should be soft and mash easily with a spoon against the side of the pan. The liquid will become red from the beans. (If the beans are not soft enough, give pressure for another 5 to 10 minutes.)

3. While beans are cooking, grind tomato sauce, onions, ginger, garlic, green chile, cashews, cumin seeds, and coriander to a smooth paste. Set aside. If needed, add 1 to 2 tablespoons of water to grind the onions.

4. In a nonstick frying pan, add the ground onion masala. Cook over medium-high heat, stirring occasionally until all the water evaporates. Add the oil and continue cooking until the onion masala colors and is thick enough to draw away from the sides and bottom of the pan in a dense mass.

5. Add the onion paste to the boiled beans and stir thoroughly. Bring to a boil and reduce heat to a simmer, 10 minutes. Stir in sugar, garam masala, and lemon juice.

6. Transfer to a serving dish and garnish with cilantro. Serve with rice or flatbread.

NOTE: *To cook in a skillet:* **Follow step 1 above. Combine drained beans, 6 cups of water, salt, and turmeric. Add ¼ teaspoon baking soda. Bring to a boil on medium-high heat. Skim off the foam after about 5 minutes with a large** slotted spoon. Reduce heat and simmer for 40 to 50 minutes, until the beans are very soft. Follow steps 3 to 6 to finish cooking.

NUTRITION INFORMATION PER SERVING:
Calories: 158; Total Fat: 7 g (Saturated Fat: 1 g); Carbohydrate: 19 g; Protein: 6 g; Fiber: 5 g; Sodium: 378 mg

---

GF, LF

Adzuki Beans
Chori

SOAK: **4 hours or longer**
PREP: **10 minutes**
COOK: **40 minutes**
MAKES: **8 servings**
SERVING SIZE: **½ cup**

Adzuki beans look like small kidney beans, but they have a distinctive flavor. I find these beans have a milder and sweeter taste than kidney beans. Serve it over rice or with flatbread.

1 cup dry adzuki beans (chori)

5 cups water

1 teaspoon salt

½ teaspoon turmeric

PASTE

¼ cup tomato sauce or 1 cup tomatoes, chopped

¾ cup onion, chopped

2 teaspoons ginger, peeled and chopped

1 teaspoon garlic, chopped

1 teaspoon green chiles, chopped, or to taste

1 tablespoon poppy seeds, optional

1 teaspoon cumin seeds

2 teaspoons ground coriander

2 tablespoons canola or vegetable oil

½ teaspoon garam masala

2 tablespoons chopped cilantro

1. Wash beans in 2 to 3 changes of water. Soak for 4 hours or overnight. Drain the water.

2. (For best results, cook in a pressure cooker. To cook in a skillet, see Note below.) In a pressure cooker, add beans, 5 cups water, salt, and turmeric. Cover with a lid and put the pressure weight in place. Once pressure develops, reduce heat and cook under pressure for 15 minutes. Cool the cooker until the pressure is removed. Open the lid carefully. Check beans for tenderness. The beans should be soft and mash easily with a spoon against the side of the pan. The liquid will become red from the beans.

3. While beans are cooking, combine tomato sauce, onions, ginger, garlic, green chiles, poppy seeds, cumin seeds, and coriander in a blender container. Grind to a smooth paste. If needed, add 1 to 2 tablespoons of water to grind the onion.

4. In a nonstick frying pan, add the ground onion masala. Cook over medium-high heat, stirring occasionally, until all the water evaporates. Add the oil and continue cooking until the onion masala colors and is thick enough to draw away from the sides and bottom of the pan in a dense mass.

5. Add the onion paste to the boiled beans and stir thoroughly. Bring to a boil and reduce heat to a simmer for 10 minutes. Stir in garam masala.

6. Transfer to a serving dish and garnish with cilantro.

NOTE: *To cook in a skillet:* Combine the soaked, drained beans, 6 cups water, and salt. Add ¼ teaspoon baking soda. Bring to a boil. Reduce heat to a low boil and simmer for 40 to 50 minutes, until beans are very tender. Continue to follow steps 3 to 6.

NUTRITION INFORMATION PER SERVING:
Calories: 122; Total Fat: 4 g (Saturated Fat: 0.5 g); Carbohydrate: 18 g; Protein: 5 g; Fiber: 4 g; Sodium: 294 mg

GF, LF

Black-Eyed Peas and Potatoes

Aloo-Lobhia

PREP: 10 minutes
COOK: 15 minutes
MAKES: 6 servings
SERVING SIZE: ½ cup

When I'm in a hurry, I love to prepare this satisfying and hearty dish. I use frozen or canned black-eyed peas; by the time the rice is cooked, so are the peas. Serve these over rice, or with flatbread.

1½ tablespoons canola or vegetable oil

½ teaspoon cumin seeds

¾ cup onion, finely chopped

1 teaspoon ginger, peeled and grated

1 cup tomatoes, chopped, or 3 tablespoons tomato sauce

½ teaspoon turmeric

1½ teaspoons ground coriander

½ teaspoon cayenne pepper, or to taste

1 tablespoon almond butter or almond meal

1½ cups frozen or boiled black-eyed peas, or 1 (16-ounce) can black-eyed peas, drained and rinsed

1 cup potatoes, peeled and cut into 1-inch pieces

¾ teaspoon salt, or to taste

2 cups water

½ teaspoon garam masala

1 teaspoon lemon or lime juice

2 tablespoons cilantro, chopped

1. Heat oil in a medium skillet on medium-high heat. Add cumin seeds and cook for a few seconds until darker brown. Add onion and fry 2 to 3 minutes until golden brown. Add ginger and tomatoes. Cover and cook for about 2 minutes. Using a potato masher or the back of a spoon, mash the tomatoes until well blended.

2. Add turmeric, coriander, cayenne pepper, and almond butter. Stir for a few seconds. Add the black-eyed peas and potatoes, and stir to coat with the onion masala. Add salt and water. Bring to a boil, reduce heat to a low boil, and simmer for about 10 minutes. Using the back of a spoon, mash a few potatoes against the pan.

3. Add garam masala and lemon juice.

4. Transfer to a serving bowl and garnish with cilantro. Serve with rice or roti.

NUTRITION INFORMATION PER SERVING:
Calories: 114; Total Fat: 4 g (Saturated Fat: 0.5 g); Carbohydrate: 17 g; Protein: 3 g; Fiber: 3 g; Sodium: 395 mg

••

Black Gram and Bengal Gram Dal

Ma Cholia Di Dal

PREP: **10 minutes**
COOK: **30 minutes**
MAKES: **12 servings**
SERVING SIZE: **½ cup**

This is a very popular dish prepared in the Punjab region. The split dals take much less time to cook than the whole urad dal. The cooked dal has a creamy and rich consistency and is great with flatbread or rice. I like to make double the batch and freeze half for those busy nights.

¾ cup (split, hulled) urad dal

¼ cup (split, hulled) chana dal

5 cups water, divided

½ teaspoon turmeric

1 teaspoon salt

SEASONING (*CHOUNK*)

3 tablespoons canola or vegetable oil

¼ teaspoon asafetida powder

½ teaspoon cumin seeds

1 cup onion, finely chopped

2 teaspoons garlic, finely chopped

1 tablespoon ginger, peeled and grated

2 teaspoons ground coriander

½ teaspoon cayenne pepper, or to taste

Lemon wedges

1. Combine urad dal and chana dal. Wash dal in 3 to 4 changes of water. Soak for 2 hours or longer. (Dal can be cooked without soaking if you don't have time and are using the pressure cooker. If cooking in a saucepan, you should soak the dal.) Drain the soaking water.

2. (For best results, cook in a pressure cooker. To cook in a skillet, see Note below.) In a pressure cooker, add washed dals, water, salt, and turmeric. Cover with a lid and put the pressure weight in place. Once pressure develops, reduce heat and cook under pressure for 15 minutes. Cool the cooker until the pressure is removed. Open the lid carefully. The dals should be soft and the water and dal should be well blended.

3. *Prepare seasoning:* While dal is cooking, heat the oil in a nonstick fry pan on medium-high heat. Add the asafetida and cumin seeds. Cook for a few seconds until cumin seeds are golden brown. Add onion and fry 2 to 3 minutes until golden brown. Add garlic, ginger, coriander, and cayenne pepper, and fry for a few seconds.

4. Add seasoning to the cooked dal. Check dal for desired consistency and add water if needed. Bring to a boil, reduce heat, and simmer dal for 5 to 10 minutes.

5. Transfer to a serving bowl and serve with lemon wedges, if desired.

NOTE: *To cook in a skillet:* Follow step 1 above to wash and soak dals. In a medium skillet, combine dals, 7 cups of water, salt, turmeric, and ¼ teaspoon baking soda. Bring to a boil, reduce heat, cover with lid, and simmer for 30 to 40 minutes until beans are soft and well blended. Finish with seasoning as in steps 3 to 5.

FREEZE: You can freeze leftover, unseasoned or seasoned dal in a freezer-safe container for up to 6 months. Thaw dal, bring to a boil, and season as in steps 3 to 5.

NUTRITION INFORMATION PER SERVING:
Calories: 96; Total Fat: 4 g (Saturated Fat: 0.5 g); Carbohydrate: 11 g; Protein: 4 g; Fiber: 3 g; Sodium: 200 mg

·.

Bengal Gram and Bottle Gourd

Chana-Lauki Dal

SOAK: 2 hours or longer
PREP: 10 minutes
COOK: 20 minutes
MAKES: 8 servings
SERVING SIZE: ½ cup

*L*auki (bottle gourd) is only available in summer, whereas zucchini is available year-round. Both work well in this dish. You can use split yellow peas instead of chana dal, but the texture of the chana dal is firmer.

¾ cup (split, hulled) chana dal, or split yellow peas

4 cups water

2 teaspoons ginger, peeled and grated

½ teaspoon turmeric

¾ teaspoon salt

2 cups bottle gourd or zucchini

SEASONING (*CHOUNK*)

1 tablespoon canola or vegetable oil

⅛ teaspoon asafetida powder

1 teaspoon cumin seeds

¾ cup onion, finely chopped

1 cup tomatoes, chopped

1 teaspoon ground coriander

½ teaspoon cayenne pepper, or to taste

½ teaspoon garam masala

½ teaspoon amchur or 1 teaspoon lemon or lime juice

2 tablespoons cilantro, chopped

1. Wash dal in 3 to 4 changes of water. Soak for 2 hours or longer. Drain the soaking water.

2. (For best results, cook in a pressure cooker. To cook in a skillet, see Note below.) In a pressure cooker, add drained dal, water, ginger, turmeric, and salt. Cover with a pressure cooker lid and put the pressure weight in place. Once pressure develops, reduce heat to medium and cook under pressure for 10 minutes. Cool the cooker until all the pressure is removed. Open the lid carefully. Check beans for tenderness. The dal should be very soft. Mash some of the beans with the back of a large spoon against the side of the pressure cooker.

3. Peel and cut the bottle gourd into 1-inch pieces. (If using zucchini, leave unpeeled and cut into 1-inch pieces.) Add the diced bottle gourd and bring mixture to a boil. Cook for 5 to 7 minutes, until the gourd is tender.

4. *Prepare seasoning while beans cook*: In a small fry pan, heat the oil on medium-high heat. Add the asafetida and cumin seeds. Cook for a few seconds, until cumin seeds are golden brown. Add onion and fry 2 to 3 minutes until golden brown. Add tomatoes and cook for 2 to 3 minutes until tomatoes are soft. Mash the tomatoes with a potato masher or the back of a large spoon. Add coriander and cayenne pepper and mix well.

5. Transfer onion mixture to the cooked dal. Add garam masala and amchur. Transfer to a serving bowl and garnish with cilantro.

NOTE: *To cook in a skillet:* Follow step 1 above. Combine drained beans, 6 cups of water, salt, and turmeric. Add ¼ teaspoon baking soda. Bring to a boil on medium-high heat. Reduce heat and simmer for 20 to 30 minutes, until the beans are very soft. Follow steps 3 to 6 to finish cooking.

GF, LF

Spinach Bengal Gram Dal

Palak Chana Dal

SOAK: 2 hours or longer (optional)
PREP: 10 minutes
COOK: 30 minutes
MAKES: 8 servings
SERVING SIZE: ½ cup

Chana dal has a nutty texture and combines well with spinach. For quick preparation and convenience, I use frozen spinach.

1 cup (split, hulled) chana dal

3 cups water

½ teaspoon turmeric

1 teaspoon salt, divided

2 tablespoons canola or vegetable oil

⅛ teaspoon asafetida powder

½ teaspoon cumin seeds

4–5 dry whole red chiles

1 cup onion, thinly sliced

2 teaspoons garlic, finely chopped

1 tablespoon ginger, peeled and grated

2 cups frozen chopped spinach, thawed, or 4 cups fresh spinach, chopped

2 teaspoons ground coriander

1 teaspoon garam masala

1. Wash dal in 3 to 4 changes of water. Soak for 2 hours or longer. (Dal can be cooked without soaking if you are using the pressure cooker. If cooking in a saucepan, soak dal beforehand.) Drain the water.

2. (For best results, cook in a skillet. To cook in a pressure cooker, see Note below.) In a medium skillet, combine washed dal, water, ½ teaspoon salt, and turmeric. Bring to a boil. Reduce heat to a low boil and simmer for 20 to 25 minutes. The dal should be tender. Do not overcook.

3. While dal is cooking, heat oil in a large nonstick fry pan on medium-high heat to near smoking point. Add the asafetida, cumin seeds, and red chiles. Cook for a few seconds until seeds are golden brown. Add onion and cook for 2 to 3 minutes until onions are light brown, stirring frequently. Add garlic and ginger, and stir for a few seconds.

4. Add thawed spinach, coriander, garam masala, and remaining ½ teaspoon salt. Stir well. Cook for 5 minutes until spinach is cooked and most of the water is absorbed.

5. Add the cooked dal and mix well. Cook for about 5 minutes. Serve hot.

NOTE: *To cook in a pressure cooker:* Wash dal as in step 1 above. In a pressure cooker, combine dal, 2 cups of water, ½ teaspoon salt, and turmeric. Cover with a pressure cooker lid and put the pressure weight in place. Once pressure develops, reduce heat to medium and cook under pressure for 4 minutes. Cool the cooker until all the pressure is removed. Open the lid carefully and check for doneness. The dal should be tender but not falling apart. Follow steps 3 to 5 to finish the dal.

···

Mixed Three Dals

Milli Dal

SOAK: 2 hours or more (optional)
PREP: 10 minutes
COOK: 20 minutes
MAKES: 8 servings
SERVING SIZE: ½ cup

This mixed dal has a nice blend of flavor. It is easy to make and is lightly seasoned.

¼ cup (split, hulled) toor dal

¼ cup (split with skin) mung dal

¼ cup (split, hulled) chana dal

3 cups water

1 teaspoon ginger, peeled and grated

½ teaspoon turmeric

1 teaspoon salt

½ teaspoon garam masala

SEASONING (*CHOUNK*)

1 tablespoon canola oil or ghee

⅛ teaspoon asafetida powder

½ teaspoon cumin seeds

1 teaspoon ground coriander

¼ teaspoon cayenne pepper, or to taste

1. Combine dals and wash in 3 to 4 changes of water. Soak for 2 hours or longer. (Dal can be cooked without soaking if you are using the pressure cooker.) Drain the soaking water.

2. (For best results, cook in a pressure cooker. To cook in a skillet, see Note below.) In a pressure cooker, combine drained dal, water, ginger, turmeric, and salt. Cover with a pressure cooker lid and put the pressure weight in place. Once pressure develops, reduce heat to medium and cook

under pressure for 5 minutes. Cool the cooker until all the pressure is removed.

3. Return dal to stove, and simmer for about 10 minutes.

4. *Prepare seasoning:* In a small fry pan, heat the oil on medium-high. Add the asafetida and cumin seeds. Cook for a few seconds until cumin seeds turn golden brown. Remove from heat and add coriander and cayenne pepper.

5. Add seasoning to the cooked dal. Transfer to a serving bowl.

NOTE: *To cook in a skillet:* Follow step 1 above to wash and soak dals. Combine drained dal, 5 cups of water, salt, and turmeric. Bring to a boil on medium-high heat. Reduce heat and simmer for 20 to 30 minutes, until the beans are very soft. Follow steps 4 to 5 to finish cooking.

NUTRITION INFORMATION PER SERVING:
Calories: 83; Total Fat: 2 g (Saturated Fat: 0 g); Carbohydrate: 12 g; Protein: 4 g; Fiber: 2 g; Sodium: 294 mg

···

Dal-Vegetable Stew

Dhan-Saak

SOAK: 2 hours or more (optional)
PREP: 10 minutes
COOK: 30 minutes
MAKES: 8 servings
SERVING SIZE: ½ cup

The first time I tasted this dal was in London. The restaurant owner told me that it was one of his popular requests from Brits—served both with chicken and without. Stew-like with a creamy consistency, this Parsi-Indian fusion dish is hearty and fragrant. In many recipes, the dal and vegetables are cooked and then strained for a creamy texture. I love making this with butternut squash. Although you can purchase *dhan-saak* masala, I use the readily available spices from my spice cabinet. Serve with rice of choice or Dried Fruit Rice (page 142).

⅓ cup (split, hulled) toor dal

⅓ cup (split, hulled) mung dal

⅓ cup pink lentils

3 cups water

1 teaspoon turmeric

1½ teaspoons salt

2 cups butternut or acorn squash, peeled and cut into 1-inch pieces

1 cup eggplant, cut into 1-inch cubes

PASTE

1 tablespoon garlic, coarsely chopped

1 tablespoon ginger, peeled and coarsely chopped

1 cup tomatoes, coarsely chopped

1 teaspoon cumin seeds

1 teaspoon garam masala

1 teaspoon ground coriander

½–1 teaspoon cayenne pepper

½ teaspoon fenugreek seeds

½ teaspoon fennel seeds

¼ cup cilantro, chopped

2 tablespoons mint leaves, chopped

1 teaspoon tamarind paste or 2 tablespoons tamarind sauce (page 25)

¼ cup water

3 tablespoons canola or vegetable oil

1 cup onion, finely chopped

1. Combine toor dal, mung dal, and lentils. Wash in 3 to 4 changes of water and drain.

2. (For best results, cook in a pressure cooker. To cook in a skillet, see Note below.) In a pressure cooker, add dal, 2 cups of water, turmeric, salt, squash, and eggplant. Cover with the lid and put the pressure weight in place. Once pressure develops, reduce heat, and cook under pressure for 5 minutes. Cool the cooker until the pressure is removed. Open the lid carefully. The beans and vegetables should be very soft. Stir a few times.

3. *In the meantime, prepare paste:* In a blender, combine garlic, ginger, tomatoes, cumin seeds, garam masala, coriander, cayenne pepper, fenugreek seeds, fennel seeds, cilantro, mint leaves, tamarind paste, and water. Grind to a smooth paste. Set aside.

4. In a large fry pan, heat oil on medium-high heat. Add onion and fry 2 to 3 minutes until golden brown. Add the paste and fry until oil separates, about 5 minutes, stirring frequently.

5. Add the dal mixture to the onion paste. Stir to coat dal mixture with the spices. Add ½ cup water, or more as needed, for desired consistency. (Mixture should have a thick, stew-like consistency.) Bring to a boil, reduce heat to a low boil, cover, and simmer for 10 minutes.

6. Serve hot over a bed of rice.

NOTE: *To cook in a skillet:* After washing dals as instructed in step 1 above, soak the dals for 2 hours or longer. Drain dals. Combine drained dals, 4 cups of water, salt, turmeric, squash, and eggplant. Bring dal to a boil, reduce heat, and simmer for 25 to 30 minutes, until the dals and vegetables are very soft. Stir to smooth consistency. Follow steps 3 to 6 to finish cooking.

NUTRITION INFORMATION PER SERVING:
Calories: 159; Total Fat: 6 g (Saturated Fat: 0.5 g); Carbohydrate: 22 g; Protein: 7 g; Fiber: 4 g; Sodium: 443 mg

....

Garlic-Flavored Mixed Dal

Lehsun Wali Dal

SOAK: 2 hours or longer (optional)
PREP: 10 minutes
COOK: 20 minutes
MAKES: 8 servings
SERVING SIZE: ½ cup

Mixing five different dals imparts a very different flavor to this dish. Since all the dals are split and dehusked, they cook up quickly. Garlic infuses the dal and adds a lot of flavor.

¼ cup (split, hulled) toor dal

3 tablespoons pink lentils

3 tablespoons (split, hulled) urad dal

3 tablespoons (split, hulled) mung dal

3 tablespoons (split, hulled) chana dal

4 cups water

2 teaspoons ginger, peeled and grated

½ teaspoon turmeric

1 teaspoon salt

2 teaspoons lemon or lime juice

SEASONING (*CHOUNK*)

1 tablespoon canola or vegetable oil

⅛ teaspoon asafetida powder

1 teaspoon cumin seeds

1 tablespoon garlic, grated

¼–½ teaspoon cayenne pepper

1. Combine all the dals and wash in 3 to 4 changes of water. Soak for about 2 hours. (Dal can be cooked without soaking if you are using the pressure cooker.) Drain the soaking water.

2. (For best results, cook in a skillet. To cook in a pressure cooker, see Note below.) In a medium saucepan, combine washed lentils, water, ginger, turmeric, and salt. Bring to a boil, reduce heat, and simmer for 15 to 20 minutes, until the lentils are completely soft and soupy.

3. *Prepare seasoning:* In a small fry pan, heat oil on medium-high heat. Add the asafetida and cumin seeds. Cook for a few seconds until cumin seeds are golden brown. Add garlic and cook for a few seconds. Remove from heat and add cayenne pepper.

4. Add seasoning to the dal. Stir in lemon juice and transfer to a serving bowl. Serve hot.

NOTE: *To cook in a pressure cooker:* Follow step 1 above. Add drained dals, 2 cups of water, ginger, turmeric, and salt. Cover with a pressure cooker lid and put the pressure weight in place. Once pressure develops, reduce heat to medium and cook under pressure for 2 minutes. Cool the cooker until all the pressure is removed. Open the lid carefully. Follow steps 2 to 4 as above.

NUTRITION INFORMATION PER SERVING:
Calories: 103; Total Fat: 2 g (Saturated Fat: 0 g); Carbohydrate: 16 g; Protein: 6 g; Fiber: 3 g; Sodium: 295 mg

....

Ginger-Spinach Pink Lentils

Adrak-Palak Dal

SOAK: 1 hour or more (optional)
PREP: 10 minutes
COOK: 30 minutes
MAKES: 8 servings
SERVING SIZE: ½ cup

Pink lentils are versatile and cook up quickly. Spinach and a hint of ginger add wonderful flavor to this dal. Serve it with rice or flatbread, or enjoy it like a soup with good, hearty whole grain bread.

¾ cup pink lentils

4 cups water

1 tablespoon ginger, peeled and grated

½ teaspoon turmeric

¾ teaspoon salt

1 cup tomatoes, finely chopped

2 cups fresh spinach, finely chopped, or 1 cup frozen spinach

SEASONING (*CHOUNK*)

2 teaspoons vegetable oil

⅛ teaspoon asafetida powder

½ teaspoon cumin seeds

1 teaspoon ground coriander

½ teaspoon cayenne pepper, or to taste

2 teaspoons lemon or lime juice

1. Wash lentils in 3 to 4 changes of water. Soak for 1 hour or longer. (Dal can be cooked without soaking if you're short on time, though the cooking time will take longer.) Drain the dal.

2. (For best results, cook in a saucepan. To cook in a pressure cooker, see Note below.) In a medium saucepan, add washed lentils, ginger, turmeric, and salt. Bring to a boil, reduce heat, and simmer for 15 to 20 minutes, until the lentils are completely soft.

3. Add the chopped tomatoes and spinach. Bring to boil. Reduce heat and simmer for 8 to 10 minutes.

4. *Prepare seasoning:* In a small fry pan, heat the oil on medium-high heat. Add the asafetida and cumin seeds. Cook for a few seconds, until cumin seeds are golden brown. Remove from heat and add coriander and cayenne pepper.

5. Add seasoning to the dal. Stir in lemon juice and transfer to a serving bowl. Serve hot.

NOTE: *To cook in a pressure cooker:* Wash lentils as in step 1 above (there is no need to soak them). In a pressure cooker, combine washed lentils, 2 cups of water, ginger, turmeric, and salt. Cover with a pressure cooker lid and put the pressure weight in place. As soon as full pressure develops, remove from heat. Cool the cooker to remove pressure. Open the lid carefully. Follow steps 2 to 4 as above.

NUTRITION INFORMATION PER SERVING:
Calories: 78; Total Fat: 2 g (Saturated Fat: 0 g); Carbohydrate: 12 g; Protein: 5 g: Fiber: 2 g; Sodium: 226 mg

---

GF, LF

Spinach Sambhar
Palak Sambhar

SOAK: **2 hours or longer (optional)**
PREP: **10 minutes**
COOK: **30 minutes**
MAKES: **6 servings**
SERVING SIZE: **½ cup**

Sambhar is the most popular way to cook dal throughout southern India. Sambhar is typically made with toor dal and has a variety of vegetables added to it. Tamarind gives sambhar its typical brown color and sour taste. There are as many variations on sambhar as there are cooks. This is one of my favorites. It's a great way to eat spinach. Serve with Quick Idli (Rice Dumplings, page 85) or plain rice.

¾ cup (split, hulled) toor dal

4 cups water, divided

1 teaspoons salt

½ teaspoon turmeric

½ cup onion, chopped into ½-inch cubes

1 cup tomato, chopped into 1-inch cubes

2 cups fresh spinach, finely chopped, or 1 cup frozen spinach

2 tablespoons sambhar powder (page 24), or purchased

1 teaspoon tamarind paste, or 2 tablespoons tamarind sauce (page 25)

SEASONING (*CHOUNK*)

2 teaspoons canola or vegetable oil

⅛ teaspoon asafetida powder

½ teaspoon mustard seeds

6–8 curry leaves, optional

1. Wash dal in 3 to 4 changes of water. Soak for 2 hours or longer. Drain the soaking water. (If you are using a pressure cooker, dal can be cooked without soaking. If cooking in a saucepan, you should soak the dal.)

2. (For best results, cook in a pressure cooker. To cook in a skillet, see Note below.) In a pressure cooker, combine washed dal, 2 cups of water, salt, and turmeric. Cover with a pressure cooker lid and put the pressure weight in place. Once the pressure is fully developed, give pressure for 5 minutes. Open the lid carefully once the pressure cooker is safe to open. Stir dal with a wire whisk a few times until smooth.

3. Return pressure cooker to the stove. Add the onion, tomatoes, spinach, and remaining 2 cups of water. Bring to a boil. Reduce heat and simmer for 6 to 7 minutes. Add sambhar powder and tamarind. Continue to simmer for an additional 5 minutes.

4. *Prepare seasoning:* In a small fry pan, heat oil on medium-high heat. Add the asafetida and mustard seeds. Cover with lid and cook for a few seconds until mustard seeds stop popping. Remove from heat and add curry leaves. Cook for a few seconds. Add seasoning to sambhar. Transfer to a serving bowl and serve hot.

NOTE: *To cook in a skillet:* Wash and soak dal as in step 1 above. Combine drained dal, 5 cups of water, salt, and turmeric. Bring to a boil on medium-high heat. Reduce heat and simmer for 20 to 30 minutes, until the beans are very soft. Follow steps 3 and 4 to finish cooking.

NUTRITION INFORMATION PER SERVING:
Calories: 114; Total Fat: 2 g (Saturated Fat: 0 g); Carbohydrate: 19 g; Protein: 6 g; Fiber: 5 g; Sodium: 402 mg

---

GF

Coconut-Vegetable Sambhar
Nariyal-Subji Sambhar

SOAK: 2 hours or longer (optional)
PREP: 10 minutes
COOK: 30 minutes
MAKES: 8 servings
SERVING SIZE: 1 cup

I used to make this sambhar the traditional way, grinding the grated coconut with water and then adding it to the sambhar. But then I discovered coconut milk. I was very happy with the results, and I now keep a can of coconut milk handy.

You can, of course, use store-bought sambhar powder to save time. I like to prepare my own sambhar powder; it lasts me for three to four batches of sambhar. It's worth the effort, and I can adjust the heat and flavor to my family's liking.

¾ cup (split, hulled) toor dal

6 cups water

1 teaspoon salt, divided

1 teaspoon turmeric

SEASONING (CHOUNK)

1 tablespoon canola or vegetable oil

⅛ teaspoon asafetida powder

½ teaspoon mustard seeds

½ teaspoon cumin seeds

6–8 curry leaves, chopped

1 cup frozen white pearl onions, or shallots, peeled

1 cup eggplant, chopped into 1-inch pieces

1 cup green peppers, chopped into1-inch pieces

1 cup green beans, chopped into 1-inch pieces, or frozen green beans

4 tablespoons sambhar powder (page 24), or purchased

½ cup coconut milk

2 teaspoons tamarind paste or 3 tablespoons tamarind sauce (page 25)

2 tablespoons cilantro, chopped

1. Wash dal in 3 to 4 changes of water. Soak for 2 hours or longer. (Dal can be cooked without soaking if you don't have time and are using the pressure cooker.) Drain the soaking water.

2. (For best results, cook in a pressure cooker. To cook in a skillet, see Note below.) In a pressure cooker, combine washed dal, 2 cups of water, ½ teaspoon salt, and turmeric. Cover with a pressure cooker lid and put the pressure weight in place. Once the pressure is fully developed, give pressure for 5 minutes. Open the lid carefully once the pressure cooker is safe to open. Stir the dal with a wire whisk a few times until smooth. Set aside.

3. *Prepare seasoning:* In a 3- to 4-quart saucepan, heat the oil on medium-high heat, to near smoking point. Add the asafetida and mustard seeds. Cover with lid, cook for a few seconds until mustard seeds pop. Add cumin seeds and curry leaves. Cook for a few seconds. Add pearl onions and eggplants and stir-fry for 1 minute. Add peppers and green beans and ½ teaspoon salt. Bring to a boil. Reduce heat to a low boil, cover with lid, and simmer for about 5 minutes.

4. Add the cooked dal to the vegetables. Add remaining 2 cups of water, sambhar powder, tamarind, and coconut milk. Bring to a boil. Reduce heat to a low boil and simmer for another 5 minutes.

5. Transfer to a serving bowl and garnish with cilantro. Serve hot with rice.

NOTE: *To cook in a skillet:* Wash and soak dal as directed in step 1 above. Combine drained dal, 5 cups of water, ½ teaspoon salt, and turmeric. Bring to a boil on medium-high heat. Reduce heat and simmer for 20 to 30 minutes, until the beans are very soft. Follow steps 3 to 5 to finish cooking.

NUTRITION INFORMATION PER SERVING:
Calories: 126; Total Fat: 5 g (Saturated Fat: 3 g); Carbohydrate: 16 g; Protein: 5 g; Fiber: 4 g; Sodium: 339 mg

Mung Bean–Tomato Dal

Sabut Mung–Tamatar Dal

SOAK: 4 hours or longer (optional)
PREP: 10 minutes
COOK: 30 minutes
MAKES: 10 servings
SERVING SIZE: ½ cup

Tomatoes and spices transform whole mung beans into a flavored stew you'll want to make again and again.

¾ cup whole mung beans

5 cups water, divided

½ teaspoon turmeric

1 teaspoon salt

2 tablespoons canola or vegetable oil

⅛ teaspoon asafetida powder

½ teaspoon cumin seeds

¾ cup onion, finely chopped

2 cups tomatoes, chopped, or ¾ cup chopped canned tomatoes

1 tablespoon ginger, peeled and grated

½ teaspoon cayenne pepper, optional

1 teaspoon garam masala

1 teaspoon lemon or lime juice

1. Wash beans in 3 to 4 changes of water. Soak for 4 hours or longer. (Dal can be cooked without soaking if you don't have time and are using the pressure cooker.)

2. (For best results, cook in a pressure cooker. To cook in a skillet, see Note below.) In a pressure cooker, combine washed beans, 4 cups of water, salt, and turmeric. Cover with a pressure cooker lid and put the pressure weight in place. Once pressure develops, reduce heat to medium and cook under pressure for 15 minutes. Cool the cooker to remove pressure. Open the lid carefully. The beans should be soft and the water and beans should be well blended.

3. While dal cooks, heat oil in a nonstick fry pan on medium-high heat. Add the asafetida and cumin seeds, cook for a few seconds until cumin seeds are golden brown. Add onion and fry 2 to 3 minutes until golden brown. Add tomatoes, ginger, and cayenne pepper, if using, and cook for 2 to 3 minutes, until tomatoes are soft.

4. Add seasoning to the cooked dal. Check for desired consistency. If necessary, add ½ to 1 cup more water. Bring to a boil, reduce heat, and simmer dal for 5 to 10 minutes. Add garam masala and lemon juice. Dal thickens as it cools.

NOTE: *To cook in a skillet:* Wash and soak beans as directed in step 1 above. In a medium skillet, combine mung beans, 7 cups of water, salt, and turmeric. Bring to a boil, reduce heat, cover with lid, and simmer for about 60 minutes. Stir periodically and adjust heat as necessary. Check for doneness and consistency. Finish with seasoning as in steps 3 to 5.

FREEZE: You can freeze dal in a freezer-safe container for up to 6 months. Thaw and bring to a boil before serving.

NUTRITION INFORMATION PER SERVING:
Calories: 90; Total Fat: 3 g (Saturated Fat: 0 g); Carbohydrate: 12 g; Protein: 4 g; Fiber: 3 g; Sodium: 235 mg

••

Zucchini-Tomato Dal

Torai-Tamatar Dal

SOAK TIME: 1 hour or longer (optional)
PREP: 10 minutes
COOK: 20 minutes
MAKES: 6 servings
SERVING SIZE: 1 cup

This is a quick, easy, and nutritious dal. Split and hulled mung dal cook up fast, like the pink lentils. I prefer the taste and texture of zucchini in this dal, as it most closely resembles torai and is available year-round. The addition of tomatoes adds a wonderful color, taste, and texture to the dal. Do not overcook the dal or the vegetables. For best results, do not prepare this dal in the pressure cooker, for it can easily become mushy.

¾ cup (split, hulled) mung dal

2 cups water

½ teaspoon turmeric

1 teaspoon salt, divided

1 tablespoon canola or vegetable oil

⅛ teaspoon asafetida powder

1 teaspoon cumin seeds

4 cups (8 ounces) zucchini, cut into ¼-inch wedges

1½ cups tomatoes, chopped, or 1 cup canned chopped tomatoes

1 teaspoon ground coriander

¼ teaspoon cayenne pepper, or to taste, or 1 teaspoon green chile, chopped

½ teaspoon garam masala

1. Wash dal in 3 to 4 changes of water, using your hands as necessary to clean the dal. Soak for 1 hour or more. Drain water. (Dal can be used without soaking, but cooking time will be longer.)

2. In a medium saucepan, combine dal, water, ½ teaspoon salt, and turmeric. Bring to a boil. Reduce heat to a low boil, cover with lid, and simmer for 10 to 15 minutes. The dal should be tender but not mushy.

3. While dal cooks, heat oil in a large, nonstick fry pan on medium-high heat to near smoking point. Add the asafetida and cumin seeds, and cook for a few seconds until seeds turn brown. Add zucchini, tomatoes, coriander, cayenne pepper, garam masala, and the remaining ½ teaspoon salt. Stir and heat until bubbling. Reduce heat, cover with lid, and cook for 5 minutes, until zucchini is tender but still crunchy.

4. Add the zucchini mixture to the cooked dal. Bring to a boil, reduce heat, and simmer for 2 minutes. Serve hot with rice or any flatbread.

NUTRITION INFORMATION PER SERVING:
Calories: 131; Total Fat: 3 g (Saturated Fat: 0 g); Carbohydrate: 21 g; Protein: 8 g; Fiber: 3 g; Sodium: 323 mg

Rice and Other Grains

RICE IS EATEN throughout India and is the primary grain eaten in southern and eastern India. Since ancient times, rice has been the staple food for three-quarters of the world's population. It is easy to grow, inexpensive, versatile, and has a long shelf life. It is a satisfying complement to almost any meal.

Regional variations in rice dishes abound, particularly in southern India, where rice is ground with beans and fermented overnight to make *idlies* (dumplings), *dosas* (crepes), and *adai* (pancakes). Then there are yogurt rice, tamarind rice, and lemon rice—these dishes can be kept at room temperature for several hours and are great for picnics, lunch boxes, and traveling.

Pulao and *Biryani* (two varieties of pilafs) are specialties of northern India. Rice (often basmati) is seasoned and mixed with a variety of vegetables, meats, nuts, and dried fruits.

Types of Rice

There are numerous types of rice available around the world. Below are the most common types of rice used in Indian dishes and featured in this book.

Long-Grain Rice: The rice most commonly eaten in India. Jasmine, is the most widely used rice though there are many other long-grain varieties as well. Long-grain rice is slightly sticky compared to basmati rice and is the perfect texture to complement most curries.

Basmati Rice: Once a hard-to-find specialty, basmati rice is now available at most natural foods stores and supermarkets. Basmati, an extra-long-grain rice, yields a mild aroma when cooked. It is less sticky than long-grain rice, and cooks up fluffy and white. It is an ideal choice for pilafs. However, it is more expensive and thus used mainly for special occasions. Nutritionally, basmati is thought to have a lower glycemic index, meaning it is more slowly absorbed into the bloodstream, and thus many people concerned with blood glucose levels find it a preferable choice. Please use this information about basmati rice with caution, as its glycemic index may change depending on how it is cooked or when eaten with other foods. The longer rice is cooked, the higher its glycemic index.

Parboiled Rice: Quick and minute rices are rarely used in Indian cooking.

Brown Rice: Brown long-grain and basmati rice are both available today. They are not traditionally used, as their strong flavor and nutty texture is overpowering and does not mix well with other foods. I have included some brown rice options. Substitute brown rice in recipes, as desired.

Other Rice: Some of the other types of rice available in Indian stores are *poha* (pounded rice) and puffed rice (*mamra* or *murmure*). *Poha* is parboiled rice that is flattened and thus cooks up in just a few minutes. *Mamra* is similar in texture to puffed rice and is primarily eaten as a snack.

Rice Noodles: Rice noodles, also called rice sticks, are readily available in supermarkets. They keep well in the pantry and take just a few minutes to prepare. They are easy to make and blend well with seasonings and other ingredients. Chinese and other Asian cuisines use rice noodles frequently. You can find fresh rice noodles in the refrigerated section of most Asian grocery stores. These noodles cook in seconds and taste fresher than the dry ones.

Other Grains: I have included a recipe using buckwheat groats (Buckwheat Pilaf, page 150), and a couscous recipe (Curried Spinach Couscous, page 150). These grains are becoming increasingly popular here in the West. They make a nice side dish or a quick meal. Enjoy them spiced and cooked with Indian seasonings.

Fluffy, Perfect Rice

Although rice is one of the simplest foods to cook, the perfect, fluffy rice can still be a challenge to achieve. I've included the correct amount of water needed to cook the rice in every recipe, but keep in mind that the heat intensity, type of pan you use, and soaking can change the rice's cooking time and consistency. Follow these steps every time you cook rice. Practice a few times and you'll have fluffy rice every time.

1. Use a wide saucepan or a skillet with a lid, large enough for the rice to expand. My general rule of thumb is a 1-quart pan for every 1 cup of rice—for example, 1 quart for 1 cup, 2 quarts for 2 cups. You can use a larger pan, but never a smaller one. If you use a smaller pan than required, you will have unevenly cooked or sticky rice, as the grains will get packed and not have

room to expand. Make sure the pan has a tight-fitting lid.

2. Wash the rice in 3 to 4 changes of water. Washing removes any starchy powder and makes the rice less sticky. To wash rice, place in a bowl and add cold water. Rub and stir the rice grains with your hand between changes of water. (Rice processed in the United States has been washed and enriched with nutrients and may not require washing. However, all rice sold in Indian and Asian stores should be washed before using.)

3. For best results, soak rice in cold water for 15 to 30 minutes. Soaking lengthens the grains and reduces the stickiness. Strain the rice and discard the water. (This step can be eliminated if you are short on time; just wash and cook rice.)

4. Add 2 cups of water for 1 cup of rice. If you're cooking 3 or more cups of rice, reduce the water by about 1 tablespoon per cup rice. For example, for 3 cups of rice use about 5 ¾ cups of water, and for 5 cups of rice use 9 ½ cups of water.

5. Bring the rice to a full boil, reduce the heat, and simmer uncovered for 12 to 15 minutes. The water should be fully absorbed. Check if the rice is done by placing 1 to 2 grains of rice on the countertop and gently pressing with a finger. The rice should be firm yet soft with no grainy texture. If the rice is not done, you will see and feel a little grain in the pressed rice. Continue to simmer for a few more minutes. Once the rice is done, remove it from the heat, cover with lid, and let stand until ready to serve.

6. Before serving, gently fluff rice with a fork. Lift rice and gently break up any lumps.

Reheating Rice

Rice tastes best when it is hot or at least at room temperature, not refrigerated. A microwave makes reheating much easier. For best results, reheat rice in a microwave-safe dish, add 1 to 2 tablespoons of water (based on the amount of rice) over the cold rice, cover with a lid, and microwave on high until steamed though. If using the stovetop, heat the water in the bottom of the pan, add rice, and steam through. Cover with lid, let sit for 2 to 3 minutes, and enjoy.

GF, LF

Basmati Rice
Basmati Chawal

SOAK TIME: 15 minutes (optional)
PREP: 5 minutes
COOK: 20 minutes
MAKES: 8 servings
SERVING SIZE: ½ cup

Basmati rice is unique in its texture and flavor. It is extra long, super white, and comes out fluffy every time. It is the preferred rice for rice pilafs such as Pea-Mushroom Pilaf (page 141). For best results, soak the rice before cooking it. Be sure not to overcook, as it will get sticky.

1 cup basmati rice

2 cups water

1. Wash rice in 2 to 3 changes of water until the water is relatively clear. Soak in cold water for 20 minutes or longer. (Soaking helps make the rice grains longer. If you don't have time, this step can be eliminated.) Drain the rice in a strainer.

2. Place rice and water in a 1-quart or larger saucepan. Bring water to a boil. Reduce heat to a simmer. Simmer for 12 to15 minutes. All the water should be absorbed. Check if rice is cooked by placing 1 or 2 grains of rice on the counter-top and gently pressing with your finger. If the rice is not cooked, you will feel the grain under your finger.

3. Remove from the heat. Cover with a lid until ready to serve. Before serving, fluff rice with a fork. Start from the sides and gradually move to the center, opening and fluffing all the rice.

NUTRITION INFORMATION PER SERVING:
Calories: 84; Total Fat: 0 g (Saturated Fat: 0 g); Carbohydrate: 19 g; Protein: 2 g; Fiber: 0 g; Sodium: 1 mg

---

GF, LF

∴∴∴∴∴∴∴∴∴∴∴∴∴∴∴∴∴∴∴∴∴∴∴∴∴∴∴∴∴∴∴∴∴

Brown Basmati Rice

Bhure Basmati Chawal

> PREP: 5 minutes
> COOK: 40 minutes
> MAKES: 8 servings
> SERVING SIZE: ½ cup

Brown basmati rice has all the flavor of white basmati rice with an extra bonus: It has a nutty texture, and all the goodness of whole grain. You can substitute brown basmati rice in some of the *pulao* recipes, but they do not absorb the flavor of spices and other ingredients as well as white rice. Serve plain brown basmati rice with any curry sauces.

1 cup brown basmati rice
2½ cups water

1. Wash rice in 2 to 3 changes of water. Drain the water. Place rice and water in a 1- to 2-quart saucepan. Bring water to a boil. Reduce heat to a simmer. Simmer for 35 to 40 minutes. All water should be absorbed. Check if rice is fully cooked, by placing 1 or 2 grains of rice on the counter-top and gently pressing with your finger. If the rice is not done, you will feel the grain under your finger.

2. Remove from the heat. Cover with a lid until ready to serve. Before serving, stir with a fork as you fluff the rice.

NUTRITION INFORMATION PER SERVING:
Calories: 86; Total Fat: 1 g (Saturated Fat: 0 g); Carbohydrate: 18 g; Protein: 2 g; Fiber: 1 g; Sodium: 2 mg

---

VARIATION: Make a wild rice and brown rice combination. Both of these rices complement each other in taste and texture and also cook in about the same amount of time. Combine ¾ cup brown basmati rice with ¼ cup wild rice. Follow the recipe as above.

•᛫•

Cumin Rice

Jeera Chawal

SOAK TIME: 15 minutes (optional)
PREP: 5 minutes
COOK: 20 minutes
MAKES: 12 servings
SERVING SIZE: ½ cup

Try this cumin-infused basmati rice at your next party instead of plain rice. It adds extra flavor and goes well with many dishes.

1½ cups basmati rice or long-grain rice

1 tablespoon canola or vegetable oil

½ teaspoon cumin seeds

2 bay leaves

3 cups water

½ teaspoon salt

1. Wash rice in 2 to 3 changes of water until the water is relatively clear. Soak in cold water for 15 minutes or longer. Drain the water.

2. Heat oil in a 2- to 3-quart saucepan over medium-high heat. Add cumin seeds and bay leaves, and cook for a few seconds until the cumin seeds are golden brown. Add drained rice and gently stir the rice for 2 to 3 minutes, coating the rice with oil.

4. Add water and salt. Bring water to a boil. Reduce heat to a simmer and cook for 12 to 15 minutes. All the water should be absorbed and the rice should be fully cooked.

3. Remove from the heat. Cover with a lid until ready to serve. Before serving, fluff rice with a fork.

NUTRITION INFORMATION PER SERVING:
Calories: 95; Total Fat: 1 g (Saturated Fat: 0 g);
Carbohydrate: 19 g; Protein: 2 g; Fiber: 0 g;
Sodium: 98 mg

•᛫•

Pea-Mushroom Pilaf

Matar-Khumb Pulao

SOAK TIME: 15 minutes
PREP: 10 minutes
COOK: 30 minutes
MAKES: 8 servings
SERVING SIZE: ½ cup

This *pulao* (pilaf) is great as a side dish or as a light meal. I often serve it as a quick and light meal accompanied by yogurt and chutney. Frozen peas make this even simpler to prepare. The whole spices, cinnamon stick, cardamom, and bay leaves, add extra flavor to the dish. The whole spices are not eaten; just push the whole spices to the side on your plate when eating.

1 cup basmati rice or brown basmati rice

½ teaspoon cumin seeds

1½-inch stick cinnamon

2 cardamom pods, split open

2 bay leaves

2 tablespoons canola or vegetable oil

½ cup onion, thinly sliced

1 cup (4 ounces) mushrooms, sliced

¾ cup frozen peas, thawed

1 teaspoon garam masala

2 cups water

1 teaspoon salt

¼ cup roasted cashews, for garnish, optional

1. Wash rice in 2 to 3 changes of water. Soak in cold water for 15 minutes or longer. Drain the soaking water.

2. Combine the cumin seeds, cinnamon stick, cardamom pods, and bay leaves in a small bowl. Set aside.

3. Heat oil in a 3-quart saucepan over medium-high heat. Add spices and fry for a few seconds until the cumin seeds are golden brown. Add onion and fry 2 to 3 minutes until golden brown. Add the mushrooms. Stir and cook for 2 to 3 minutes until mushrooms are wilted.

4. Add rice and peas. Gently stir the rice to coat the oil. Cook for 1 minute. Add garam masala, water, and salt. Stir gently to mix.

5. Bring to a boil and reduce heat to a simmer. Simmer for 12 to 15 minutes, until rice is cooked and the water is absorbed. Cover with a lid until ready to serve.

6. Before serving, gently stir and fluff rice with a fork. Garnish with cashews, if desired.

NUTRITION INFORMATION PER SERVING:
Calories: 131; Total Fat: 4 g (Saturated Fat: 0 g); Carbohydrate: 21 g; Protein: 3 g; Fiber: 1 g; Sodium: 306 mg

---

GF

··

Dried Fruit Rice
Meva Chawal

SOAK TIME: **15 minutes**
PREP: **10 minutes**
COOK: **20 minutes**
MAKES: **8 servings**
SERVING SIZE: **½ cup**

Nuts make any dish special; this one has several types, along with dried fruit. Make this rice dish for any special occasion, or use it to dress up any meal.

1 cup basmati rice

½ teaspoon cumin seeds

2 cloves

1½-inch stick cinnamon

2 cardamom pods

2 bay leaves

2 tablespoons canola or vegetable oil

¼ cup sliced almonds

2 tablespoons raisins

2 cups water, divided

½ teaspoon salt

Pinch of saffron

¼ cup roasted cashew halves

2 tablespoons pistachio nuts

¼ cup (sweetened) coconut flakes

1. Wash rice in 2 to 3 changes of water. Soak in cold water for 15 minutes or longer. Drain the soaking water.

2. Combine cumin seeds, cinnamon stick, cloves, cardamom, and bay leaves in a small bowl. Set aside.

3. Heat oil in a large fry pan over medium-high heat. Add the sliced almonds and cook for 1 minute until the almonds are light brown. Remove with a slotted spoon and set aside.

4. Add spices to same pan and fry for a few seconds until the cumin seeds are golden brown. (All the spices will puff up.) Add strained rice and raisins. Gently stir the rice to coat with the oil, and cook for 1 minute.

5. Add water and salt. Bring water to a boil and reduce heat. Simmer for 12 to 15 minutes, until rice is cooked.

6. While rice is cooking, soak saffron threads in 2 tablespoons warm water.

7. Add the roasted almonds, cashews, pistachios, and coconut. Drizzle the saffron mixture over the rice. Cover with lid until ready to serve. Gently stir and fluff rice with a fork, mixing in the nuts.

NUTRITION INFORMATION PER SERVING:
Calories: 131; Total Fat: 6 g (Saturated Fat: 1 g); Carbohydrate: 16 g; Protein: 3 g; Fiber: 1 g; Sodium: 107 mg

---

GF

···

Black Bean Pilaf

Kalli Khichri

PREP: **5 minutes**
COOK: **20 minutes**
MAKES: **6 servings**
SERVING SIZE: **1 cup**

*K*hichri, which brings together beans and rice, has a porridge-like consistency. Think of it as a one-dish meal like a casserole. Khichri is often served with plain yogurt, *papad*, and Indian pickles. For a satisfying vegan meal, I suggest serving it with a soup of your choice. This pilaf-like *khichri* is made with split (with husk) urad dal and is black in color—thus named *kalli* (black) *khichri*.

1 cup long-grain rice
¾ cup (split with husk) urad dal
2 teaspoons ginger, peeled and finely grated
1 teaspoon salt
3¾ cups water
Olive oil or ghee, optional

1. Combine rice and dal and wash in 3 to 4 changes of water, lightly rubbing the grains between your fingers, until water is relatively clear. Strain and set aside.

2. In a 3- to 4-quart saucepan, combine strained rice mixture, ginger, salt, and water. Bring to a boil. Reduce heat and simmer for 10 to 12 minutes until most of the water is absorbed. Cover with lid, and continue to cook for another 8 to 10 minutes, until the dal is fully cooked. Leave covered until ready to serve.

3. Serve hot and drizzle with oil or ghee, if desired, on each individual serving. Enjoy with soup and Indian pickles.

NUTRITION INFORMATION PER SERVING:
Calories: 201; Total Fat: 1 g (Saturated Fat: 0 g); Carbohydrate: 40 g; Protein: 9 g; Fiber: 5 g; Sodium: 399 mg

---

Tomato Rice

Tamatari Chawal

SOAK TIME: **15 minutes (optional)**
PREP: **10 minutes**
COOK: **30 minutes**
MAKES: **8 Servings**
SERVING SIZE: **½ cup**

Cherry tomatoes give this dish an elegant appeal. Although you can use any type of tomatoes, choose cherry tomatoes if they're available. This is a wonderful dish to make in the summer, when tomatoes are in ample supply.

1 cup basmati rice or brown basmati rice

2 cups water

2 tablespoons canola or vegetable oil

1 teaspoon cumin seeds

1 cup onion, thinly sliced

1 cup green peppers, finely chopped

2 cups (8 ounces) cherry tomatoes, halved

¼ teaspoon cayenne pepper, or to taste

1 teaspoon salt

1. Wash rice in 2 to 3 changes of water, until the water is relatively clear. Soak in cold water for 15 minutes or longer. (Soaking can be eliminated if in a hurry.) Drain the rice in a strainer; set aside.

2. In a small saucepan, combine drained rice and 2 cups water. Bring to a boil. Reduce heat to medium and simmer for 12 to 15 minutes until the rice is cooked. Let rice cool for about 15 minutes.

3. While rice is cooling, heat oil in a heavy skillet over medium-high heat. Add cumin seeds and cook for a few seconds until the cumin seeds are golden brown. Add onion and fry 2 to 3 minutes until golden brown. Add green peppers and cook for about 2 minutes. Add tomatoes and cook for another 2 to 3 minutes. Add cayenne pepper and salt. Mix well.

4. Fluff rice with fork. Add rice to tomato mixture. Stir gently in a lifting and turning motion, taking care not to break the rice.

5. Transfer to a serving bowl. Cover until ready to serve. Before serving, fluff rice again gently.

NUTRITION INFORMATION PER SERVING: Calories: 132; Total Fat: 4 g (Saturated Fat: 0.5 g); Carbohydrate: 22 g; Protein: 2 g; Fiber: 1 g; Sodium: 295 mg

Bean-Vegetable Porridge

Subji Khichri

PREP: **10 minutes**
COOK: **40 minutes**
MAKES: **10 servings**
SERVING SIZE: **¾ cup**

*K*hichri is a light meal often served with a porridge-like consistency. Mung dal is considered to be the easiest dal to digest, and thus this *khichri* is often eaten as a light and easy-to-digest meal. A hot bowl of *khichri* is sometimes a comfort food for me, very satisfying and nourishing. I like this *khichri* with or without vegetables. It tastes great served with mango or lime pickles, roasted *papad*, and plain yogurt.

¾ cup long-grain rice

⅔ cup split (with husk) mung dal

2 tablespoons canola or vegetable oil

½ teaspoon asafetida powder

1 teaspoon cumin seeds

3–4 cloves

1 tablespoon ginger, peeled and grated

½ teaspoon turmeric

1 teaspoon salt

6 cups water

2 cups cauliflower, cut into 1-inch florets

½ cup carrot, diced into ¼-inch pieces

½ cup green beans, cut into ½-inch pieces

1 teaspoon garam masala

Olive oil for garnish, optional

1. Combine rice and mung dal. Wash in 3 to 4 changes of water, using your hands to rub the grains. Strain and set aside.

2. Heat the oil in a heavy skillet over medium-high heat. Add asafetida, cumin seeds, and cloves. Cook for a few seconds until cumin seeds are golden brown. Add ginger and stir.

3. Add the strained rice and mung dal. Add turmeric, salt, and water. Bring to a boil. Reduce heat and partially cover with a lid. Simmer for 15 minutes, stirring occasionally.

4. Add the cauliflower, carrots, and beans. Bring to a boil. Cover with lid and continue to simmer for 10 to 15 minutes. The rice and vegetables should be well blended. Stir in garam masala. If needed, stir in more water for desired consistency.

5. Serve hot. Drizzle some oil over each serving, if desired.

VARIATIONS: 1. If desired, use 2 cups frozen mixed vegetables in place of the cauliflower, carrots, and green beans.
2. Make plain *khichri*, eliminating all the vegetables. When you're not feeling well, this one may be most appealing.

NUTRITION INFORMATION PER SERVING:
Calories: 134; Total Fat: 3 g (Saturated Fat: 0.5 g); Carbohydrate: 22 g; Protein: 5 g; Fiber: 3 g; Sodium: 247 mg

---

·······································

Eggplant Rice Pilaf

Vangi Bhat

PREP: **10 minutes**
COOK: **20 minutes**
MAKES: **6 servings**
SERVING SIZE: **1 cup**

When my daughter first ate this rice dish at our friend Simi's house, she asked me to make it at home. Simi graciously shared her recipe. The eggplant and chana dal spice mixture give it a unique flavor and texture. If you prefer, try it with spinach instead of eggplant.

1 cup long-grain rice

2½ cups water, divided

1½ teaspoons salt, divided

½ pound eggplant or Japanese long eggplant

¼ cup canola or vegetable oil

½ teaspoon mustard seeds

8–10 curry leaves

1 cup onion, cut into 1-inch dice

4 tablespoons vangi bhat masala (at right), or purchased

¼ cup roasted cashews or peanuts, optional

1. Wash rice in 2 to 3 changes of water. Soak in cold water for 15 minutes. Drain the water.

2. In a small saucepan, combine drained rice, 2 cups of water, and 1 teaspoon salt. Bring to a boil. Reduce heat to medium and simmer for 12 to 15 minutes, until the rice is fully cooked. Fluff with a fork. Cool rice slightly.

3. Cut the eggplant into 1-inch cubes just before cooking, as they turn brown very quickly. Set aside.

4. Heat oil in a large nonstick fry pan on medium-high heat. Add mustard seeds, cover with lid to keep mustard seeds from popping out, and cook for a few seconds, until mustard seeds stop popping. Add curry leaves and cook for a few seconds. Add onion and fry 2 to 3 minutes until golden brown. Add eggplant and fry for 5 minutes. Add the remaining ½ cup water and ½ teaspoon salt. Cover with lid and simmer for 5 to 7 minutes until eggplant is tender.

5. Add vangi bhat masala. Stir well to coat the eggplant. Remove from heat.

6. Fluff cooled rice with a fork and add to the eggplant mixture. In a lifting and turning motion, carefully mix rice and eggplant mixture (avoid breaking the rice).

7. Transfer to a serving platter and garnish with roasted cashews, if desired.

NUTRITION INFORMATION PER SERVING:
Calories: 247; Total Fat: 10 g (Saturated Fat: 1 g); Carbohydrate: 35 g; Protein: 5 g; Fiber: 3 g; Sodium: 587 mg

---

VANGI BHAT MASALA

MAKES: **¾ cup**

½ teaspoon canola or vegetable oil

½ cup (split, hulled) chana dal

¼ cup (split, hulled) urad dal

4 dried red chiles, or to taste

1 tablespoon coriander seeds

6 cloves

1 1-inch cinnamon stick

1. In a small fry pan, heat oil on medium heat. Add dal, red chiles, coriander seeds, cloves, and cinnamon stick. Stirring frequently, roast for 3 to 4 minutes until the dals turn golden brown. Transfer to a plate and cool.

2. Grind in a spice grinder or a small blender jar to a coarse powder. Store in an airtight container.

••

Tamarind Rice Pilaf

Imli Chawal

SOAK TIME: 15 minutes (optional)
PREP: 10 minutes
COOK: 40 minutes
MAKES: 8 servings
SERVING SIZE: ½ cup

This is a southern Indian specialty served on special occasions. It is best enjoyed at room temperature. Making your own tamarind masala takes time but is well worth the effort. Once you make it, it will keep for up to six months. If you love the recipe, as I do, double the tamarind masala and mix it with leftover rice anytime for a quick meal.

1 cup long-grain rice

2 cups water

¼ cup tamarind rice masala (at right), or purchased

2 tablespoons cilantro, chopped

3 tablespoons roasted Spanish peanuts

1 tablespoon coconut, finely grated, optional

1. Wash rice in 2 to 3 changes of water. Soak in cold water for 15 minutes. Drain the water.

2. In a small saucepan, combine drained rice and water. Bring to a boil. Reduce heat to medium and simmer for 12 to 15 minutes, until the rice is cooked.

3. Fluff the rice with a fork and spread in a serving tray. Let cool to room temperature.

4. Add tamarind rice masala and mix into rice using a gentle lifting and turning motion. Avoid breaking the rice. If necessary, you may need to use your hands to thoroughly mix in the masala.

5. Garnish with cilantro, peanuts, and coconut, if desired.

NUTRITION INFORMATION PER SERVING:
Calories: 138; Total Fat: 4 g (Saturated Fat: 4 g); Carbohydrate: 22 g; Protein: 3 g; Fiber: 1 g; Sodium: 350 mg

---

TAMARIND RICE MASALA

MAKES: 1 cup masala

For best results, use dry reconstituted tamarind sauce for this masala. Although some people use tamarind paste, I feel the dry tamarind gives a better color and flavor. This is enough masala for 3 to 4 recipes.

⅓ cup coriander seeds

⅓ cup sesame seeds

5–8 dried red chiles, or to taste

¼ cup canola or vegetable oil

1 teaspoon mustard seeds

⅛ teaspoon asafetida

½ teaspoon cumin seeds

½ cup (split, hulled) chana dal

8–10 curry leaves, chopped

1½ cups tamarind sauce (page 25)

¼ teaspoon turmeric

5 teaspoons salt

1 tablespoon brown sugar

1. Heat a small fry pan on medium heat. Dry-roast coriander seeds, sesame seeds, and red chiles for 2 to 3 minutes until the sesame seeds are light brown. Transfer to a plate and cool to room temperature.

2. In a spice grinder or a small blender jar, grind sesame seed mixture. Set aside.

3. Heat oil in a skillet on medium-high heat. Add the mustard seeds, and cook for a few seconds until mustard seeds stop popping (use a lid to prevent seeds from popping out). Add asafetida, cumin seeds, chana dal, and curry leaves, and cook for a few seconds. Add tamarind sauce and cook for about 10 minutes. Stir in the sesame seed mixture, turmeric, salt, and brown sugar. Cook until most of the water is evaporated, 12 to 20 minutes, stirring frequently and adjusting heat as needed. The masala is ready when the oil rises to the top. Cool to room temperature and store in a bottle. Store in refrigerator for up to 6 months.

GF, LF

••

Lemon Rice Noodles

Neembu Savai

PREP: **10 minutes**
COOK: **10 minutes**
MAKES: **6 servings**
SERVING SIZE: **1 cup**

Rice noodles make this dish particularly easy and quick to make. Chana dal and peanuts add a nice crunchy texture to the soft noodles. Dried rice noodles are readily available at most supermarkets, but if you can find refrigerated rice noodles (commonly sold at Asian grocery stores), use them. They add freshness to this bright yellow, tart dish.

½ package of rice noodles (8 ounces), or fresh (refrigerated) rice noodles

1¼ teaspoons salt, divided

2 tablespoons canola or vegetable oil

1 teaspoon brown mustard seeds

3 tablespoons (split, hulled) chana dal

8–10 curry leaves or 2 tablespoons cilantro, chopped

2–3 dried red chiles

¼ teaspoon turmeric

2 tablespoons lemon or lime juice

¼ cup roasted Spanish peanuts, optional

1. Break the noodles into 2-inch pieces. In a large skillet, boil 12 cups (3 quarts) water. Add 1 teaspoon salt. Add rice noodles. Return to a boil and cook for about 3 minutes until the noodles are cooked. Drain the water. Set aside. (If using fresh rice noodles, cook for only 20 seconds and drain.)

2. In a separate skillet, heat oil on medium-high heat. Add mustard seeds, cover with lid, and cook for a few seconds until the seeds stop popping. Add chana dal, curry leaves, and dried red chiles. Cook for a few seconds, until the chana dal is light brown.

3. Add the noodles, turmeric, and ¼ teaspoon salt. Stir well to coat the noodles. Cover and steam through.

4. Remove from heat, cover, and let sit for 10 minutes. Stir in lemon juice. Transfer to a serving bowl and garnish with peanuts, if using.

NOTE: These noodles are great at room temperature. If refrigerated and you wish to reheat them, for best results add more lemon juice, to taste.

NUTRITION INFORMATION PER SERVING:
Calories: 198; Total Fat: 5 g (Saturated Fat: 0.5 g); Carbohydrate: 35 g; Protein: 2 g; Fiber: 1 g; Sodium: 295 mg

Chickpeas and Rice Noodles

Chane Aur Savai

PREP: **10 minutes**
COOK: **10 minutes**
MAKES: **6 servings**
SERVING SIZE: **1 cup**

Make this one-dish meal when you're in a hurry. Using rice noodles and canned chickpeas makes it remarkably quick and simple.

½ package (8 ounces) dried rice noodles, or fresh (refrigerated) rice noodles

1¼ teaspoons salt

2 tablespoons canola or vegetable oil

½ teaspoon cumin seeds

1 cup onion, finely chopped

1 (16-ounce) can chickpeas, drained and rinsed

1 cup carrot, peeled and diced

¼ teaspoon cayenne pepper, or to taste, or 1 teaspoon green chile

½ cup water

1 teaspoon lemon or lime juice

2 tablespoons cilantro, chopped

¼ cup Spanish peanuts, roasted, optional

1. Break noodles into 2-inch pieces. In a large skillet, boil 12 cups (3 quarts) water. Add 1 teaspoon salt. Add rice noodles to boiling water. Boil for about 2 minutes. Drain the water. (If using fresh rice noodles, cook for only 20 seconds and drain.)

2. In a separate skillet, heat oil on medium-high heat. Add cumin seeds and cook for a few seconds until golden brown. Add onion and fry 2 to 3 minutes until golden brown. Add the drained chickpeas and chopped carrots. Stir in remaining ¼ teaspoon salt and cayenne pepper. Add water. Cover and cook for 4 to 5 minutes, until carrots are tender.

3. Add the drained noodles. Stir well to coat the noodles. Cover and steam through. Remove from heat and stir in lemon juice. Cover until ready to serve.

4. Transfer to a serving bowl and garnish with cilantro and peanuts, if desired.

NUTRITION INFORMATION PER SERVING:
Calories: 275; Total Fat: 6 g (Saturated Fat: 0.5 g); Carbohydrate: 49 g; Protein: 6 g; Fiber: 5 g; Sodium: 382 mg

---

VARIATION: If desired, use 2 cups of mixed vegetables in place of chickpeas and carrots in step 2. Finish recipe as above.

••

Buckwheat Pilaf

Kuttu Pulao

PREP: **10 minutes**
COOK: **20 minutes**
MAKES: **6 servings**
SERVING SIZE: **1 cup**

Buckwheat groats and flour (*kuttu*) have gained significant popularity in the West in recent years. Buckwheat is not wheat—nor is it a grain for that matter. Rather, it is the seed of the broadleaf plant. It is high in protein and fiber, is gluten-free, and is often used as a grain substitute.

1 cup buckwheat hulled groats or long-grain rice

3 cups water, divided

1 teaspoon salt, divided

1 medium onion, finely chopped

½ teaspoon cumin seeds

3 tablespoons canola or vegetable oil

½ cup potatoes, peeled and diced into ¼-inch pieces

½ cup carrot, peeled and diced into ¼-inch pieces★

½ cup frozen peas★

¼ cup raisins

½ teaspoon garam masala

¼ cup roasted Spanish peanuts

1. In a 2-quart saucepan, combine the groats, 2 cups of water, and ½ teaspoon salt. Bring to a boil. Reduce heat to a simmer. Simmer for 12 to 14 minutes, until all the water is absorbed and the groats are soft. Cover with lid and set aside.

★Substitute 1 cup frozen peas and carrots for the fresh peas and carrots.

2. In a blender jar, mix 2 tablespoons water, onion, and cumin seeds. Grind to a smooth paste. Set aside.

3. Heat oil in a heavy, large nonstick skillet on medium-high heat. Add onion mixture. Stirring frequently, cook onion masala for 5 to 7 minutes, until most of the water is evaporated.

4. Add chopped potatoes, carrot, peas, raisins, and remaining ½ teaspoon salt. Mix well. Add remaining 1 cup water, bring to a boil, and reduce heat. Cover with a lid and simmer until potatoes are tender, 7 to 8 minutes.

5. Add the cooked groats and garam masala. Stir gently with a spatula. Cover with a lid and steam through for 2 to 3 minutes.

6. Remove from the heat. Cover and let stand until ready to serve. Fluff with a fork before serving and transfer to a serving platter. Garnish with peanuts.

NUTRITION INFORMATION PER SERVING:
Calories: 156; Total Fat: 6 g (Saturated Fat: 0.5 g); Carbohydrate: 23 g; Protein: 4 g; Fiber: 3 g; Sodium: 311 mg

•••

Curried Spinach Couscous

Palak Couscous

PREP: **10 minutes**
COOK: **15 minutes**
MAKES: **6 servings**
SERVING SIZE: **½ cup**

Recently, couscous has become very popular in America, with the increase in international and fusion cuisines. Couscous is a spherical granule typically made from wheat semolina, and then coated them with finely ground wheat flour. (It is not to be confused with *khus khus* of India, which are poppy seeds.) Serve instead of rice, topped with vegetable curries, or as a side dish. This spinach couscous is a nice complement with any soup or salad.

1 cup couscous

1 tablespoon canola or vegetable oil

½ cup spring onions, finely chopped

1 teaspoon ginger, peeled and finely grated

1 teaspoon ground cumin

¼ teaspoon turmeric

½ teaspoon cayenne pepper, optional

2 tablespoons mint leaves, chopped, or cilantro

3 cups fresh spinach, chopped, or 1½ cups frozen spinach

¾ teaspoon salt

1 teaspoon sugar

2 cups water

1. Heat a large nonstick fry pan on medium-high heat. Add couscous and lightly roast for about 5 minutes, stirring occasionally. Remove to a plate and set aside.

2. In the same fry pan, heat oil. Add spring onions and fry for 2 to 3 minutes until transparent. Add ginger, cumin, turmeric, cayenne pepper, and mint leaves; stir well.

3. Add spinach, salt, and sugar. Cook for 1 to 2 minutes, stirring constantly, coating the spinach with spices, until the spinach is wilted. Add water. Bring to a boil.

4. Add couscous, bring mixture to a boil. Reduce heat to simmer, cover with lid, and cook for 7 to 8 minutes, until all the water is absorbed and couscous is cooked. Stir to fluff the couscous.

5. Transfer to a serving bowl. Cover with a lid until ready to serve. Before serving, fluff couscous again.

NUTRITION INFORMATION PER SERVING:
Calories: 138; Total Fat: 3 g (Saturated Fat: 0 g); Carbohydrate: 24 g; Protein: 4 g; Fiber: 2 g; Sodium: 307 mg

Flatbreads

FLATBREADS PLAY A fundamental role in Indian cooking, just as loaf breads do in Western cuisines. Wheat is the staple food in northern India, and flatbreads are served at most meals. Indian breads are unleavened, flat, and usually made of whole grain. They are very different in taste and texture from oven-baked, leavened loaves. Probably the bread closest to Indian flatbreads is Mexican tortillas—but in shape only, as the taste and texture are very different. The scope of Indian flatbreads is unmatched by any other cuisine. They are easy, quick, and fun to prepare and absolutely delicious to eat.

Wheat is the most common type of grain used to make a variety of flatbreads. Other grains such as millet (*bajra*), sorghum (*jawar*), and corn (*makka*) are also used occasionally (see Types of Flour, page 155). A variety of wheat flatbreads are eaten at most meals. Rolling them perfectly round may take a little practice, but then again, they taste great whatever shape they are. Different flours, shaping techniques, and cooking sources produce a variety of taste and textures.

Flatbreads for All Occasions

From daily bread (roti) to festive bread (*puri*), Indian breads can be broken down into four basic types, each one defined by how it's cooked.

Pan-Baked Flatbread

The most prevalent and nutritious variety, and the daily bread of India, is roti, also known as *phulka* in some regions, or *chapatti* in Westernized homes. It is made with whole wheat flour.

The everyday plain roti is made on a *tava* (flat iron griddle). It is beautifully simple. You mix whole wheat flour and water, roll the dough into a thin circle, cook it on the heated *tava* for 1 to 2 minutes, and it's ready to eat. The cooked roti may be buttered, for flavor and moistness. For variations, different grains, spices, herbs, vegetables, beans, and nuts are used.

The roti is served hot off the griddle (hot translates to *garam*). It's soft and pliable and great for scooping up vegetables and dals. Traditionally, as well as today in India whenever possible, the roti is made fresh and comes to you one by one when you sit down to eat. A mother instinctively knows the value of hot roti, and takes pride in making them hot and fresh for her family (*garam, garam*, as we would say). After she feeds the family hot roti, she makes the last two for herself and joins the family. This might sound subservient to a non-Indian, but it's ingrained in the Indian culture. There is nothing as satisfying and wholesome as hot roti. For the sake of time, I rarely serve them this way. But I do make all the roti just before we sit down to eat. They are still fresh and hot but not served one by one. Roti can also be kept and eaten later.

Pan-Fried Flatbread

The next most popular flatbread after the roti is *paratha*. In my repertoire of flatbreads, *parathas* take the cake. When I was growing up, *paratha*

was made for breakfast and dinner. Things changed over the years, and *parathas* were served more and more occasionally as the family became increasingly health-conscious.

Most *parathas* are made with whole wheat flour, rolled into a small circle, lightly oiled, folded and rolled out again. They are then lightly fried on a hot *tava*. They are layered, flaky, and tender. Most *parathas* are eaten plain—that is, they have nothing added to them. Even plain *parathas* make meals more special and taste better and richer with curries. *Parathas* keep well, and thus are great for lunch boxes, traveling, and picnics.

Parathas can be stuffed with spicy potatoes, grated radishes, and onions. Just when I think I've eaten every possible type of *paratha*, I am surprised with a new stuffing and a new flavor. My kids' favorite is Potato-Stuffed Flatbread (*Aloo Paratha*, page 160), and my vote goes to Daikon-Stuffed Flatbread (*Mooli Paratha*, page 163). Try all the recipes and see which one you like the best. Trust me, making the decision won't be easy.

Deep-Fried Flatbreads

It seems wrong to call the deep-fried bread known as *puri* a flatbread, since it puffs up like a balloon in the hot oil, but within seconds it loses its steam and gently falls flat. *Puri* is a festive bread made on holidays and for special celebrations, weddings, parties, and banquets. Sometimes on weekends, especially if I have company over, I will serve hot *puri* and potato curry for brunch. It is sure to bring a satisfied smile from the guests as well the family.

Most *puri*s are plain with just a hint of salt, and like rotis, they are used to scoop up flavorful curries. They keep better than *parathas* and thus are often taken when traveling long distances. They are a standard at Indian picnics. Stuffed or flavored *puris* are also popular. *Kachories* are a variation of stuffed *puri* served at special occasions for breakfast, snacks, or with a meal.

Bhatura originates from the Punjab region. It is made with leavened white flour and is often considered a street food. In Delhi and other large northern Indian cities, you can get amazing *chole-bhature* (*bhatura* with spicy chickpeas) at roadside stands.

Tandoor or Oven Flatbreads

Tandoor is a clay oven that originated from the Punjab region in India. But its roots lie in the Middle East when Persians migrated to India in the 1300s. *Tandoori* breads have become the most popular Indian flatbreads in the world today. Most Indian restaurants around the world flaunt a *tandoor*, often within the view of customers, and make wonderful hot bread called *naan*.

Naan is rarely made in Indian homes, for it does require a *tandoor*, and is made with white flour and thus is not considered healthy. You can make acceptable naan in your oven (see Sesame Seed Naan, page 166). Naan can also be flavored with spices and filled with vegetables or cheese, but the most popular is plain naan.

TYPES OF FLOUR

Wheat is the staple food of northern Indians and the most common type of grain used to make a variety of rotis. Other grains such as millet are occasionally used.

WHOLE WHEAT FLOUR
Use roti-atta or white whole wheat flour.

The whole wheat flour (*atta*) used to make Indian flatbreads is made of a different variety of wheat that grinds up finer and is lighter in color than the regular whole wheat flour available in the United States. Most stores that carry Indian groceries carry durum wheat flour (which comes from Canada), which makes softer Indian flatbreads. It comes under several names, all of which mean the same thing: roti flour or roti-atta, or chapatti flour or chapatti-atta.

These days, you will find white whole wheat flour in most supermarkets or natural foods stores. The white whole wheat flour is made from an albino variety of wheat, which is lighter in color; has a sweeter, milder flavor; and has a softer texture. It has all the nutritional value and fiber of regular whole wheat flour. The regular whole wheat flour is made with red wheat, which is darker in color and has a slightly bitter taste. White whole wheat flour comes closest to the roti-atta available in the Indian stores. It is the best substitute, although you can also combine regular whole wheat flour (three parts) with all-purpose flour (one part) to make a variety of flatbreads in this book. To avoid confusion, I have used the term *roti-atta* (or white whole wheat flour) in all the recipes.

Making Dough

Dough can be made by hand in a shallow bowl, or in a food processor. Electric bread machines are not suitable for Indian flatbreads, as they do not require rising or baking. A food processor is great for making most wheat doughs, and I use it all the time. It takes less time and makes smoother dough in a fraction of the time.

Storing Dough

Make all the flatbreads per recipe or refrigerate the dough and make fresh flatbreads, as needed. I usually make enough dough for at least two batches and refrigerate the extra dough in an airtight bowl. The cold dough takes a little more effort to roll out, as it will be stiff, but this will not affect the quality of the finished flatbread.

The dough will keep for up to three days in the refrigerator. Roti-atta will stay pretty close to its original color, but the white whole wheat flour and the regular whole wheat flour will turn darker in color.

OTHER FLOURS

Millet (*bajra*), sorghum (*jawar*), corn (*makka*), and buckwheat (*kuttu*) flour recipes are also included in this book. The rotis made with these flours are hearty and best served hot. They do not keep well. These flours are gluten-free, whole grain, rich in nutrients, and high in fiber. Sometimes wheat flour is mixed with these flours to make a softer roti. I have kept the recipes in this book gluten-free.

All of the recipes have been tested with both Indian flours and supermarket flours. However, wherever possible, use millet or sorghum flour purchased from an Indian grocery store rather than a supermarket. They are ground much finer, which makes the dough easier to handle.

Grilled Flatbread

Roti

PREP: 10 minutes
COOK: 15 minutes
MAKES: 12 servings
SERVING SIZE: 1 roti

Roti, also called *chapatti* or *phulka*, is basic everyday Indian bread. It is made with roti-atta (whole wheat flour), which is similar to white whole wheat flour available in supermarkets (see Types of Flour, page 155). If possible, try to use roti-atta from Indian grocery stores. It works best and is cheaper than white whole wheat flour.

> 2 cups roti-atta, or white whole wheat flour, plus additional for rolling
>
> 1¼ cups water
>
> 2 teaspoons canola oil or ghee, optional

1. In a mixing bowl or food processor, place flour. Make a well in the center of the flour. Add water gradually as you mix dough. (Depending on the type of flour, the amount of water needed may vary slightly.) The dough should be soft and easy to roll into a ball. Knead the dough for 1 to 2 minutes until smooth and elastic. Cover and let sit for 10 minutes or longer.

2. Place ½ cup flour for rolling in a shallow container and set aside.

3. Divide dough into 12 balls. Roll each ball between palms of your hands in a circular motion until the dough is smooth. Press to flatten.

4. Heat *tava*/iron griddle or a heavy fry pan on medium to medium-high heat. Adjust heat as needed. If *tava* is too hot, roti will burn and stick to the *tava*, and if not hot enough, the roti will take a long time to cook and become dry.

5. Roll each flat ball in the flour. Roll into approximately 6-inch-round flatbreads.

6. Place the roti on the heated *tava*. Cook for 1 to 2 minutes until roti colors and becomes firm and easy to pick up. Turn over and cook roti on the other side. Cook for a few seconds, until light brown spots appear on the underside. Turn back to the first side. With a folded kitchen towel, press the roti down gently but firmly. The roti will puff as you press it.

7. If desired, lightly brush top of roti with oil. Oiling keeps the rotis softer and moist. Serve immediately or place in an airtight container to serve later.

NUTRITION INFORMATION PER SERVING:
Calories: 68; Total Fat: 0 g (Saturated Fat: 0 g); Carbohydrate: 15 g; Protein: 3 g; Fiber: 2 g; Sodium: 1 mg

---

Veggie Wrap

Roti-Subji Roll

PREP: 10 minutes
COOK: 25 minutes
MAKES: 8 servings
SERVING SIZE: 1 roll

Similar to a wrap, roti rolls are a fun way to enjoy roti and vegetables all in one. If you like, serve them with Cucumber-Tomato Salad (page 193) and chutney of choice.

DOUGH

> 2 cups roti-atta, or white whole wheat flour, plus additional for rolling
>
> ½ teaspoon salt
>
> 2 tablespoons canola or vegetable oil
>
> 1¼ cups water

FILLING

- 2 tablespoons canola or vegetable oil
- ½ teaspoon cumin seeds
- 6 cups cauliflower, cut into ½-inch florets
- 1½ cups potatoes, peeled and cut into ½-inch pieces
- 2 teaspoons ginger, peeled and grated
- ½ teaspoon turmeric
- 1 teaspoon salt
- ½ teaspoon cayenne pepper, or to taste
- 2 teaspoons ground coriander
- ¼ cup water
- ½ teaspoon amchur or 1 teaspoon lemon juice
- ½ teaspoon garam masala
- 2 tablespoons cilantro, finely chopped

1. In a mixing bowl or food processor, combine flour and salt. Mix in the oil. Make a well in the center of the flour. Add water gradually as you mix dough. (Depending on the type of flour, the amount of water needed may vary slightly.) The dough should be soft and easy to roll into a ball. Knead the dough for 1 to 2 minutes until smooth and elastic. Cover and let stand for 10 minutes or longer.

2. *While dough rests, prepare filling:* Heat oil in a nonstick skillet over medium-high heat. Add cumin seeds and fry for a few seconds until seeds are golden brown. Add cauliflower, potatoes, and ginger, and stir. Add turmeric, salt, cayenne pepper, coriander, and water, and stir thoroughly to coat vegetables. Bring to a boil, cover with lid, and reduce heat. Simmer for 8 to 10 minutes, until potatoes are tender. If there is any liquid accumulated in the bottom of the vegetables, open the lid and simmer until liquid evaporates. Sprinkle with amchur and garam masala. Stir in cilantro. Set aside.

3. Heat *tava*/iron griddle or a heavy fry pan on medium heat. Adjust heat as needed. If *tava* is too hot, the roti will burn and stick to the *tava*, and if it's not hot enough, it will a take a long time to cook and become dry.

4. Place about ½ cup flour for rolling in a shallow container and set aside.

5. Divide dough into 8 balls. Roll each ball between palms of your hands in a circular motion until the dough is smooth. Press to flatten. Roll each flat ball in the flour, then roll into approximately an 8- to 9-inch circle.

6. Place the roti on the heated *tava*. Cook roti for a few seconds until it colors and becomes firm and easy to pick up. Turn over and cook for a few seconds, until light brown spots appear on the underside. Place about ½ cup filling in the center of the circle in a log shape, leaving at least 1 inch on sides of filling. Roll small side over the filling, and then fold both long sides over each other. Fold like a wrap.

7. Serve immediately, with chutney of choice.

NOTE: The stuffed roti rolls will become soft. Prepare only what you need and refrigerate the dough and filling separately until ready to use.

NUTRITION INFORMATION PER SERVING:
Calories: 204; Total Fat: 8 g (Saturated Fat: 0.5 g); Carbohydrate: 31 g; Protein: 6 g; Fiber: 6 g; Sodium: 462 mg

LF

··

Flaxseed Flatbread

Flaxseed Roti

PREP: 10 minutes
COOK: 15 minutes
MAKES: 8 servings
SERVING SIZE: 1 roti

Flaxseeds are high in omega-3 fatty acids and are known to lower cholesterol. Flaxseeds need to be ground before adding to recipes. They add a nutty taste and texture to the roti, and *besan* complements the protein, making this dish healthful and delicious.

1½ cups roti-atta, or white whole wheat flour, plus additional for rolling

⅓ cup besan (or soy flour)

2 tablespoons flaxseeds, ground

¼ teaspoon salt

¾ cup water

1 tablespoon canola oil or ghee, optional

1. In a mixing bowl or food processor, combine flour, besan, flaxseeds, and salt. Make a well in the center of the flour. Add water gradually as you mix dough. (Depending on the type of flour, the amount of water needed may vary slightly.) The dough should be soft and easy to roll into a ball. Knead the dough for 1 to 2 minutes until smooth and elastic. Cover and let stand for 10 minutes or longer.

2. Place ¼ cup flour for rolling in a shallow container.

3. Divide dough into 8 balls. Roll each ball between the palms of your hands in a circular motion until the dough is smooth. Press to flatten.

4. Heat *tava*/iron griddle or a heavy fry pan on medium to medium-high heat. (Adjust heat as needed. If *tava* is too hot, the roti will burn and stick to the *tava*, and if not hot enough, it will take a long time to cook and become dry.)

5. Roll each flat ball in the flour. Using flour as needed, roll into approximately 6-inch-round flatbreads.

6. Place roti on the heated *tava*. Cook for a few seconds until it colors and becomes firm and easy to pick up. Turn over and cook for a few seconds, until light brown spots appear on the underside. Turn roti back over and press down gently but firmly with a folded kitchen towel. The roti will puff as you press it.

7. If desired, lightly brush top of roti with oil. Oiling keeps the roti softer and moist. Serve immediately or place in an airtight container to serve later.

NUTRITION INFORMATION PER SERVING:
Calories: 104; Total Fat: 2 g (Saturated Fat: 0 g); Carbohydrate: 19 g; Protein: 4 g; Fiber: 4 g; Sodium: 77 mg

Pan-Fried Flatbread

Paratha

PREP: 10 minutes

COOK: 20 minutes

MAKES: 8 servings

SERVING SIZE: 1 *paratha*

I'm quite partial to this bread. I like them any way, from hot off the griddle to cold leftovers. They are great for any meal, with a curried dish or plain with just a little butter and salt.

> 2 cups roti-atta, or white whole wheat flour, plus additional for rolling
>
> 1¼ cups water
>
> 2–3 tablespoons canola or vegetable oil

1. In a mixing bowl or food processor, place flour. Make a well in the center of the flour. Add water gradually as you mix dough. (Depending on the type of flour, the amount of water needed may vary slightly.) The dough should be soft and easy to roll into a ball. Knead the dough for 1 to 2 minutes until smooth and elastic. Cover and let sit for 10 minutes or longer.

2. Place about ½ cup flour for rolling in a round shallow container.

3. Divide dough into 8 balls. Roll each ball between the palms of your hands in a circular motion until the dough is smooth. Press to flatten. Roll each ball in the dry flour.

4. Heat *tava*/iron griddle or a heavy fry pan on medium to medium-high heat. (Adjust heat as needed. If *tava* is too hot, the *paratha* will burn and stick to the *tava*, and if not hot enough, it will take a long time to cook and become dry.)

5. Roll out each ball to about a 3-inch circle. Brush the circle on the top with oil. Fold the circle in half and press lightly. Brush the top of the half circle with oil again and fold in half, making a triangle. Pick up the triangle and roll in flour. Roll the triangle into an approximately 6-inch triangle, dusting with flour as needed. (Use only the amount of flour you need to easily roll the bread. Excess flour will burn on the griddle, and creates smoke.)

6. Pick up the triangle, dust off extra flour, and place it carefully on the heated *tava*. Cook for a few seconds until underside colors and *paratha* becomes firm and easy to pick up. Turn *paratha* over and cook for a few seconds, until light brown spots appear on the underside.

7. Using a large spoon, oil top of the bread with ½ teaspoon oil. Turn over and oil bottom. Using the spoon, press the *paratha* in a circular motion. The *paratha* will puff. Cook until light brown on both sides. Serve immediately or place in an airtight container to serve later.

NUTRITION INFORMATION PER SERVING:

Calories: 133; Total Fat: 4 g (Saturated Fat: 0.5 g); Carbohydrate: 22 g; Protein: 4 g; Fiber: 4 g; Sodium: 2 mg

---

Potato-Stuffed Flatbread

Aloo Paratha

PREP: 20 minutes

COOK: 40 minutes

MAKES: 10 servings

SERVING SIZE: 1 *paratha*

This is the most popular stuffed pan-fried flatbread, loved by children and adults alike. They are great hot or cold. Make them for breakfast or dinner. They are also great for a picnic or traveling. Take them along instead of a sandwich—simply roll and eat. If making them for children, omit the green chiles and cayenne pepper. Serve them with plain yogurt, Indian pickles, or plain.

DOUGH

2 cups roti-atta, or white whole wheat flour, plus additional for rolling

½ teaspoon salt

1¼ cups water

3–4 tablespoons canola or vegetable oil

FILLING

3 medium potatoes (about 3 cups), boiled

½ teaspoon salt

½ teaspoon cayenne pepper, or to taste

2 teaspoons green chiles, finely chopped, or to taste

1 teaspoon ground coriander

½ teaspoon amchur

1. In a mixing bowl or food processor, combine flour and salt. Make a well in the center of the flour. Gradually add water. (Depending on the type of flour, the amount of water needed may vary slightly.) The dough should be soft and easy to roll into a ball. Knead the dough for 1 to 2 minutes until smooth and elastic. Cover and let stand until ready to use.

2. Peel the boiled potatoes. On a plate, mash the potatoes with your hands. The potatoes should be lumpy with some ¼-inch pieces. Add salt, cayenne pepper, green chiles, coriander, and amchur. Mix well and set aside.

3. Place ½ cup flour for rolling in a shallow container.

4. Divide dough into 8 balls. Roll each ball with the palms of your hands in a circular motion until the dough is smooth. Press to flatten. Roll each flat ball in the flour. Roll out each ball into

an approximately 3-inch circle. Place about ¼ cup of the filling in the center and gather the edges of the circle and join together. Seal the edges tightly and flatten with the palm of your hand. Pick up the filled ball and roll in the flour again. Place the filled side down and roll out to a 6-inch circle. (Use only the amount of flour you need to easily roll the dough. Excess flour on the griddle burns and creates smoke.)

5. Heat *tava*/iron griddle or a heavy fry pan on medium heat. Adjust heat as needed. If *tava* is too hot, the *paratha* will burn and stick to the *tava*, and if not hot enough, it will take a long time to cook and become dry.

6. Lightly oil the preheated griddle and wipe off excess. Place one filled *paratha* on the griddle. Cook for 1 to 2 minutes, until bottom colors and the *paratha* becomes firm and easy to pick up. Turn over with a flat spatula and cook until light brown spots appear on the underside. (While one is cooking, fill and roll the next one.)

7. Using a large soup or serving spoon, lightly oil the top of the *paratha* with ½ teaspoon oil, turn over, and oil the second side. Using the spoon or the spatula, press the *paratha* several times. This helps the *paratha* brown evenly. Cook until golden brown on both sides.

8. Serve immediately or place in an airtight container to serve later.

NOTE: Cooked *parathas* can be kept at room temperature for up to 8 hours. If planning to serve later, refrigerate cooked *parathas* and enjoy cold or reheat on the griddle. *Parathas* can also be frozen; thaw in refrigerator and reheat before serving.

·:

Onion-Stuffed Flatbread

Pyaj Paratha

PREP: 20 minutes
COOK: 40 minutes
MAKES: 8 servings
SERVING SIZE: 1 *paratha*

These *parathas* are a perennial favorite, for there are always onions in the house. For breakfast or dinner, you'll love these flatbreads, either with a curry dish or just by themselves.

DOUGH

2 cups roti-atta, or white whole wheat flour, plus additional for rolling

½ teaspoon salt

1¼ cups water

3–4 tablespoons canola or vegetable oil

FILLING

2 cups red or white onion, finely chopped

½ teaspoon cayenne pepper, optional

1–2 teaspoons green chiles, finely chopped, optional

1 teaspoon ground coriander

½ teaspoon *amchur*

Salt, to taste

1. In a mixing bowl or food processor, combine flour and salt. Make a well in the center of the flour. Gradually add water as you mix dough. (Depending on the type of flour, the amount of water needed may vary slightly.) Knead the dough for 1 to 2 minutes until smooth and elastic. Cover and let stand for 10 minutes or longer.

2. Mix together chopped onion, cayenne pepper, green chiles, coriander, and *amchur*. Mix well and set aside. (Do not add salt here, as it will make the filling too wet.)

3. Place ½ cup flour for rolling in a shallow container.

4. Divide dough into 8 balls. Roll each ball with the palms of your hands in a circular motion until the dough is smooth. Press to flatten. Roll each flat ball in the flour.

5. Heat *tava*/iron griddle or a heavy fry pan on medium heat. Adjust heat as needed. If *tava* is too hot, the *paratha* will burn and stick to the *tava*, and if not hot enough, it will take a long time to cook and become dry.

6. Roll out each ball into an approximately 3-inch circle. Place about 2 tablespoons of the onion filling in the center and sprinkle lightly with salt, if desired. Gather the edges of the circle and join together. Crimp the edges tightly and flatten with the palm of your hand. Pick up the filled ball and roll again in the flour. Place the filled side down and roll out again to a 6-inch circle. (Use only the amount of flour you need to easily roll the dough. Excess flour on the griddle burns and creates smoke.)

7. Lightly oil the preheated griddle and wipe off the oil. Place one filled *paratha* on the griddle. Cook for 1 to 2 minutes, until bottom colors and *paratha* becomes firm and easy to pick up. Turn over with a flat spatula and cook until light brown spots appear on the underside. (While one is cooking, fill and roll the next one.)

8. Using a large soup or serving spoon, lightly oil the top of the *paratha* with ½ teaspoon oil. Turn over and oil the second side. Using the spoon or the spatula, press the *paratha* several times. This helps the *paratha* brown evenly. Cook until golden brown on both sides.

9. Serve immediately or place in an airtight container to serve later. When the *paratha* is hot, it is crunchy, but once cooled, the moisture from the onions will soften it. Enjoy them hot or cold.

NOTE: Cooked *parathas* can be kept at room temperature for about 4 hours. If planning to serve later, refrigerate cooked *parathas* and enjoy cold or reheat on the griddle. *Parathas* can also be frozen for up to 3 months; thaw in refrigerator and reheat before serving.

NUTRITION INFORMATION PER SERVING:
Calories: 164; Total Fat: 6 g (Saturated Fat: 0.5 g); Carbohydrate: 26 g; Protein: 5 g; Fiber: 4 g; Sodium: 148 mg

Daikon-Stuffed Flatbread

Mooli Paratha

PREP: **20 minutes**
COOK: **40 minutes**
MAKES: **8 servings**
SERVING SIZE: **1** *paratha*

Just writing this recipe takes me back home; it is one of those comfort foods for me. In winter, long white radishes (called daikon) are tender and sweet. On Sunday mornings my dad would dig fresh ones out of his garden, wash them, grate them, and squeeze out the water; now they were ready for Mom to make the *parathas*. These flatbreads are crunchy on the outside with tender, sweet, and spicy daikons on the inside. They are best eaten hot off the griddle; the longer they sit, the softer they become. Enjoy them with Indian pickles or chutneys.

DOUGH

　2 cups roti-atta, or white whole wheat flour, plus additional for rolling

　½ teaspoon salt

　1¼ cups water

　3–4 tablespoons canola or vegetable oil

FILLING

　2 cups daikon or carrot, grated

　½ teaspoon cayenne pepper, optional

　1–2 teaspoons green chiles, finely chopped, optional

　2 teaspoons ground coriander

　½ teaspoon amchur

　Salt, to taste

1. In a mixing bowl or food processor, combine flour and salt. Make a well in the center of the flour. Gradually add water as you mix dough. (Depending on the type of flour, the amount of water needed may vary slightly.) The dough should be soft and easy to roll into a ball. Knead the dough for 1 to 2 minutes until smooth and elastic. Dough should resemble bread dough in consistency and smoothness. Cover and let stand for 10 minutes or longer.

2. Squeeze the grated daikon between your palms or place in a towel and twist, to remove the excess water. Discard the water. Place the squeezed daikon in a bowl. Mix in cayenne pepper, green chiles, coriander, and amchur. Mix well. Divide filling into 8 (¼-cup) equal portions. Set aside.

3. Place ½ cup flour for rolling in a shallow container.

4. Divide dough into 16 small balls. Roll each ball with the palms of your hands in a circular motion until the dough is smooth. Press to flatten. Roll each flat ball in the dry flour.

5. You will need two dough balls for each *paratha*. Roll out each ball into a 3-inch circle. Place about ¼ cup of the filling on one circle, spreading evenly. Sprinkle the filling with salt. Place the second 3-inch circle on top of the filling. Press firmly your palm and seal the edges of the two circles together. Lift the filled circle, dust it with flour on both sides, and roll out to a 6-inch circle. (Use only the amount of flour you need to easily roll the dough. Excess flour on the griddle burns and creates smoke.)

6. Heat *tava*/iron griddle or a heavy fry pan on medium-high heat. Adjust heat as needed. If *tava* is too hot, the *paratha* will burn and stick to the *tava*, and if not hot enough, it will take a long time to cook and become dry.

7. Lightly oil the preheated griddle and wipe off excess. Place one filled *paratha* on the griddle. Cook for 1 to 2 minutes, until bottom colors and *paratha* becomes firm and easy to pick up. Turn over with a flat spatula and cook until light brown spots appear on the underside. (While one is cooking, fill and roll the next one.)

8. Using a large soup or serving spoon, lightly oil the top of the *paratha* with ½ teaspoon oil. Turn it over and oil the second side. Using the spoon or the spatula, press the *paratha* several times. This helps the *paratha* brown evenly. Cook until golden brown on both sides.

9. Serve immediately or store in an airtight container.

NUTRITION INFORMATION PER SERVING:
Calories: 160; Total Fat: 6 g (Saturated Fat: 1 g); Carbohydrate: 24 g; Protein: 5 g; Fiber: 5 g; Sodium: 160 mg

---

Spinach Flatbread
Palak Paratha

PREP: 10 minutes
COOK: 25 minutes
MAKES: 8 servings
SERVING SIZE: 1 *paratha*

Make these *parathas* with spinach or *methi* (fenugreek) leaves. *Methi* leaves are more pungent and slightly bitter, with a distinct flavor and aroma—their flavor takes a little getting used to. You can even mix spinach and *methi* leaves in any portion for a different taste. Fresh spinach is best for this recipe, but you can use frozen too.

2 cups roti-atta, or white whole wheat flour, plus additional for rolling

1 teaspoon salt

½ teaspoon cayenne pepper, or to taste

1½ cups spinach (loosely packed), chopped, or fresh fenugreek (methi) leaves, chopped

¾ cup water

2 tablespoons canola or vegetable oil

1. In a mixing bowl, combine flour, salt, cayenne pepper, and spinach. (Do not make this dough in a food processor.) Make a well in the center of the flour. Gradually add water as you mix dough. (Depending on the type of flour and the moisture in spinach, the amount of water needed may vary slightly.) The dough should be soft and easy to roll into a ball. Knead the dough for 1 to 2 minutes until smooth and elastic. Cover and let stand for 10 minutes or longer.

2. Place ½ cup flour for rolling in a shallow container.

3. Heat *tava*/iron griddle or a heavy fry pan on medium-high heat. Adjust heat as needed. If *tava* is too hot, the *paratha* will burn and stick to the *tava*, and if not hot enough, it will take a long time to cook and become dry.

4. Divide dough into 8 balls. Roll each ball with the palms of your hands in a circular motion until the dough is smooth. Press to flatten. Roll each flattened ball in the flour. Roll out each ball into a 3-inch circle. Brush the top of the circle with oil. Fold in half and press lightly. Brush the top of the half circle with oil and fold in half again, making a triangle. Pick up the triangle and roll in flour. Roll the triangle into a 6-inch triangle, dusting with flour as needed. (Use only the amount of flour you need to easily roll the bread. Excess flour on the griddle burns and creates smoke.)

5. Lightly oil the preheated griddle and wipe off excess. Pick up the triangle, dust off extra flour, and place on the heated griddle. Cook for 1 minute until bottom colors and *paratha* becomes firm and easy to pick up. Turn *paratha* over and cook until light brown spots appear on the underside, about 1 minute.

6. Using a large spoon, lightly oil the top of the *paratha* with ½ teaspoon oil. Turn over and oil the other side. Using the large spoon or spatula, press the *paratha* in a circular motion. It will puff in some places. Cook until light brown on both sides. The longer you cook it, the crispier it will become. If you're going to eat it right away, make it crispy. But if you're going to eat them later, keep them soft; the crispy ones will become dry.

7. Serve immediately or place in an airtight container to serve later. Enjoy the *parathas* plain, with or without Indian pickles, or serve them with any curry dish.

NOTE: Cooked *parathas* can be kept at room temperature for about 8 hours. If planning to serve later, refrigerate *parathas* and enjoy cold or reheat on the griddle. *Parathas* can also be frozen; thaw in refrigerator and reheat before serving.

NUTRITION INFORMATION PER SERVING:
Calories: 134; Total Fat: 4 g (Saturated Fat: 0.5 g); Carbohydrate: 22 g; Protein: 4 g; Fiber: 4 g; Sodium: 224 mg

---

Fried Bread
Puri

PREP: 15 minutes
COOK: 30 minutes
MAKES: 10 servings
SERVING SIZE: 2 *puris*

*P*uris make any meal a celebration. Everyone, young and old, loves *puris*. Although you can make them alone, they are easier to make with two people—one to fry and one to roll the dough. I sometimes make them with *ajwain* (carom seeds) and sometimes without—whatever the mood calls for.

2 cups roti-atta, or white whole wheat flour

½ teaspoon salt

¾ teaspoon ajwain, optional

1 cup water

2 teaspoons canola or vegetable oil

Canola or vegetable oil for frying

1. In a mixing bowl or food processor, combine flour, salt, and ajwain, if using. Make a well in the center of the flour. Gradually add water as you mix dough. (Depending on the type of flour, the amount of water needed may vary slightly.) Knead the dough for 1 to 2 minutes until smooth and elastic. Dough is slightly harder than roti dough in consistency. Cover and let stand for 10 minutes or longer.

2. Lightly oil your hands. Divide the dough into 20 balls. Roll each ball between the palms of your hands in a circular motion until smooth. Press to flatten.

3. Heat 3 inches oil in a *karahi*/wok or skillet on high heat. Oil is ready when a little bit of batter dropped in the oil rises to the top right away (about 400°F).

4. On a lightly oiled surface, roll out each ball to a 3-inch circle. (If you are frying alone, roll out all the *puris* and place between towels to prevent drying. If you have help in frying, one person can roll the *puris* and the other one can fry.

5. Carefully drop one *puri* at a time into the hot oil. Using a large flat frying spatula, turn the *puri* as it rises to the top. Lightly press with the spatula and it will puff into a ball. Turn the *puri* again and lightly brown both sides.

6. Drain the *puri* on the side of the *karahi* and place on several layers of paper towels. Continue frying one at a time, making sure the oil is hot.

7. Serve immediately as puffed breads or store in an airtight container. As the *puri* cools, it will deflate. While they are still slightly warm, place them in an airtight container. Or stack them on top of each other and wrap them in aluminum foil.

> NOTE: If the *puris* are at room temperature, it is best not to warm them since they can dry out quickly. Serve them with hot curry instead. If refrigerated, place the *puris*, stacked and tightly wrapped in aluminum foil, in a preheated 350°F oven for 10 minutes. Do not overheat the *puris*, as they will become dry.

NUTRITION INFORMATION PER SERVING:
Calories: 152; Total Fat: 8 g (Saturated Fat: 0.5 g); Carbohydrate: 17 g; Protein: 3 g; Fiber: 3 g; Sodium: 118 mg

···

Sesame Seed Naan
Til Wale Naan

RISE DOUGH: 3 to 4 hours
PREP: 15 minutes
COOK: 15 minutes
MAKES: 8 servings
SERVING SIZE: 1 naan

If you have eaten in an Indian restaurant, you're familiar with naan—the most popular flatbread freshly baked in a *tandoor* (clay) oven. Enjoy all the flavor of restaurant naan in your oven. Use all-purpose flour for the best flavor. But for convenience or when in a hurry, I have made them using self-rising flour (see Variation, below). Sesame seeds add a wonderful taste and aroma to this bread.

1 teaspoon active dry yeast
2 teaspoons sugar
1 cup lukewarm water, divided
3 cups all-purpose flour
½ teaspoon salt
3 tablespoons canola or vegetable oil
2 tablespoons sesame seeds

1. Dissolve yeast and sugar in ¼ cup lukewarm water. Set aside.

2. In a medium mixing bowl or food processor, combine flour, salt, and oil.

3. Add yeast mixture to flour and mix. Add the remaining ¾ cup of water, and make dough. The dough should be soft and easy to roll into a ball. Knead the dough for 1 to 2 minutes until smooth and elastic.

4. Transfer dough to a bowl and coat lightly with oil to prevent drying. Cover with a towel and let sit for 3 to 4 hours at room temperature.

5. Divide dough into 8 equal portions. Roll between the palms of your hands to make smooth balls. Cover with dry towel and let rise for about 20 minutes.

6. Preheat oven to 450°F. Once oven is heated, turn the oven to broil. (If you have a pizza stone, heat stone on the middle rack.)

7. Dip each ball into the sesame seeds. On a lightly oiled surface, roll out each ball to a 7- or 8-inch oval or teardrop shape. Roll out all the naan before cooking, as the process in the oven goes very fast.

8. Place 3 to 4 pieces of naan on an ungreased baking sheet or directly on the pizza stone. Prick with fork a few times. Broil in the middle of the oven for 2 to 3 minutes until they are slightly puffed and become lightly browned. Turn over and broil for another 1 to 2 minutes. Do not overcook the naan, as it will become dry. (If you're using a pizza stone, you may not need to turn over the naan, as it will cook on both sides at the same time.)

9. Brush the sesame seed side lightly with oil, if desired. Serve immediately or store in an airtight container.

NUTRITION INFORMATION PER SERVING:
Calories: 235; Total Fat: 7 g (Saturated Fat: 0.5 g); Carbohydrate: 38 g; Protein: 5 g; Fiber: 2 g; Sodium: 147 mg

---

VARIATION: For instant naan, combine 3 cups self-rising flour and 2 teaspoons sugar. Mix in 3 tablespoons oil. Add 1 cup lukewarm water to make smooth dough. Lightly coat the dough with oil, to prevent it from drying. Cover and let rise for 15 minutes. Follow from step 5 on to prepare the naan.

··

Stretchy Fried Bread
Bhatura

RISING TIME: 3 to 4 hours
PREP: 10 minutes
COOK: 30 minutes
MAKES: 18 servings
SERVING SIZE: 1 *bhatura*

This stretchy bread, made with all-purpose flour, is a specialty of the Punjab region, where roadside stands sell it along with *Chole* (Blackened Spicy Chickpeas, page 121). My brother and sisters all requested *Chole-Bhature* for their special birthday meal. My mother made the best *bhatura*, and now my kids and nieces and nephews—the next generation—also want *chole-bhature* on their birthdays. The process of making *bhature* is easier and faster with two people—one person rolls and the other fries. Keep the oil on high heat; *bhatura* do not fry well in an electric, temperature-controlled fryer.

½ teaspoon active dry yeast

1 teaspoon sugar

1¼ cups lukewarm water, divided

3 cups all-purpose flour

Canola or vegetable oil for frying

1. In a small bowl, dissolve yeast and sugar in ¼ cup lukewarm water.

2. In a medium mixing bowl or food processor, combine flour and yeast mixture. Add the remaining lukewarm water and make dough. The dough should be soft and easy to roll into a ball. Knead the dough for 1 to 2 minutes until smooth and elastic.

3. Lightly oil top of the dough to prevent drying. Cover dough with a towel, place in a warm place, and let rise for 3 to 4 hours, until doubled in volume.

4. Oil hands and divide dough into 18 equal portions. Roll between the palms of your hands to make smooth balls. Cover with dry towel and let rise for about 20 minutes.

5. Heat 3 inches oil in a *karahi*/wok or skillet on high heat. Oil is ready when a little bit of batter dropped in the oil immediately rises to the top (about 400°F).

6. On a lightly oiled surface, roll out each ball to a 5-inch circle. (The dough might want to stretch back; do the best you can.) Carefully drop the *bhatura* into the hot oil. Using a large flat frying spatula, turn the *bhatura* as it puffs. Slightly brown both sides.

7. Drain the *bhatura* on several layers of paper towels. Continue frying 1 at a time. Serve immediately or store in an airtight container.

NUTRITION INFORMATION PER SERVING:
Calories: 132; Total Fat: 6 g (Saturated Fat: 0.5 g); Carbohydrate: 16 g; Protein: 2 g; Fiber: 1 g; Sodium: 0 mg

---

GF, LF

Sorghum Flatbread
Jawar Roti

PREP: 15 minutes
COOK: 20 minutes
MAKES: 4–6 servings
SERVING SIZE: 1 roti

These rotis are wonderfully hearty and satisfying. Serve them with any curry dish; I like them best with a soupy dal. They tend to be a little dry, thus hot curry sauce for dipping is perfect. If you're on a gluten-free diet, this recipe is great and can be made quickly.

1½ cups sorghum flour (*jawar atta*), plus additional for rolling

½ cup boiled potatoes, mashed

½ cup spring onions with greens, finely chopped

½ teaspoon salt

¼ teaspoon cayenne pepper, or to taste

1 teaspoon cornstarch

½ teaspoon baking powder

7–8 tablespoons hot water*

1 tablespoon olive oil or ghee, optional

1. In a mixing bowl, combine flour, mashed boiled potatoes, spring onions, salt, cayenne pepper, cornstarch, and baking powder. Gradually add the water. (The amount of water needed may vary slightly based on the type of flour used.) Mix the dough well with your hands; it should be soft and easy to roll into a ball. (The sorghum flour is not easy to knead, since it does not have any gluten.) Cover with a towel and let sit for 10 minutes or longer.

*If you're using *jawar* flour from an Indian store, it is very fine. Use tap water. If you're using sorghum flour from a supermarket, it is slightly coarser, so use hot water.

2. Place about ¼ cup flour for rolling in a shallow container.

3. Heat *tava*/iron griddle or a heavy fry pan on medium heat. Lightly oil the surface and wipe off excess. Adjust heat as needed. If *tava* is too hot, the roti will burn and stick to the *tava*, and if not hot enough, it will a take a long time to cook and become dry.

4. Divide dough into 4 to 6 balls. Roll each ball between the palms of your hands in a circular motion until the dough is smooth. Lightly oil hands, if needed, to prevent sticking.

5. Roll out the roti between two sheets of wax paper. Line the counter with a 6-inch-square piece of wax paper and sprinkle with flour. Place the dough ball in the center. Place another 6-inch square of wax paper on top of dough. Lightly roll out each ball into a 4–5-inch-round flatbread.

6. Remove the top wax paper and pick up the bread with the bottom wax paper (carefully dust off any excess flour on the bread) and flip it carefully onto the heated *tava*. Remove wax paper. Cook for 1 minute, until roti becomes firm and easy to pick up. Turn over with a flat turner and cook on the other side until light brown on the underside, 1 minute.

7. If you are using an electric stove, heat a burner on high and place a wire rack directly on the coils, creating a little space between the coils and the rack. If you have a gas stove, place the wire rack on the stove rack. Using full heat, place the bread directly on the wire rack. Grill roti on direct heat on both sides, turning with tongs.

8. Lightly brush top of roti with oil. Oiling keeps the roti softer and moist. Serve immediately or place in an airtight container to serve later.

NOTE: These rotis are best eaten hot or within a few hours of preparing, as they do not keep well.

NUTRITION INFORMATION PER SERVING:
Calories: 147; Total Fat: 0 g (Saturated Fat: 0 g); Carbohydrate: 31 g; Protein: 5 g; Fiber: 4 g; Sodium: 284 mg

---

GF, LF

Millet-Potato Flatbread
Bajra-Aloo Roti

PREP: 10 minutes
COOK: 20 minutes
MAKES: 8 servings
SERVING SIZE: 1 roti

If you like millet flour but don't know what to do with it, try these flatbreads. Boiled potatoes make this traditional *bajra-roti* moist and hearty. Millet flour naturally does not have any gluten, and thus is tricky to work with. Using wax paper to roll out the dough makes the job a bit easier.

2 cups millet flour (*bajra atta*), plus additional for rolling

½ teaspoon salt

½ teaspoon cayenne pepper, or to taste

1 cup boiled potatoes, mashed

2 tablespoons cilantro, chopped

1 cup warm water*

1 tablespoon olive oil or ghee, optional

*If you're using millet flour from an Indian grocery store, it is ground very fine; use tap water. If you're using millet flour from a regular grocery store, it tends to be coarser, so use hot water.

1. In a mixing bowl, combine millet flour, salt, and cayenne pepper. Mix in the mashed potatoes. Gradually add water. (The amount of water needed may vary slightly based on the type of flour used.) Mix the dough well with your hands; it should be soft and easy to roll into a ball. The millet flour is not easy to knead, since it does not have any gluten. Cover with a towel and let sit for about 10 minutes.

2. Place about ¼ cup flour for rolling in a shallow container.

3. Heat *tava*/iron griddle or a heavy fry pan on medium heat. Lightly oil the surface and wipe off the excess. Adjust heat as needed. If *tava* is too hot, the roti will burn and stick to the *tava*, and if not hot enough, it will a take a long time to cook and become dry.

4. Divide dough into 8 balls. Roll each ball between the palms of your hands in a circular motion until the dough is smooth. Lightly oil hands, if needed, to prevent sticking.

5. Roll out the roti between two sheets of wax paper. Line the counter with a 6- to 8-inch-square piece of wax paper and sprinkle with flour. Place the dough ball in the center. Place another piece of wax paper on top. Roll out the dough into a 6-inch-round flatbread. (First pat the bread flat with your palms as much as you can and then lightly roll with the rolling pin.)

6. Remove the top wax paper and pick up the bread with the bottom wax paper. Carefully dust off any excess flour on the bread and flip the roti carefully onto the heated griddle. Remove the top wax paper. Cook for about 1 minute, until it becomes firm and easy to pick up. Turn over with a flat turner and cook until light brown on the underside, 1 minute.

7. If using an electric stove, heat a burner on high and place a wire rack directly on the coils, creating a little space between the coils and the rack. If using a gas stove, place the wire rack on the stove rack. Using full heat, place the bread directly on the wire rack. Grill roti on direct heat on both sides, turning with tongs.

8. Lightly brush top of roti with oil. Oiling keeps the roti softer and moist. Serve immediately or place in an airtight container to serve later.

NOTE: These rotis are best eaten hot or within a few hours of preparing, as they do not keep well.

NUTRITION INFORMATION PER SERVING:
Calories: 203; Total Fat: 2 g (Saturated Fat: 0 g); Carbohydrate: 40 g; Protein: 8 g; Fiber: 5 g; Sodium: 149 mg

Corn Flatbread

Makka Roti

PREP: 10 minutes
COOK: 30 minutes
MAKES: 6 servings
SERVING SIZE: 1 roti

I make these roti with cornmeal. They come out crunchy on the outside and soft on the inside. A specialty of Punjab, these take time to make and the process is a little messy. The flour tends to be sticky; when you're done, soak the counter for a few minutes before you wipe it clean. Serve with Spinach and Tofu (page 174) or Mixed Greens (page 112).

2 cups water

1½ cups yellow cornmeal

2 tablespoons canola oil or ghee

1. In a medium skillet, boil water. Gradually add cornmeal, stirring continuously. Remove from heat, cover with lid, and let sit for 20 minutes or longer. Open the lid and cool.

2. Using a potato masher, mash the dough until it is smooth, making sure to remove all lumps.

3. Divide the dough into 6 parts. Oil your hands and roll each ball between the palms of your hands in a circular motion until the dough is smooth. Press to flatten. Lightly oil each ball.

4. Heat *tava*/iron griddle or a heavy fry pan on medium-high heat. Lightly oil the griddle and wipe off excess. Adjust heat as needed. If *tava* is too hot, the roti will burn and stick to the *tava*, and if not hot enough, it will a take a long time to cook and become dry.

5. Line the counter with an 8-inch-square piece of wax paper. Place the oiled ball in the center of the wax paper. Place another piece of wax paper on top. Roll dough into a 6-inch round.

6. Remove the top wax paper and pick up the bread with the bottom wax paper. Flip it carefully onto the heated griddle. Remove the top wax paper. Cook for 2 to 3 minutes, until it becomes firm and easy to pick up. Turn over with a flat spatula and cook roti on the other side, until light brown spots appear on the underside, another 2 to 3 minutes.

7. If you are using an electric stove, heat a burner on high and place a wire rack directly on the coils, creating a space between the coils and the rack. If you have a gas stove, place the wire rack on the stove rack. Using full heat, place the bread directly on the wire rack. Grill roti on direct heat on both sides, turning with tongs.

8. Lightly brush top of roti with oil. Oiling keeps the roti softer and moist. Serve immediately, or place in an airtight container to serve later.

NOTE: Since corn roti take a long time to cook, I often use two griddles to speed up the process. These are best eaten within a few hours of preparing, as they do not keep well.

NUTRITION INFORMATION PER SERVING:
Calories: 145; Total Fat: 6 g (Saturated Fat: 0.5 g); Carbohydrate: 22 g; Protein: 3 g; Fiber: 0 g; Sodium: 1 mg

Soy Products

I HAVE INCLUDED ONLY a few soy recipes in this book, but they feature a cross section of soy products and will add an excellent variety to your repertoire.

Soybeans, soy flour, soymilk, and soy granules are not new to Indian cuisine. Back in the early 1970s, soy products were introduced in India. My mother was actually one of the recipe testers at the G. B. Pant University of Agriculture and Technology, Pantnagar, Uttaranchal. There was a group of eight women who tested recipes for everything from appetizers to desserts using soy products. They published a book with some 250 recipes. Pant University was one of the agriculture universities chosen by the Indian Agriculture Department to test and integrate soy products into the Indian market. At that time, my friends and I would go down to the local coop and have a glass of cold soymilk. Today, many shops carry cold plain and flavored soymilk among their line of beverages.

Soybeans and soy products occasionally require some flavoring, herbs, and/or spices to enhance their flavor or mask a "beanie" taste. In general, soybeans, soymilk, soy yogurt, texturized vegetable protein (TVP, or soy granules), and tofu all integrate well into Indian dishes.

Tofu

Tofu works well as a substitute in *paneer* (fresh Indian cheese) dishes. Use extra-firm tofu, as it holds up better in the curry sauce and is closer to the texture of *paneer*. Tofu by itself is relatively bland and absorbs the flavor of the curry sauce. Most tofu comes packaged in water. Remove the tofu from water, cut into cubes or strips, or grate, as desired, and place on a dry kitchen towel or paper towels to help remove excess water. Tofu has a sponge-like quality, so when you remove the excess moisture, it can better soak up the curry sauce, marinade, or spices, intensifying its flavor. Pea-and-Tofu Curry (page 176) and Spinach and Tofu (at right) are crowd pleasers.

> Tofu is typically packaged in water, which should be discarded prior to use. If you use only part of the tofu, place the remainder in an airtight container, cover with fresh water, and store in the refrigerator. If you change the water daily, the tofu will stay fresh for up to five days.

Soymilk and Soy Yogurt

Soymilk can be substituted for milk in some dishes, but it will have a different taste and texture. Soy yogurt has a very different texture from that of milk yogurt. It works well in sweetened beverages such as Mango Yogurt Drink (page 182). On the other hand, in vegetable salty *raita* (yogurt dish) it requires extra seasonings and lemon juice to bring out the traditional *raita* flavor; see Cucumber-Yogurt Sauce (page 180).

Textured Vegetable Protein (TVP)

TVP is a processed soy-based product made from defatted soy flour that's cooked under pressure and extruded through a machine. It's available in a dry form as granules, flakes, and chunks. The chunks are available as soy-*baddiyan* or nuggets in Indian grocery stores. The chunks can be added to the curry sauce for a high-protein dish. TVP products are easily hydrated in hot liquids.

GF

Spinach and Tofu
Palak-Tofu

PREP: 10 minutes
COOK: 40 minutes
MAKES: 8 servings
SERVING SIZE: ½ cup

Whether you're a spinach enthusiast or not, this variation on the standard Indian restaurant dish known as *Saag-Paneer* is a must-try. Traditionally, it is made with *paneer* (homemade cheese) and cream, making it high in fat and calories. Extra-firm tofu is an excellent substitute for the *paneer*, as you will soon discover. For convenience, I always use frozen spinach for this recipe.

1 pound frozen chopped spinach, or fresh spinach, coarsely chopped

1 teaspoon salt

½ teaspoon turmeric

1 cup water, divided

1½ cups (10 ounces) extra-firm tofu

2 tablespoons besan or cornmeal

2 tablespoons canola or vegetable oil

½ teaspoon cumin seeds

4–6 dried red chiles

1 cup onion, finely chopped

1 tablespoon ginger, peeled and grated

2 teaspoons garlic, finely chopped

½ teaspoon cayenne pepper, or to taste

1. In a heavy skillet, place spinach, turmeric, salt, and ½ cup water. Bring to a boil over medium-high heat. Reduce heat, cover, and simmer for 5 minutes. Open lid and cool slightly.

2. While spinach mixture cools, cut tofu into 1-inch squares and lay them on a towel to remove excess water.

3. In a blender jar, place the cooled spinach mixture and coarsely grind.

4. Return the coarsely ground spinach to the skillet. In a separate bowl, combine besan with remaining ½ cup water. Stir besan mixture into the spinach. Cover with a lid and cook on medium heat until spinach is simmering. (Caution: Before stirring, remove the skillet from the heat and carefully remove the lid. The spinach tends to splatter and can burn.) Reduce heat and simmer for 20 minutes. A longer cooking time adds flavor to the spinach.

5. *While spinach mixture cooks, prepare seasoning:* In a medium fry pan, heat oil on medium-high heat, add cumin seeds and dried red chiles, and cook for a few seconds, until seeds and chiles turn brown. Add onion and fry 2 to 3 minutes until golden brown. Add ginger and garlic and fry for another minute. Remove from heat, add the cayenne pepper, and cook for a few seconds.

6. Remove spinach from the heat, add tofu pieces and the seasoning, and stir gently to avoid breaking the tofu. Cover with a lid and return to the stove. Continue to simmer for another 5 minutes. Leave covered until ready to serve.

7. Transfer to a serving bowl and serve hot with flatbread or rice.

NUTRITION INFORMATION PER SERVING:
Calories: 109; Total Fat: 7 g (Saturated Fat: 0.5 g); Carbohydrate: 6 g; Protein: 8 g; Fiber: 3 g; Sodium: 299 mg

·:·

Pea-and-Tofu Curry

Matar-Tofu

PREP: 10 minutes
COOK: 30 minutes
MAKES: 10 servings
SERVING SIZE: ¾ cup

Matar-paneer is an essential dish in most Indian restaurants, loved by adults and children alike. The traditional version is typically made with yogurt and/or cream, along with *paneer* (homemade cheese). If you have time, prepare this dish a few hours before you plan to serve it, since it tastes better as the flavors merge and absorb in the tofu. It also makes great leftovers.

2 cups (10 ounces) extra-firm tofu

2 cups frozen peas

1 cup onion, coarsely chopped

1 tablespoon ginger, peeled and chopped

1 teaspoon garlic

1 teaspoon green chile, chopped, or to taste, or ½ teaspoon cayenne pepper

½ cup tomato sauce

1 teaspoon cumin seeds

2 tablespoons almond meal, or 1 tablespoon almond butter

1 tablespoon white poppy seeds

½ teaspoon turmeric

2 teaspoons ground coriander

3 tablespoons canola or vegetable oil, divided

2½ cups water

1 teaspoon salt

¾ teaspoon garam masala

2 tablespoons cilantro, chopped

1. Cut tofu into ½- to ¾-inch squares and lay them on a towel for 10 minutes to remove excess water. Thaw frozen peas by soaking in cold water.

2. In a blender jar, grind onion, ginger, garlic, green chile, tomato sauce, cumin seeds, almond meal, poppy seeds, turmeric, and coriander to a smooth paste. Set aside. (If necessary, add 1 to 2 tablespoons water to help grind the masala.)

3. Heat 1 tablespoon oil in a heavy skillet over medium-high heat. Add the tofu pieces in a single layer. Cook until light brown on one side, turn over and brown the other side, about 2 to 3 minutes on each side. Remove the tofu to a plate and set aside.

4. In the same skillet, add the onion mixture. Cook until most of the liquid has evaporated, stirring occasionally. Add the remaining 2 tablespoons of oil and cook until mixture is thick enough to draw away from the sides and bottom of the pan in a dense mass and the oil starts to separate, making the masala shiny. Add water and bring to a boil.

5. Add peas, salt, and tofu pieces. Bring the mixture to a boil, reduce heat, and simmer for 10 minutes. Add garam masala and cilantro. Transfer to a serving bowl.

NUTRITION INFORMATION PER SERVING:
Calories: 151; Total Fat: 10 g (Saturated Fat: 1 g); Carbohydrate: 8 g; Protein: 10 g; Fiber: 3 g; Sodium: 334 mg

Kale-Tofu Pilaf

Saag-Tofu Pulao

PREP: 10 minutes
COOK: 20 minutes
MAKES: 6 servings
SERVING SIZE: 1 cup

This rice dish is easy to make and is loaded with nutrients. Kale is high in beta-carotene (vitamin A compound), vitamin C, and minerals such as iron, manganese, calcium, and potassium. Tofu adds the protein and all the goodness of soy. The grated tofu blends well with the rice, and the kale adds a nice texture and flavor. Enjoy it with Cilantro Chutney (page 185) and a bowl of soup for a complete meal.

1 cup long-grain or basmati rice

2½ cups water, divided

1 teaspoon salt, divided

2 cups (10 ounces) extra-firm tofu

2 tablespoons canola or vegetable oil

1 cup onion, thinly sliced

½ teaspoon ground cumin

4 cups fresh kale (loosely packed) or spinach, finely chopped

½ teaspoon cayenne pepper, or to taste

1 teaspoon garam masala

1. Wash rice in 2 to 3 changes of water, rubbing the rice with your fingers, until the water is relatively clear. Soak in cold water for 15 minutes or longer. Drain the rice in a strainer; set aside.

2. In a 1- to 2-quart saucepan, place drained rice, 2 cups water, and ½ teaspoon salt. Bring to a boil. Reduce heat to medium and simmer for 12 to 15 minutes, until the rice is fully cooked. Let cool for 5 minutes or longer. Fluff with a fork.

3. While rice cooks, grate the tofu and spread on a towel to absorb the water.

4. Heat oil in a large nonstick fry pan on medium-high heat. Add the onion and fry for 2 to 3 minutes until light brown. Add the cumin and stir.

5. Add grated tofu and fry for 1 to 2 minutes. Add kale and fry for 1 to 2 minutes. Add remaining ½ teaspoon salt, cayenne pepper, garam masala, and remaining ½ cup water. Stir, cover with lid, and simmer for 5 minutes.

6. Add fluffed rice to the kale mixture. Stir well with spatula. Cover with lid. Steam through for 3 to 4 minutes. Leave covered until ready to serve. Fluff with fork again before serving.

NUTRITION INFORMATION PER SERVING:
Calories: 255; Total Fat: 9 g (Saturated Fat: 1 g); Carbohydrate: 37 g; Protein: 11 g; Fiber: 3 g; Sodium: 416 mg

Scrambled Tofu

Tofu Ki Bhuji

PREP: 10 minutes
COOK: 5 minutes
MAKES: 2 servings
SERVING SIZE: ½ cup

This dish is for anyone who misses eggs, or for anyone who wants something substantial and high in protein for breakfast. Tofu has an enormous advantage in that it absorbs the flavors of spices and other ingredients, making it very versatile. Extra-firm tofu grates easily and maintains its texture. Serve with toast or any flatbread.

1 cup extra-firm tofu

1 tablespoon canola or vegetable oil

¼ cup onion, finely chopped

¼ cup mushrooms, thinly sliced

¼ cup green peppers, finely chopped

¼ cup tomato, finely chopped

2 tablespoons cilantro, finely chopped

Pinch of turmeric

¼ teaspoon black salt or table salt

⅛ teaspoon black pepper

1. Grate tofu and spread it on a towel to remove excess water.

2. Heat oil in a nonstick fry pan on medium-high heat. Add the chopped onion and cook for 1 to 2 minutes, until translucent. Add mushrooms and cook for 1 to 2 minutes. Add green peppers, tomatoes, and cilantro and cook for another minute.

3. Add grated tofu and scramble mixture together. Add turmeric, salt, and black pepper. Stir for 1 minute and remove from heat. Serve hot.

NUTRITION INFORMATION PER SERVING:
Calories: 262; Total Fat: 18 g (Saturated Fat: 2 g); Carbohydrate: 9 g; Protein: 21 g; Fiber: 4 g; Sodium: 311 mg

---

GF

Soy Granules and Cabbage Snack
Soy-Gobhi Uppama

PREP: **10 minutes**
COOK: **15 minutes**
MAKES: **4 servings**
SERVING SIZE: **½ cup**

Quick and easy to make, this high-protein dish is great for breakfast or dinner. *Uppama* is typically made with cream of wheat and has a very distinctive texture and flavor. The seasonings transform the texturized vegetable protein, and the cabbage adds moisture, making this a great anytime dish.

1¼ cups water, divided

¾ cup texturized vegetable protein (TVP or soy granules)

2 tablespoons canola or vegetable oil

½ teaspoon brown mustard seeds

10–12 curry leaves

1 teaspoon (split, hulled) chana dal

¾ cup onion, finely chopped

1–2 teaspoons green chiles, finely chopped

¾ cup carrot, grated

2 cups cabbage, finely chopped

½ teaspoon salt

Lemon wedges, optional

1. In a small skillet, boil 1 cup water. Add TVP. Remove from heat and let sit for 5 minutes or more.

2. In a medium skillet, heat oil on medium-high heat. Add mustard seeds, cover with lid, and cook the seeds for a few seconds, until they stop popping. Add curry leaves and chana dal, fry for a few seconds, and add the onions.

3. Fry onion for 2 to 3 minutes until golden brown. Add green chiles, carrots, and cabbage.

Add the remaining ¼ cup water and salt. Cover with lid. Reduce heat to medium and cook for 3 to 5 minutes, until carrots are tender.

4. Add the hydrated TVP. Stir well and fry for 2 to 3 minutes. Remove from heat.

5. Cover and let stand until ready to serve. Serve with lemon wedges, if desired.

NUTRITION INFORMATION PER SERVING:
Calories: 149; Total Fat: 8 g (Saturated Fat: 0.5 g); Carbohydrate: 13 g; Protein: 7 g; Fiber: 5 g; Sodium: 322 mg

---

GF

Soy Cutlets
Soy Ki Tikki

PREP: 10 minutes
COOK: 20 minutes
MAKES: 6 servings
SERVING SIZE: 2 patties

Vegetable patties are great for a snack or appetizer. The texturized vegetable protein blends well with the vegetables without changing the taste of the traditional cutlets. I like to make sandwiches with the leftover cutlets.

1 cup water

½ cup texturized vegetable protein (TVP or soy granules)

1 tablespoon canola or vegetable oil

½ cup scallions, chopped

¾ cup grated carrot

1 teaspoon ginger, peeled and finely grated

1–2 teaspoons green chile, finely chopped

1 medium potato (about 1 cup), boiled

½ teaspoon salt

¼ teaspoon ground black pepper

½ teaspoon garam masala

1 tablespoon cilantro, finely chopped

1 tablespoon cornstarch

½ cup bread crumbs

Canola or vegetable oil for frying

1. In a small skillet, boil 1 cup of water. Add TVP, remove from heat, and let sit for 5 minutes. Drain in a strainer and let cool. Place cooled TVP in the center of a kitchen towel and squeeze out excess water. Place in a medium bowl and set aside.

2. Heat 1 tablespoon of oil in a small fry pan over medium-high heat. Add the scallions and fry for 1 minute. Add the grated carrot, ginger, and green chiles. Cover and cook for 2 minutes. Remove from heat and let sit, covered, for 5 minutes. Open lid and cool completely.

3. Peel and mash the boiled potato. Set aside.

4. Add the carrot mixture and mashed potato to the TVP. Add salt, black pepper, garam masala, cilantro, and cornstarch. Mix well with hands. The mixture should come together as soft dough. Divide into 12 portions.

5. Place bread crumbs on a plate. Make 12 round or oval patties, 2 inches round and 1 inch thick. Roll patties in bread crumbs and set aside.

6. Heat 3 inches oil in a *karahi*/wok or skillet on high heat. Oil is ready when a little bit of dough dropped in the oil rises to the top right away (about 400°F).

7. Add 4 to 6 patties at a time. Fry for 3 to 5 minutes, until golden brown on one side. Turn patties over, and fry for 2 to 3 minutes until golden brown. Drain on paper towels.

8. Serve hot with your favorite chutney or ketchup.

GF

Cumin-Cilantro Edamame
Hare Soy Ki Subji

PREP: 5 minutes
COOK: 10 minutes
MAKES: 4 servings
SERVING SIZE: ½ cup

Fresh green soybeans have become popular, thanks to their nutritional value as well as their sweet, tender flavor. Mildly seasoned with cumin and cilantro, these nutty edamame are a nutritious substitute for green beans. For convenience, use frozen edamame, if they're available.

1 tablespoon olive or canola oil

½ teaspoon cumin seeds

12 ounces frozen edamame, or seeded fresh edamame

¼ teaspoon turmeric

¼ teaspoon salt

¼ teaspoon cayenne pepper, or to taste

½ cup water

1 teaspoon lemon or lime juice

¼ cup cilantro, chopped

1. In a medium nonstick fry pan, heat oil on medium–high heat. Add cumin seeds and cook for a few seconds, until golden brown. Add edamame and stir.

2. Stir in turmeric, salt, and cayenne pepper.

3. Add water. Cover with lid. Reduce heat and simmer for 5 to 7 minutes, until edamame is tender.

4. Transfer to a serving bowl and stir in lemon juice and cilantro. Serve warm or cold.

GF, LF

Cucumber-Yogurt Sauce
Kheere Ka Raita

PREP: 5 minutes
COOK: 0 minutes
MAKES: 4 servings
SERVING SIZE: ½ cup

A *raita* is a yogurt-based dish, served as a meal accompaniment. *Raita* can be made with a variety of vegetables or fruits added to the yogurt. The most popular is cucumber *raita*, made here using soy yogurt. Lemon juice and spices help bring out the traditional tart taste and flavor in this raita.

1 cup plain soy yogurt

1 cup cucumber, peeled and grated

2 tablespoons chopped cilantro

½ teaspoon roasted cumin powder (page 25)

½ teaspoon chaat masala (page 24), or purchased

2 teaspoons lemon or lime juice

1. In a small bowl, whip soy yogurt. Add the grated cucumber.

2. Add cilantro, cumin powder, chaat masala, and lemon juice. Mix well. Refrigerate for 10 minutes or longer.

Almond Spicy Drink

Thandai

PREP: 20 minutes
COOK: None
MARINATE: 2 to 8 hours
MAKES: 4 servings
SERVING SIZE: 1 cup

*T*handai is associated with the spring festival known as Holi, a festival of color that is very popular in northern India. *Thandai* is condidered to be cooling, and is served all summer long. With so many ingredients, it is a complicated drink with a spicy-creamy flavor. You can buy *thandai* mixes, but they are not as good as this concoction. (Spiked *thandai*, featuring marijuana leaves, is sometimes enjoyed at Holi celebrations—but for that variation, you're on your own.)

¼ cup slivered almonds

1 tablespoon pumpkin seeds

2 tablespoons white poppy seeds

2 teaspoons fennel seeds

6 green cardamom pods

½ teaspoon peppercorns

4 cups soymilk

⅓ cup sugar

½ teaspoon rose water

Crushed ice

Organic dried or fresh red rose petals, for garnish, optional

1. In a spice grinder, combine almonds, pumpkin seeds, poppy seeds, fennel seeds, cardamom pods, and peppercorns. Grind to a smooth consistency.

2. In a small bowl, mix soymilk, almond paste, sugar, and rose water. Combine using a wire whisk. Refrigerate for 2 to 8 hours. (You can serve it right away, but the longer you let it rest, the more the flavor intensifies.)

3. Strain the milk (use general kitchen strainer not a tea strainer) into a pitcher. Squeeze out all the milk and discard the pulp. Serve over crushed ice and garnish with rose petals, if desired.

NUTRITION INFORMATION PER SERVING:
Calories: 238; Total Fat: 9 g (Saturated Fat: 1 g); Carbohydrate: 31 g; Protein: 9 g; Fiber: 2 g; Sodium: 120 mg

---

Spiced Chai Latte

Masala Chai

PREP: 5 minutes
COOK: 5 minutes
MAKES: 2 servings
SERVING SIZE: 1 cup

*C*hai—brewed tea with milk and sugar—is well known to most Westerners today. In India, chai is a matter of personal taste and preference, just as coffee is to coffee lovers. Some like it plain, while others prefer it with spices (masala chai). Chai latte has more milk than typical chai.

1¼ cups water

1 teaspoon chai masala (page 182) or purchased

2 tea bags or 2 teaspoons black tea leaves

1 cup soymilk

2 tablespoons sugar, or to taste

1. In a small saucepan, boil water with chai masala. Add tea bags, reduce heat, and simmer for 2 minutes. Remove from heat and steep tea for 3 to 5 minutes.

2. Add soymilk and sugar, return to stove, and bring to a boil. Remove tea bags and strain tea into a cup or teapot. Serve hot.

NOTE: Chai can be made in a microwave. Just remember to make strong brewed tea and reheat after adding milk and sugar.

NUTRITION INFORMATION PER SERVING:
Calories: 104; Total Fat: 2 g (Saturated Fat: 0.5 g); Carbohydrate: 19 g; Protein: 3 g; Fiber: 0 g; Sodium: 59 mg

CHAI MASALA

MAKES: ¼ cup

Although you can purchase chai masala, you'll love this version. It takes just a few minutes, so you can grind fresh masala whenever you need it.

1 tablespoon cardamom seeds

2 tablespoons ground ginger

½ teaspoon cinnamon

8 whole cloves

1 teaspoon black peppercorns

¼ teaspoon fennel seeds

In a spice grinder, combine all the spices and grind until fine. Store in an airtight container for up to 6 months.

Mango Yogurt Drink

Aam Lassi

PREP: 5 minutes
COOK: 5 minutes
MAKES: 2 servings
SERVING SIZE: 1½ cups

This is a variation on the traditional—and popular—yogurt drink known as *lassi*, which is often served at Indian restaurants. Lime juice adds tartness to the soy yogurt and helps to bring out the traditional sweet-and-sour taste of *lassi*.

1 cup plain soy yogurt

1 cup water

1 cup fresh or frozen mango chunks

2 tablespoons sugar or sugar substitute equivalent

2 teaspoons lemon or lime juice

Crushed ice cubes

In a blender jar, combine soy yogurt, water, mango chunks, sugar, and lemon juice. Blend until well combined and mixture is the consistency of a smoothie. Serve over ice.

NOTE: If the mango has too many stringy fibers (as some mangoes do), strain the *lassi* and discard the fiber.

NUTRITION INFORMATION PER SERVING:
Calories: 226; Total Fat: 3 g (Saturated Fat: 0.5 g); Carbohydrate: 48 g; Protein: 5 g; Fiber: 2 g; Sodium: 48 mg

Salads and Chutneys

‧‧

SALAD, PER SE, is not typically an Indian meal. That's not to say that raw vegetables are not commonplace. In fact, a few pieces of cucumber, tomato, onion, and radish often grace a meal. Typically these vegetables, along with a fruit such as papaya, mango, or melon, are simply sliced and served raw alongside a meal, as a relish. You want to keep them as plain as possible—at the most, with a squeeze of lemon or lime, a sprinkle of salt, and black pepper—and enjoy a slice between bites, as a palate cleanser.

In my family, my dad was so fond of these crunchy vegetables that he would cut them himself at almost every lunch and dinner. After he retired, Mom put him officially in charge of that process. These fresh fruits and vegetables are served for their freshness and crunch as much as for their nutritional value.

That said, there are other salads that are made by marinating in lemon/lime juice or vinegar, or they are lightly seasoned with oil, spices, and herbs. The most prevalent salad served with Indian meals is called *kachumber*, which literally translates to "minced vegetables." My friend's husband Suresh makes the best *kachumber*. I think he puts everything in the salad except the kitchen sink. He patiently dices all the vegetables and some crunchy fruits into ¼-inch pieces and ever so lightly seasons them, such as Peanut-Mung Salad (page 192). You will find a variety of fresh and seasoned salads in this section to complement any meal.

Chutneys and pickles are as Indian as curries. The concept of chutneys is no longer new to the Western world; they have become as well-known as salsa. Indian chutneys are typically piquant—with all its synonyms, *hot*, *spicy*, *tangy*, and *sharp*—palate-pleasing condiments that liven up any dish. They can also be sweet and mild. Chutney can be fresh ground or preserved. You will find them in most Indian restaurants as a condiment. I have included some of the most popular chutneys in this section, including the quintessential cilantro chutney, which is probably the most popular chutney enjoyed in Indian homes around the world. I grind a couple of batches of cilantro chutney at a time and freeze it in small containers, so that I can always have some handy.

Indian pickles are unique to the cuisine. They are an acquired taste; Indians love them, but many non-Indians find them too strange, intense, or stinky. Just remember that a little bit goes a long way! For best results, just dab your food into the pickle or take only a smidgen. Pickles are preserved meticulously when the fruit or vegetable is in season. A few jars of pickles—mango, chili, and/or lemon—are just as much a part of an Indian pantry as spices. Until recently, each family made their own pickles and kept them in 5- to 8-gallon ceramic jars and guarded them with a vengeance. Only a designated person was allowed to dip into those jars, for a very simple reason: If you mishandled the pickles—for example, if you put a dirty or wet spoon in the jar—you could ruin a year's supply.

Today, Indians buy store-bought pickles as needed, as they are available year-round. As with any specialty, there is nothing like homemade pickles. My mother makes the most incredible pickles, and until a few years ago used to give us a jar of her best. Now, I have to buy the pickles or make my own if I want the same flavors. Because it is hard to find the right pickling mango, I did not include pickle recipes in this book. However, I have included preserved chutneys, such as Mango Chutney (page 187) and Cran-Apple Chutney (page 188).

GF, LF

Tamarind Chutney
Imli Chutney

PREP: **30 minutes**
COOK: **20 minutes**
MAKES: **1 cup, or 48 servings**
SERVING SIZE: **1 teaspoon**

Good tamarind chutney is essential for chaat (page 24) and a great condiment for many savory snacks, including fritters and samosas. It adds a sweet-and-sour taste and perks up the flavor of any dish. I always keep a jar of tamarind chutney in the refrigerator, since it's too time-consuming to make at the last minute. If you're in a hurry, use Amchur Chutney (page 187).

1¼ cup tamarind sauce (page 25)
¾ teaspoon salt
½ cup brown sugar
½ teaspoon cayenne pepper, or to taste
½ teaspoon roasted cumin powder (page 25)
1 tablespoon dates, chopped, or golden raisins, optional

1. Heat tamarind sauce in a medium-heavy saucepan. Add salt, brown sugar, cayenne pepper, and cumin powder. Stir until the sugar is dissolved. Heat on medium heat, stirring occasionally. Bring to a boil, reduce heat, and simmer for 5 to 7 minutes. Add the dates. Remove from heat and cool to room temperature. The chutney will thicken as it cools.

2. Serve immediately or refrigerate in an airtight container for up to 1 month. If desired, freeze part of it for up to 6 months.

NUTRITION INFORMATION PER SERVING:
Calories: 9; Total Fat: 0 g (Saturated Fat: 0 g); Carbohydrate: 2 g; Protein: 0 g; Fiber: 0 g; Sodium: 37 mg

GF, LF

Cilantro Chutney
Dhania Chutney

PREP: 10 minutes
COOK: 0 minutes
MAKES: 1 cup, or 48 servings
SERVING SIZE: 1 teaspoon

The quintessential chutney, much like ketchup, cilantro chutney is ubiquitous and goes with everything. It keeps well in the refrigerator for up to two weeks, but it will change color to a dull green. I often double the batch and freeze it in small containers, to maintain the bright green color.

3 cups (3 ounces) cilantro, with stems

½ cup onion, coarsely chopped

1 tablespoon ginger, peeled and chopped

½ teaspoon cumin seeds

2–3 teaspoons green chiles, coarsely chopped

1 teaspoon salt

3 tablespoons lemon or lime juice

1–2 tablespoons water

1. Clean coriander of any discolored leaves and stems. Cut about 1 inch from the tips of the stems. Leave the rest of the stems intact. Wash thoroughly in 2 to 3 changes of water to remove any dirt.

2. Place cilantro, onion, ginger, cumin seeds, green chiles, salt, and lemon juice, in a blender jar and grind to a smooth paste. Add 1 to 2 tablespoons water, as needed, to help grind the chutney.

3. Serve immediately or refrigerate in an airtight container for up to 2 weeks.

NOTE: Cilantro Chutney can be frozen for up to 6 months. Frozen chutney maintains its bright green color. Thaw in refrigerator beforte serving.

NUTRITION INFORMATION PER SERVING:
Calories: 1; Total Fat: 0 g (Saturated Fat: 0 g); Carbohydrate: 0 g; Protein: 0 g; Fiber: 0 g; Sodium: 44 mg

GF

Coconut Chutney
Nariyal Chutney

PREP: 20 minutes
COOK: 5 minutes
MAKES: 1 cup, or 20 servings
SERVING SIZE: 1 tablespoon

Coconut chutney is as prevalent in southern India as cilantro chutney is in the north. It is versatile and goes with a variety of dishes such as *idli, dosa, vada,* and *dhokla.* Once you taste it, you'll use it with everything.

¼ cup (split, hulled) chana dal

2–3 dry red chiles

½ cup fresh or frozen coconut, grated

½ cup cilantro, loosely packed with stems

1 teaspoon ginger, peeled and chopped

½ teaspoon salt

⅔ cup water

2 teaspoons tamarind paste or 3 tablespoons tamarind sauce (page 25)

1. In a small fry pan, dry-roast chana dal and red chiles over medium heat for 3 to 5 minutes until the dal turns reddish brown. Transfer to a plate and cool.

2. In a blender jar, place chana dal and chiles, coconut, cilantro, ginger, salt, water, and tamarind paste. Blend to a smooth consistency.

3. Transfer to a serving dish. Serve immediately or cover and refrigerate until ready to serve. Will keep covered in refrigerator for up to 2 weeks.

NOTE: Coconut chutney can be frozen for up to 6 months. Thaw overnight in refrigerator or at room temperature for about 4 hours.

NUTRITION INFORMATION PER SERVING:
Calories: 16; Total Fat: 1 g (Saturated Fat: 0.5 g); Carbohydrate: 2 g; Protein: 1 g; Fiber: 0 g; Sodium: 59 mg

---

GF

••

Tomato-Coconut Chutney

Tamatar-Nariyal Chutney

PREP: 10 minutes
COOK: 15 minutes
MAKES: 1½ cups, or 24 servings
SERVING SIZE: 1 tablespoon

Tomatoes add a wonderful fresh taste to this chutney. It goes especially well with southern Indian dishes such as Mung Bean Crepes (page 83) and Bean-Rice Pancakes (page 84), although once you taste it you'll want to serve it with everything. Traditionally, this chutney is seasoned at the end, but I often skip this step without compromising the flavor.

2 tablespoons canola or vegetable oil
⅓ cup (split, hulled) chana dal

2 teaspoons (split, hulled) urad dal
1 tablespoon coriander seeds
1 teaspoon cumin seeds
2–4 dried red chiles
½ onion, chopped
2 teaspoons garlic, chopped
1 tablespoon ginger, peeled and chopped
1½ cups tomatoes, chopped
½ cup coconut, grated
1 teaspoon salt
¼ cup cilantro, chopped
½ cup water

SEASONING (*CHOUNK*) (OPTIONAL)
1 teaspoon canola or vegetable oil
½ teaspoon brown mustard seeds
7–9 curry leaves, chopped

1. Heat oil in a small 2-quart skillet on medium heat. Add chana dal, urad dal, coriander seeds, cumin seeds, and red chiles. Roast the ingredients for 4 to 5 minutes, stirring constantly, until the chana dal is golden brown.

2. Add onion, garlic, and ginger. Cook for 1 to 2 minutes, until onions are transparent. Add tomatoes and coconut. Cook for about 3 minutes, until the tomatoes are slightly soft. Remove from heat and add salt and cilantro. Cool for about 10 minutes.

3. In a blender, combine tomato mixture and water. Blend until smooth. Transfer to a serving container.

4. *Prepare seasoning, if desired:* Heat oil in a nonstick fry pan on medium-high heat. Add the mustard seeds, cover with lid to prevent seeds from splattering, and cook for a few seconds until the mustard seeds stop popping. Add the curry

leaves and cook for a few seconds. Add the seasoning to the chutney.

5. Serve immediately or cover and refrigerate, for up to 1 week. This chutney does not freeze well.

NUTRITION INFORMATION PER SERVING:
Calories: 31; Total Fat: 2 g (Saturated Fat: 0.5 g); Carbohydrate: 3 g; Protein: 1 g; Fiber: 1 g; Sodium: 98 mg

---

3. Cool chutney and store in an airtight jar. Keeps in refrigerator for up to 1 month.

NUTRITION INFORMATION PER SERVING:
Calories: 13; Total Fat: 0 g (Saturated Fat: 0 g); Carbohydrate: 3 g; Protein: 0 g; Fiber: 0 g; Sodium: 145 mg

---

GF, LF

Mango Chutney
Aam Chutney

MARINADE: 8 hours or overnight
PREP: 10 minutes
COOK: 15 minutes
MAKES: 1 1/2 cups, or 72 servings
SERVING SIZE: 1 teaspoon

This chutney falls in the Indian pickle category; it is preserved and will keep for months at room temperature. Mango chutney is full of flavor; a little bit goes a long way. Enjoy it with snacks like Stick Crackers (page 59), or as a condiment with flatbreads. There are many varieties of mango chutney out there, but you'll want to try this one.

3½ cups peeled, pitted, and sliced raw mango, cut into 1-inch strips

1½ tablespoons salt

1½ cups sugar

1 teaspoon fennel seeds

½ teaspoon fenugreek seeds

½ teaspoon kalonji

1 teaspoon cayenne pepper

⅓ cup vinegar

1. *Important:* Measure mango slices after discarding peel and pits. In a glass bowl with lid, mix mango slices and salt. Let sit at room temperature for 8 hours or overnight.

GF, LF

Instant Sweet-and-Sour Chutney
Amchur Chutney

PREP: 5 minutes
COOK: 10 minutes
MAKES: ¾ cup, or 12 servings
SERVING SIZE: 1 tablespoon

This sweet-and-sour chutney is made with *amchur* (dry mango powder) and is a quick substitute for tamarind chutney.

2 tablespoons amchur

¾ teaspoon salt

2 ½ tablespoons sugar

¾ cup water

½ teaspoon roasted cumin powder (page 25)

½ teaspoon cayenne pepper

¼ teaspoon ground ginger

1 tablespoon golden raisins

1. In a small saucepan, mix amchur, salt, sugar, and water until well blended. Bring to a boil over medium heat.

2. Add cumin powder, cayenne pepper, ginger, and raisins. Reduce heat and simmer for about 5 minutes.

2. Strain the mango slices over a large bowl, squeezing the mango slices slightly with a large spoon to remove all the juices. Reserve the juices and set aside. Spread the mango on a clean cloth, and let sit for 1 hour.

3. Blend half of the mango slices in a blender to the consistency of applesauce. Do not add any water.

4. In a medium saucepan, place sugar and the reserved mango juices. Cook on medium heat for about 5 minutes, until syrup is very thick.

5. Add the mango slices and the mango sauce. Bring to a boil. Add fennel seeds, fenugreek seeds, kalonji, and cayenne pepper. Adjust heat as necessary and simmer for 5 to 8 minutes, until mango slices are tender.

6. Add vinegar and cook for another 3 to 5 minutes, until chutney is thick. Chutney will thicken further as it cools.

7. Cool the chutney completely. Store in an airtight jar.

> TIP: This chutney is more like a preserve and will keep in a cool, dry place for up to 6 months. It is important to use a clean spoon when dipping into the chutney, and do not return the leftover chutney to the same container. If desired, refrigerate the chutney.

NUTRITION INFORMATION PER SERVING:
Calories: 22; Total Fat: 0 g (Saturated Fat: 0 g); Carbohydrate: 5 g; Protein: 0 g; Fiber: 0 g; Sodium: 145 mg

---

Cran-Apple Chutney
Cranberries-Sev Chutney

PREP: 10 minutes
COOK: 30 minutes
MAKES: 2 cups, or 96 servings
SERVING SIZE: 1 teaspoon

This chutney is similar in consistency to apple jam. This recipe is a twist on the traditional Indian apple chutney. Cranberries add a wonderful color and taste. From what I know, cranberries are not found in India. For traditional taste, use the golden raisins. It will keep at room temperature for up to one month, and can be refrigerated for longer storage.

1½ pounds tart apples, such as Granny Smith

½ cup dried cranberries or golden raisins

2 cups sugar

2 teaspoons salt

½ teaspoon cayenne pepper, or to taste

½ teaspoon black peppercorns, coarsely ground

2 teaspoons ginger, peeled and grated, or ½ teaspoon ground ginger

2 teaspoons fennel seeds

1 cinnamon stick

½ teaspoon fenugreek seeds

⅓ cup apple cider vinegar

1. Peel, core, and slice apples. In a food processor, coarsely chop apple slices.

2. In a heavy stainless steel sauce pan, combine apples, dried cranberries, sugar, salt, cayenne pepper, black pepper, ginger, fennel seeds, cinnamon stick, and fenugreek seeds. Heat on medium heat, stirring occasionally, until sugar is dissolved. Bring mixture to a boil.

3. Reduce heat and simmer for 20 to 30 minutes. Stir frequently, adjusting heat as needed to avoid sticking to the bottom of the pan. The consistency of the chutney will become thick, like jam.

4. Add vinegar and cook for another 2 to 3 minutes. Chutney will continue to thicken as it cools.

5. Cool the chutney completely. Store in an airtight jar.

NUTRITION INFORMATION PER SERVING:
Calories: 22; Total Fat: 0 g (Saturated Fat: 0 g); Carbohydrate: 6 g; Protein: 0 g; Fiber: 0 g; Sodium: 49 mg

---

GF

Cabbage-Peanut Salad
Bund Gobhi-Mungfali Salad

PREP: **10 minutes**
COOK: **10 minutes**
MAKES: **4 servings**
SERVING SIZE: **½ cup**

Peanuts add a distinctive texture to mildly sour-and-sweet cabbage. Make this salad with red or green cabbage. My daughter serves this salad with pasta dishes and sandwiches.

2 tablespoons olive or canola oil

1 tablespoon sesame seeds

1 cup red onion, thinly sliced

2 cups cabbage, thinly sliced

1 cup yellow or green pepper, thinly sliced

1 tablespoon vinegar, distilled

½ teaspoon salt

½ teaspoon black pepper, coarsely ground, or to taste

2 teaspoons sugar

2 tablespoons dry-roasted unsalted peanuts, coarsely ground

1. Heat oil in a nonstick medium fry pan on medium-high heat. Add sesame seeds and onion. Fry for 1 to 2 minutes until onions are transparent.

2. Add the cabbage and peppers. Stir well to coat with oil. Cook for 3 to 5 minutes until cabbage is tender but still crunchy.

3. Stir in vinegar, salt, black pepper, and sugar. Cook for 1 minute. Transfer to a serving dish and garnish with peanuts.

NUTRITION INFORMATION PER SERVING:
Calories: 138; Total Fat: 10 g (Saturated Fat: 1.5 g); Carbohydrate: 11 g; Protein: 3 g; Fiber: 3 g; Sodium: 301 mg

---

GF, LF

Onion-Ginger Relish
Pyaj-Adrak Sirka Wala

MARINADE: **2 hours or longer**
PREP: **10 minutes**
COOK: **0 minutes**
MAKES: **24 servings**
SERVING SIZE: **1 tablespoon**

The health benefits of ginger are well reflected in Indian food traditions. In winter, ginger is often eaten in salads and brewed in tea to ward off infections. At our house a jar of marinated ginger (with or without onion) would sit at the dining table throughout winter. Just a few strips are eaten with a meal for both flavor and health benefits.

1 cup red onion, thinly sliced

1 cup ginger, peeled and cut into thin strips (julienne)

1 teaspoon salt

¼ cup vinegar

In a bowl or jar, mix together onion, ginger, salt, and vinegar. Marinate for 2 hours or more before serving. Store in an airtight jar. Relish will keep at room temperature for up to 3 days. For best results, store in refrigerator for up to 2 weeks.

NUTRITION INFORMATION PER SERVING:
Calories: 2; Total Fat: 0 g (Saturated Fat: 0 g); Carbohydrate: 1 g; Protein: 0 g; Fiber: 0 g; Sodium: 49 mg

GF, LF

·•·

Chickpea Salad

Kabuli Chana Salad

PREP: 10 minutes
COOK: 0 minutes
MAKES: 4 servings
SERVING SIZE: ½ cup

Crunchy cucumbers add a nice crunch to soft chickpeas. I sometimes make this salad just for myself when I'm busy writing, for it's easy and nourishing. Serve this on cup-shaped lettuce leaves or any lettuce leaves for a gourmet appeal.

1 (16-ounce) can chickpeas

1 cup cucumbers, chopped into ¼-inch pieces

¼ cup onion, finely chopped

½ cup green bell pepper, finely chopped

2 tablespoons cilantro, finely chopped

2 tablespoons lemon or lime juice

½ teaspoon salt

½ teaspoon roasted cumin powder (page 25)

¼ teaspoon black pepper

1 teaspoon sugar

¼ teaspoon cayenne pepper, optional

1½ cups cherry tomatoes, halved

Cup-shaped lettuce leaves such as buttercup or any lettuce leaves

Cilantro sprigs, for garnish, optional

1. Drain and rinse chickpeas. In a medium bowl, combine drained chickpeas, cucumbers, onion, bell pepper, and cilantro. Add the lemon juice, salt, cumin powder, black pepper, sugar, and cayenne pepper, if using. Toss well. Marinate for about 20 minutes.

2. Toss in the tomato halves.

3. Place 2 to 3 lettuce leaves on 4 small serving plates. Scoop in the chickpea mixture and garnish with cilantro sprigs, if desired.

NUTRITION INFORMATION PER SERVING:
Calories: 158; Total Fat: 2 g (Saturated Fat: 0 g); Carbohydrate: 28 g; Protein: 8 g; Fiber: 8 g; Sodium: 472 mg

GF, LF

·•·

Sprouted Mung Salad

Ankurit Mung Salad

PREP: 15 minutes
COOK: 10 minutes
MAKES: 8 servings
SERVING SIZE: ¾ cup

When my sister-in-law was visiting from India, she noticed that I had frozen sprouted mung beans in my freezer and a pomegranate in my fruit bowl, so she asked if she could make a salad. It was an instant hit, and I always think of her when I make this dish.

1 cup sprouted mung beans (page 26)

1 cup water, divided

1 cup fresh or frozen corn

¼ cup onion, finely chopped

¼ cup cilantro, finely chopped

½ cup green bell pepper, finely chopped

1 cup tomatoes, chopped into ¼-inch pieces

1 cup apple, finely chopped

¼ cup pomegranate seeds

¾ teaspoon salt

1 teaspoon roasted cumin powder (page 25)

¼ – ½ teaspoon cayenne pepper

3 – 4 tablespoons lemon or lime juice

¼ cup roasted Spanish peanuts

1. In a small pan, boil the sprouted mung beans with ½ cup water. Simmer for 3 to 4 minutes until slightly soft. Drain and cool the beans for a few minutes.

2. In a separate small pan, boil the corn with ½ cup water. Simmer for 5 to 6 minutes, until corn is cooked. Drain and cool the corn for a few minutes.

3. In a medium bowl, mix the cooked sprouts and corn. Add the chopped onion, cilantro, bell pepper, tomatoes, apples, and pomegranate seeds. Toss well to combine all ingredients.

4. Sprinkle mixture with the salt, cumin powder, and cayenne pepper. Stir in the lemon juice. Garnish with peanuts just before serving.

TIP: This salad has a lot of ingredients; feel free to substitute or delete if you don't have something on hand.

NUTRITION INFORMATION PER SERVING:
Calories: 107; Total Fat: 3 g (Saturated Fat: 0.5 g); Carbohydrate: 17 g; Protein: 5 g; Fiber: 3 g; Sodium: 245 mg

···

Beet-Kohlrabi Salad
Chukunder-Ganth Gobhi Salad

PREP: 10 minutes
COOK: 10 minutes
MARINATE: 1 hour
MAKES: 4 servings
SERVING SIZE: ½ cup

Crunchy, sweet, and sour, this salad is colorful, interesting, and refreshing. I love making this salad in the summer when beets and kohlrabi are fresh at the farmers' market. Serve it as a side dish or on a bed of lettuce.

2–3 beets (8 ounces)

½ cup kohlrabi, peeled and diced into ¼-inch pieces

1 cup cucumber, cut into ¼-inch dice

DRESSING

1 tablespoon distilled vinegar

1 tablespoon olive or canola oil

1 teaspoon sugar

¼ teaspoon salt

¼ teaspoon black pepper

¼ teaspoon roasted cumin powder (page 25)

1. Peel beets and cut in half.

2. In a small skillet, add beets. Cover with water and bring to a boil. Reduce heat and simmer for 5 to 7 minutes, until beets are slightly tender. Drain water and cool until beets are easy to handle.

3. *While beets cool, make dressing:* Combine vinegar, oil, sugar, salt, pepper, and cumin powder. Set aside.

4. Cut beets into 1/4-inch pieces. In a small bowl, combine beets, kohlrabi, and cucumbers.

Toss in the dressing. Cover and refrigerate for 1 to 2 hours. Serve chilled.

NUTRITION INFORMATION PER SERVING:
Calories: 61; Total Fat: 4 g (Saturated Fat: 0.5 g); Carbohydrate: 7 g; Protein: 1 g; Fiber: 2 g; Sodium: 182 mg

---

GF

··

Peanut-Mung Salad
Mungfali-Mung Salad

SOAK TIME: 2 hours or longer
PREP: 30 minutes
COOK: 5 minutes
MAKES: 10 servings
SERVING SIZE: ½ cup

This salad is a Mumbai version of *kachumber* (chopped salad). It is also the speciality of my friends Vandana and Suresh. Suresh is famous for meticulously chopping all the vegetables into bite-size pieces. My husband and I often make a meal out of it; the many vegetables and fruits make it filling and nutritious.

¼ cup (split, hulled) mung dal

½ cup raw peanuts with skin

1 cup water, divided

1 teaspoon salt, divided

1½ cups green, yellow, and red peppers, finely chopped into ¼-inch pieces

¾ cup cucumbers, peeled and cut into ½-inch pieces

¾ cup carrot, diced into ¼-inch pieces

1 cup tomatoes, chopped into ¼-inch pieces

1 cup apple, peeled and chopped into ½-inch pieces

¼ cup raw mango, peeled and finely chopped into ½-inch pieces

2 tablespoons cilantro, finely chopped

½ teaspoon roasted cumin powder (page 25)

1 teaspoon chaat masala (page 24), or purchased

1 tablespoon lemon or lime juice

SEASONING (*CHOUNK*)
2 teaspoons olive or canola oil
1 teaspoon sesame seeds
7–8 curry leaves

1. Wash the mung dal in 3 to 4 changes of water, until water is relatively clear. Soak for 2 hours or more. In a separate bowl, soak the peanuts. Drain the soaked mung and soaked peanuts.

2. In a small pan, boil the mung with ½ cup water and ¼ teaspoon salt. Simmer for 2 to 3 minutes. (Mung can also be cooked in the microwave, for 2 minutes on high.) Drain the water and cool the beans.

3. In a separate small pan, boil the peanuts with ½ cup water and ¼ teaspoon salt. Simmer for 2 minutes. Drain peanuts and cool. (Or microwave for 2 minutes on high.)

4. In a medium bowl, combine peppers, cucumbers, carrots, tomatoes, apple, mango, and cilantro. Add cooled mung and peanuts and mix to combine.

5. Sprinkle mixture with salt, cumin powder, chaat masala, and lemon juice. Stir well and set aside.

6. *Prepare seasoning:* Heat oil in a small skillet on medium heat. Add sesame seeds and curry leaves. Cover with lid. Cook for a few seconds, until the seeds stop splattering. The seeds will become light brown. Add seasoning to salad. Toss well.

7. Marinate at room temperature for 20 to 40 minutes before serving.

NUTRITION INFORMATION PER SERVING:
Calories: 94; Total Fat: 5 g (Saturated Fat: 0.5 g); Carbohydrate: 10 g; Protein: 4 g; Fiber: 2 g; Sodium: 144 mg

GF, LF

Cucumber-Tomato Salad

Kheera-Tamatar Salad

PREP: 10 minutes
COOK: 0 minutes
MAKES: 4 servings
SERVING SIZE: ½ cup

This is a really simple and versatile salad. The crunch of the cucumbers and the sweetness of the tomatoes make it a nice accompaniment to any meal.

1 cup cucumber, peeled and diced into ½-inch pieces

1 cup cherry tomatoes, halved, or chopped tomatoes

2 teaspoons lemon or lime juice

⅛ teaspoon black pepper, or to taste, coarsely ground

¼ teaspoon black salt

Salt, to taste

1. In a small bowl, combine the diced cucumbers and tomatoes. Stir in lemon juice and black pepper.

2. Just before serving, stir in the black pepper and salt, to taste. (Salt makes the vegetables soft and watery, so it's best to add the salt just before serving.)

NUTRITION INFORMATION PER SERVING:
Calories: 11; Total Fat: 0 g (Saturated Fat: 0 g); Carbohydrate: 2 g; Protein: 1 g; Fiber: 1 g; Sodium: 142 mg

Desserts

"LIFE IS SHORT, eat dessert first." I think most Indians subscribe to that saying. Eating sweets galore is tradition, from ancient temples to modern celebrations. In fact, at wedding parties it is considered a sign of status and hospitality to serve guests a few pieces of *mithai* (dessert) on an individual plate—before dinner!

Indian sweets are quite different from Western desserts. The variety of sweets available is remarkably wide, and in many cases there are no Western equivalents. Some of the basic categories are *barfi*, *halwa*, *laddu*, and *kheer*. Traditionally, chocolate is not an ingredient in Indian desserts, although today you'll find chocolate *barfi* as sweets makers (*halwai*) try to cater to the younger generation.

Because Indians do not use eggs in desserts and ovens were not typically found in Indian kitchens, baked goods are not part of the Indian dessert repertoire. With the migration of Zoroastrians (called Parsis) in the 1500s, and the British in the 1700s, baked goods have been around for a while, but only recently (in the last forty years) have bakeries proliferated in India. The two baked recipes I've included—Whole Wheat Cookies (page 202) and Cardamom Cookies (page 203)— have been around for a long time and have a distinct flavor and texture.

The Indian equivalent to the baker and bakery of the Western world are *halwai* and *halwai* shop. A visit to the *halwai* shop is as fun as going to a sensational French bakery. The *halwai* shop is lined with trays of beautifully displayed sweets—the white, gold, and green *barfi* are layered like a wall of bricks, the round *laddu* are neatly stacked in a pyramid shape, and the *halwa* sprinkled with nuts are kept hot in a large, round skillet. And right outside the shop, the *halwai* himself skillfully makes hot *jalebi*—my personal favorite—in a large shallow fryer, then dunks them in syrup. Eat a plate of hot *jalebi* at the *halwai* shop and bring a sackful home for the family.

The primary source of sweetener in Indian desserts is white crystallized cane sugar. Sugarcane has been cultivated for centuries and is abundant in India. Whenever sugarcane was fresh harvested, we would have some delivered to the house. It would be our afternoon snack. Just imagine peeling sugarcane with your teeth (that took talent and strong side teeth!) and biting into the juicy and succulent fruit. You chew and chew until all the juices are sucked out, and then (and only then) you spit out the husk. It's pure sugar ecstasy. To eat sugarcane you have to stand up, bending about 20 degrees so that the juices don't drip out of your mouth and onto your clothes. Even now when I go to India and sugarcane is available, I love to bite into some just for the fun of it. Somehow the newer generation of kids doesn't eat it like we did. With all the freshly squeezed sugarcane juice that's available these days, I guess the younger generation doesn't like to get dirty or work too hard for their treats. Now they get five times the sugar without any effort (does this sound familiar?).

White crystallized sugar is the final version of the sugarcane processing. There are other in-between stages of purifying sugar that are rarely used today, though one popular by-product is jaggery, also called *gur*. It's not as shelf-stable as sugar, although it is now available throughout the year. Desserts made with jaggery have a very different taste and texture from those made with sugar. It is rich in molasses and has a soft texture. Brown sugar, as available in this country, is a reverse process of adding molasses to the finished white sugar and thus does not give the same finished results. Jaggery is now available in Indian grocery stores. If you can find jaggery, try both versions and decide which texture you like better. Honey is rarely, if ever, used as a sweetener in Indian desserts. Based on Ayurvedic practices (the science of herbal medicine), which are ingrained in Indian cooking, honey is not to be boiled, for it affects the flavor and develops toxicity. This works well with vegan practices, as honey is an animal product.

Other than sugar, the main ingredients in traditional Indian desserts are milk and ghee—not ideal if you're cooking vegan, to say the least. Over the years, vegetable oil and shortening have replaced ghee in many desserts. Vegetable oil is used because of health concerns, and shortening is used because it's cheaper. This is very similar to how the desserts have changed in the United States. Here, we use shortening for cost reasons and oil or margarine instead of butter for health reasons.

Overall, coming up with good vegan Indian desserts without using milk and ghee has been a challenge. I have not included any milk desserts in this book. I chose not to substitute soymilk except in the Whole Wheat Cookies (page 202), for it used very little and would not alter the taste of the finished product. That is not to say you cannot make *kheer* or *halwa* with soymilk; just use the recipes from my previous book, *New Indian Home Cooking* and substitute the milk. In this book I have provided only recipes that were easily made with vegan ingredients. The recipes have been tested with shortening, but I also give an option for ghee or butter where it might make a difference in taste. Choose the ingredient you're most comfortable with.

In India, as in the United States, desserts are typically high in fat and calories. I've cut down on the fat wherever possible, without compromising taste. Enjoy a small piece or a bite occasionally, for everything fits into a healthy diet.

Types of Desserts (*Mithai*)

I've attempted to simplify the wide array of Indian desserts, which are called *mithai*. Most are cooked on the stovetop; the four main categories are *barfi*, *laddu*, *halwa*, and *kheer*. Then there are other *mithais* that do not fall into these categories, such as *jalebi*, *gulab jamun*, and *rasagulla*, which I'll call others.

Barfi is either square- or diamond-shaped and is made with a variety of ingredients. The closest thing that I can use to describe its appearance is fudge. The majority of *barfi* are made with super evaporated milk. Then there are nut *barfi* (see Almond Barfi, page 204) and *barfi* made from different beans, grains, and even vegetables. The majority of *barfi* use milk or ghee as one of the major ingredients. *Barfi* are often lined with a thin layer of edible silver foil called *vark*, which is more like a garnish and makes the *barfi* glitter. Very occasionally, edible gold foil is also used, but only on special requests from wealthy customers.

Laddu is a round ball that looks quite a bit like a chocolate truffle. The most common *laddu* is *boondi laddu*. It is made with *besan* (chickpea flour) that is fried into tiny balls, soaked in syrup, and formed into balls. *Halwai* makes the best *boondi laddu* versus homemade, that is. Then there are *laddu* made with whole wheat flour (*atta*) or *besan* (chickpea flour). These *laddus*, although available at a *halwai* shop, are often made at home using family recipes.

Halwa varieties are limitless. The most popular *halwa* is made with cream of wheat and is served in temples as communion. The best way to describe *halwa* is a very thick pudding. The majority of *halwas* use ghee and milk as the main ingredients. Carrot *halwa*, mung bean *halwa*, and Almond Halwa (page 203) are some of the most popular *halwas*.

Kheer literally translates to "pudding" but should not be confused with Western pudding, as it has a very different taste and texture. Indian *kheers* are primarily made with milk and are not in the scope of this book. Anything can go into a *kheer*, rice being the most common. You can make *kheer* using soymilk, if desired.

Other Mithai: There is an array of *mithai* that do not fall into the above four categories, such as Indian Funnel Cakes (page 200), a pretzel-shaped dessert soaked in syrup, *gulab jamun* (milk balls swimming in syrup), and *rasagulla* (fresh cheese boiled in syrup).

Crunchy Blossom Pastries

Chirote

PREP: 10 minutes
COOK: 50 minutes
MAKES: 20 servings
SERVING SIZE: 2 *chirote*

*C*hirote, also called *khaja*, is a layered, flaky, and crunchy pastry. These are fun to make, serve, and eat. Sprinkled with powdered sugar, these elegant, blossom-like pastries look beautiful on the table. They are lightly sweet, as the only sugar is the powdered sugar on the top.

DOUGH

> 2 cups all-purpose flour
> ¼ cup shortening or unsalted butter
> ½ cup plus 1 tablespoon water

FILLING

> 3 tablespoons rice flour, plus additional for sprinkling
> ¼ teaspoon cardamom powder
> 3 tablespoons shortening or unsalted butter, melted
> Canola oil for frying
> ⅓ cup powdered sugar

1. *Prepare dough:* In a bowl, mix flour and shortening until the flour becomes a little crumbly and the shortening is well blended. Gradually add ½ cup water. Gather the dough in your hands. If the dough is dry or crumbly, add 1 more tablespoon of water and mix. Turn dough onto a floured surface and knead for about 3 minutes, or until dough becomes smooth and soft. Divide dough into 3 equal portions and roll each into a smooth ball. Cover with a towel and let rest for about 10 minutes.

2. *Prepare filling:* In a small bowl, combine rice flour and cardamom powder. Set aside.

3. In a separate microwave small bowl, melt the shortening and set aside. (You may need to re-melt shortening as you work.)

4. On a clean counter, roll out one of the dough balls, dusting with flour as needed, to an 11-by-16-inch sheet. Using a pastry brush, spread a thin layer of melted shortening (about 1 tablespoon) on the top of dough sheet. Sprinkle a thin layer of rice flour (about 1 tablespoon) on the shortening. If necessary, spread the flour evenly with your fingers.

5. Starting from one edge roll the dough into a tight scroll. (From the beginning, roll tightly, keeping the roll as straight as possible.) Starting from the center toward the ends, gently squeeze the scroll, stretching and compacting it into a 20-inch rope. Cover and set the rope aside. Shape the remaining 2 balls.

6. Cut each pastry rope into 13 to 14 pieces (about 1½ inches long). Place each piece cut side down and press gently on the top with your palm, making a flat disc. With a rolling pin, gently roll each disc into a 2½- to 3-inch circle. Cover with a dry cloth.

7. Heat 2 to 3 inches of oil in a *karahi*/wok or a flat skillet on medium heat. (Or use electric skillet and heat oil to 300°F.) The oil is ready when a small amount of dough dropped in oil rises to the top right away.

8. Carefully slide in several *chirote* at a time in a single layer. Fry for 3 to 4 minutes on each side, turning only once or twice, until light brown on each side. Using a slotted spoon, remove pastries from oil and drain on paper towels.

9. Sift pastries with a generous amount of sugar.

10. Continue frying and powdering the pastries in batches. Cool completely and store in an airtight container.

NUTRITION INFORMATION PER SERVING:
Calories: 111; Total Fat: 6 g (Saturated Fat: 1 g); Carbohydrate: 13 g; Protein: 2 g; Fiber: 0 g; Sodium: 0 mg

---

GF

··:···:··

Peanut Brittle

Chikki

PREP: 10 minutes
COOK: 10 minutes
MAKES: 20 servings
SERVING SIZE: 1 1-inch piece

Chikki is typically made with peanuts and is similar to peanut brittle in appearance. However, *chikki* is traditionally made with jaggery (page 20) and has a very different taste and texture to brittle. Jaggery is now readily available in most Indian grocery stores. You can substitute brown sugar, if desired (see Variation).

1 cup raw peanuts with shell (Spanish peanuts)

⅓ cup water

1½ cups (about 10 ounces) jaggery, grated and packed (page 20)

1. Preheat a large nonstick fry pan on medium heat. Add the peanuts and dry-roast, stirring frequently for about 5 minutes, until light brown. Remove onto a plate.

2. Lightly oil a plate or cookie sheet and set aside.

3. Put some cold water in a plate and set near the stove.

4. In the same fry pan, add water and jaggery. Bring to a boil on medium heat, stirring occa-

sionally. Within a few minutes, the syrup will start to bubble and thicken. Pour a drop of syrup into the plate of water; the syrup should turn into a ball right away. Pick up the ball and roll between your fingers. It should be easy to roll into a soft ball. It should not be sticky on your fingers or brittle. (Or, cook mixture to 260°F on a candy thermometer.)

5. Remove from heat, add the peanuts, and stir to coat.

6. Pour mixture onto a greased plate. The peanuts should spread themselves. If necessary, spread the peanuts in a single layer using a butter knife. Cool completely.

7. Break *chikki* into about 1 to 1½-inch pieces. Store in an airtight container.

NUTRITION INFORMATION PER SERVING:
Calories: 105; Total Fat: 4 g (Saturated Fat: 0.5 g); Carbohydrate: 18 g; Protein: 2 g; Fiber: 1 g; Sodium: 36 mg

---

VARIATION: Using brown sugar in place of jaggery requires slightly different ingredients and method:

1 cup raw peanuts with shell

½ cup light corn syrup

¼ cup water

1 cup dark brown sugar

1 tablespoon canola or vegetable oil or butter

⅛ teaspoon baking soda

1. Follow steps 1 to 3, as above.

2. *To make syrup:* Combine corn syrup, water, and brown sugar on medium heat. Stir until sugar is dissolved. Stir in oil. Cook for about 10 minutes, stirring frequently and adjusting heat as needed to avoid burning. The syrup will start to bubble and thicken. Pour a drop of syrup onto the plate with water; the syrup should turn into a ball right away. Pick up the ball and roll between your fingers. It should be easy to roll into a soft ball. It should not be sticky on your fingers or brittle. (Or, cook mixture to 280°F on a candy thermometer.)

3. Remove mixture from heat. Add the peanuts and baking soda and lightly stir to coat the peanuts. Follow steps 6 and 7, as above.

:·:

Indian Funnel Cakes
Instant Jalebi

PREP: 10 minutes
COOK: 60 minutes
MAKES: 12 servings
SERVING SIZE: 2 *jalebies*

Imagine my delight when I discovered funnel cakes at the Iowa State Fair . . . and my disappointment when I bit into them. Don't get me wrong—I love funnel cakes, but they're just not *jalebi*. Hot *jalebi* is, by far, my favorite dessert. Crunchy on the outside and filled with syrup on the inside, they are one of the most popular sweets in India. Like doughnuts in America, they are available fresh and hot in the morning for breakfast.

Jalebi batter is typically fermented overnight with a buttermilk base. In contrast, these instant—and vegan—*jalebies* require no fermenting, no overnight prepping, and of course no milk product. But they are just as good if not better than most *jalebies* I've had. It may take you a while to master the traditional *jalebi* shape, but don't worry, any shape will work.

1 cup all-purpose flour

1 tablespoon besan

½ teaspoon baking powder

¼ teaspoon cream of tartar

¾ cup water

1 tablespoon melted shortening or ghee

1 teaspoon lemon or lime juice

SYRUP

2 cups sugar

1⅓ cups water

⅛ teaspoon saffron or a few drops of yellow food color

1 teaspoon rose water, optional

3–4 drops yellow food color, optional

Canola oil for frying

1. Use a cone-shaped thick pastry bag and cut about ¼-inch at the bottom of cone to dispense the batter. Set aside. (Or, use a thick plastic storage bag prepped as above.)

2. In a mixing bowl, combine flour, besan, baking powder, and cream of tartar. Add water and mix with hand mixer (about 50 strokes) or electric mixer for about 2 minutes. Add melted shortening and lemon juice and mix gently with a large spoon. Mixture should fall from spoon in a ribbon-like flow. (If needed, add 1 more tablespoon of water and stir well.) Let sit for about 10 minutes.

3. *While batter rests, prepare syrup:* In a small skillet, combine sugar and water and stir until sugar is dissolved. Bring syrup to a boil over medium-high heat. Cook for about 5 minutes. The syrup will reach about 210°F on a candy thermometer. Let cool slightly.

4. Heat 2 inches of oil in a *karahi*/wok or a flat skillet on medium heat. (Or use electric skillet and heat oil to 325°F.) The oil is ready when a small amount of dough dropped in oil rises to the top right away.

5. Transfer the batter into the pastry bag. Twist the top for easy dispensing.

6. Squeezing the batter directly into the hot oil, make a 2-inch circle and cross over it like a pretzel. Continue making 3 to 4 pretzel shapes, joined together in a strip. Fry as many *jalebi* as you can in a single layer. Fry 5 minutes on each side until golden brown. Drain on paper towels for about 2 minutes.

7. Add *jalebi* to the warm syrup (about 150°F on a candy thermometer). You might need to heat the syrup periodically to keep it warm. Soak for 2 to 3 minutes until the syrup is absorbed into *jalebi*. Remove *jalebi* with tongs, draining excess syrup.

8. Transfer to a serving platter and serve warm or at room temperature. Store leftover *jalebi* in an airtight container at room temperature for up to 3 days.

NUTRITION INFORMATION PER SERVING:
Calories: 172; Total Fat: 4 g (Saturated Fat: 0.5 g); Carbohydrate: 33 g; Protein: 1 g; Fiber: 0 g; Sodium: 21 mg

GF

Coconut-Cream Bananas
Nariyal Kela

PREP: **10 minutes**
COOK: **20 minutes**
MAKES: **8 servings**
SERVING SIZE: **½ banana**

Coconut and bananas give this dessert a tropical appeal. The nuts add a nice crunch.

¾ cup coconut milk

⅓ cup sugar

1 teaspoon cornstarch

4 firm, ripe bananas

2 tablespoons canola oil or ghee

¼ cup raw cashews

2 tablespoons pistachios

2 tablespoons sweetened coconut flakes

1. In a small skillet, combine coconut milk, sugar, and cornstarch until well blended. Cook on medium heat, stirring constantly for 3 to 5 minutes, until the milk is bubbly and thickened. Set aside.

2. Peel and cut the bananas in half.

3. Heat oil on medium heat in a nonstick fry pan. Add the bananas and cook for 3 to 5 minutes, turning the bananas to brown all sides.

4. Transfer the bananas to a serving platter and pour the coconut cream over the warm bananas.

5. Chill in refrigerator for 2 to 4 hours. Garnish with cashews, pistachios, and coconut. Serve cold.

NUTRITION INFORMATION PER SERVING:
Calories: 203; Total Fat: 12 g (Saturated Fat: 5 g); Carbohydrate: 26 g; Protein: 1 g; Fiber: 1 g; Sodium: 14 mg

Tropical Fruit Salad

Phal Ki Chaat

PREP: 15 minutes
COOK: 0 minutes
MAKES: 6 servings
SERVING SIZE: ¾ cup

In India, fruit salads are eaten more like a snack than a dessert and are often called fruit chaat. Chaat masala and lemon juice add a little zip to this fruit salad.

1 banana, sliced

2 cups ripe mango, diced into 1-inch pieces

1 cup ripe papaya, diced into 1-inch pieces

1 cup pineapple, cut into ½-inch pieces

1 cup green or red seedless grapes, halved

1 orange, juiced (about ½ cup)

1 tablespoon lemon or lime juice

¼ teaspoon salt

½ teaspoon chaat masala (page 24), or purchased

2 tablespoons walnuts or pecans, dry-roasted, coarsely chopped

1. In a serving bowl, mix together all the fruit.

2. In a separate small bowl, mix together orange juice, lemon juice, salt, and chaat masala. Pour over the fruit. Mix gently. Cover and refrigerate for about 2 hours.

3. Before serving, garnish with walnuts. Serve cold.

NUTRITION INFORMATION PER SERVING:
Calories: 120; Total Fat: 2 g (Saturated Fat: 0 g); Carbohydrate: 28 g; Protein: 2 g; Fiber: 3 g; Sodium: 135 mg

Whole Wheat Cookies

Atte-Ke Biscuits

PREP: 10 minutes
COOK: 12 to 15 minutes
MAKES: 30 servings
SERVING SIZE: 2 cookies

When I was growing up in India, my mother would often order these cookies from a local bakery. She would send whole wheat flour (*atta*) and butter in the morning and by afternoon we would get a large tin, full of fresh baked cookies (called biscuits in India). Indians no longer supply bakeries with their own ingredients, but back in those days, you wanted to make sure the best supplies were used. A few years ago, I wanted to replicate that taste and started experimenting and came pretty close to what I remember from those cookie tins all those years ago. The biscuits are exceptionally crunchy and are great with tea or milk.

2¼ cups roti-atta, or white whole wheat flour

1 teaspoon baking powder

½ teaspoon salt

1 cup shortening or butter

1¼ cups sugar

¼ cup soymilk

1 teaspoon vanilla

1. In a small bowl, combine flour, baking powder, and salt. Set aside.

2. In a large mixing bowl, beat shortening with an electric mixer on medium to high speed for 30 seconds. Add sugar and beat for another 30 seconds. Add milk and vanilla, and beat until combined. Add flour mixture. Beat mixture; when dough becomes tough to work with, stir in the remaining flour with a large wooden spoon.

3. Divide dough into 4 pieces. Shape each into a 6-inch log. Cover and refrigerate for 20 to 30 minutes.

4. Preheat oven to 375°F.

5. Using a sharp knife, cut dough logs into ¼-inch-thick slices. Place cookies 1 inch apart on ungreased cookie sheets.

6. Bake for 8 to 10 minutes until edges are light brown. Carefully transfer cookies to a wire rack. Cool completely. Store in an airtight container.

NUTRITION INFORMATION PER SERVING:
Calories: 124; Total Fat: 7 g (Saturated Fat: 2 g); Carbohydrate: 15 g; Protein: 1 g; Fiber: 1 g; Sodium: 57 mg

---

···

Cardamom Cookies
Naan-Khatai

PREP: 10 minutes
BAKE: 10 to 12 minutes
MAKES: 24 servings
SERVING SIZE: 1 cookie

These round, flaky cookies are very popular in north India, especially in the Muslim neighborhoods, where they are a specialty.

2 cups all-purpose flour
½ teaspoon baking powder
½ teaspoon cardamom powder
1 cup shortening or butter
1 cup powdered sugar
1 teaspoon vanilla or rose water
24 raw whole almonds, optional

1. In a small bowl, combine flour, baking powder, and cardamom powder. Set aside.

2. In a large mixing bowl, beat shortening with an electric mixer on medium to high speed for 30 seconds. Add powdered sugar and vanilla and

beat for 1 minute, until light and fluffy. Add flour mixture. Beat mixture; when dough becomes tough to work with, stir in the remaining flour with a large wooden spoon.

3. Cover the dough with plastic wrap and refrigerate for 20 to 30 minutes.

4. Preheat oven to 375°F.

5. Roll dough into 1-inch balls and place them 1 inch apart on an ungreased cookie sheet. Press an almond, if using, into the center of each cookie or make a little depression with a tip of your finger.

6. Bake for 8 to 10 minutes, until the cookies are light brown. Carefully transfer cookies to a wire rack. Cool completely. Store in an airtight container.

NUTRITION INFORMATION PER SERVING:
Calories: 133; Total Fat: 9 g (Saturated Fat: 2 g); Carbohydrate: 13 g; Protein: 1g; Fiber: 0 g; Sodium: 11 mg

---

GF

···

Almond Halwa
Badam Halwa

PREP: 5 minutes
COOK: 10 minutes
MAKES: 6 servings
SERVING SIZE: ¼ cup

Almond *halwa* (*badam halwa*) is one of the richest *halwa* in terms of taste, flavor, and calories. It's like marzipan, creamy and delectable. A little bit goes a long way—¼ cup is a good portion. Serve in small bowls. For convenience, use almond meal, if available. Or, grind the raw almonds in a spice grinder to a fine powder (you can grind it in a blender but it takes longer and will not come out as fine).

¾ cup sugar

½ cup water

2 tablespoons canola or vegetable oil

1½ cups ground almond meal, or 1½ cups slivered almonds, finely ground

⅛ teaspoon cardamom powder

1 tablespoon slivered almonds, for garnish, optional

1. In a bowl, mix sugar and water. Set aside.

2. Mix oil and almond powder in a medium nonstick skillet. Stirring constantly, roast on medium heat until golden brown.

3. Carefully add the sugared water (stand back, as the water will bubble and can spill over). Reduce heat and simmer for 5 to 7 minutes, until water is absorbed.

4. Transfer to a serving container and sprinkle with cardamom powder. Garnish with slivered almonds, if desired.

NUTRITION INFORMATION PER SERVING:
Calories: 254; Total Fat: 10 g (Saturated Fat: 1 g); Carbohydrate: 11 g; Protein: 0 g; Fiber: 0 g; Sodium: 2 mg

GF

Almond Barfi
Badam Barfi

PREP: 5 minutes
COOK: 20 minutes
MAKES: 24 servings
SERVING SIZE: 1 piece

Almond meal is now readily available, and is convenient to use. However, it is relatively expensive. I typically grind slivered almonds in a coffee grinder; it does not take much time, is less expensive, and I can grind it finer than the purchased almond meal. Almond *barfi* is nutritious and delicious, for a dessert. *Vark* is silver foil, added for decoration, and is optional.

1¼ cups sugar

¾ cup water

1¾ cups ground almond meal, or 1 ½ cups slivered almonds, finely ground

3–4 *vark* (edible silver foil), optional

1. Put some cold water in a plate and set near the stove.

2. In a large skillet, combine sugar and water. Cook over medium heat, bring to a boil, and simmer for 8 to 10 minutes until the syrup reaches the soft-ball stage. (To test for the soft-ball stage, pour a drop of syrup into the plate with water; the syrup should turn into a ball right away. Pick up the ball and roll between your fingers. It should easily roll into a soft ball. It should not be sticky on your fingers or brittle. (Or, cook to 200°F on a candy thermometer.)

3. Remove from heat. Add almond powder and mix well. Cool for 8 to 10 minutes, mixing occasionally to prevent drying. The almond mix-

ture will thicken as it cools. The mixture should still be warm but cool enough to touch.

4. Stir the almond mixture thoroughly and pour onto a clean, dry counter or a pastry board. It will have dough-like consistency. Knead for 2 to 3 minutes and form a smooth flat ball.

5. Place flattened ball in center of parchment paper. Put another sheet of parchment paper on top. Roll out to ⅓-inch thickness with a rolling pin. Remove the top parchment paper.

6. If using silver foil, carefully place on dough. The silver foil is very delicate and it will stick to the *barfi* immediately. Once placed, it cannot be removed.

7. Cut dough into 1-inch vertical strips, then cut 1½-inch diagonal strips, making diamond shapes. Carefully remove the *barfi* from the parchment paper and place in a single layer on a plate or tray.

8. Allow the *barfi* to air-dry for 20 to 30 minutes before storing in an airtight container. The *barfi* can be served immediately, kept at room temperature for up to 2 weeks, refrigerated for a month, or frozen for later use.

NUTRITION INFORMATION PER SERVING:
Calories: 74; Total Fat: 2 g (Saturated Fat: 0 g); Carbohydrate: 13 g; Protein: 3 g; Fiber: 0 g; Sodium: 1 mg

---

Doughnut Holes
Gulgule

PREP: 5 minutes
COOK: 20 minutes
MAKES: 8 servings
SERVING SIZE: 5 pieces

The easiest way to explain this dessert is that they look like doughnut holes—but of course taste completely different. *Gulgule* are often made as communion food for *pooja* (prayer) during festivals. I often make these at *Diwali* (festival of light) time during one of the *poojas*.

1 cup roti-atta, or white whole wheat flour
⅔ cup sugar
1 tablespoon fennel seeds
⅔ cup water
Canola oil for frying

1. In a small mixing bowl, mix flour, sugar, and fennel seeds. Add water and make a stiff batter. Let sit for about 10 minutes.

2. While batter rests, heat oil in a *karahi*/wok on medium heat or electric fryer to 300°F. Oil is ready when a small amount of dough dropped into the oil slowly rises to the top.

3. Drop 1 teaspoon of batter into the oil. Quickly drop several additional teaspoons of batter into the oil in a single layer. Fry for 8 to 10 minutes, until the *gulgule* are golden brown.

4. Drain the *gulgule* on a paper towel. Cool before serving.

NUTRITION INFORMATION PER SERVING:
Calories: 147; Total Fat: 4 g (Saturated Fat: 0 g); Carbohydrate: 28 g; Protein: 2 g; Fiber: 2 g; Sodium: 1 mg

---

Coconut-Mango Rice

Nariyal-Aam Ke Chawal

PREP: 10 minutes

COOK: 20 minutes

MAKES: 8 servings

SERVING SIZE: ½ cup

Sweetened rice is served as a dessert or a side dish. The sweet and smooth taste of mango and the hint of coconut turn this dish into an exotic dessert.

1 cup basmati rice

1 tablespoon canola oil or ghee

3–4 whole cardamom pods

3–4 cloves

2 cups water

¼ teaspoon saffron threads

½ cup coconut milk

1 cup sugar

2 tablespoons sweetened coconut flakes

3 ripe sweet mangoes

1. Wash rice in 2 to 3 changes of water. Soak in cold water for about 15 minutes, then drain.

2. Heat oil in 2- to 3-quart saucepan on medium-high heat. Split open cardamom pods. Add pods and the cloves to oil, and cook for a few seconds until the spices puff. Add the rice and stir for 1 to 2 minutes to coat with oil.

3. Add water and saffron threads and bring to a boil. Reduce heat to medium and simmer for 12 to 15 minutes, until the rice is cooked and all water is absorbed.

4. In a separate small saucepan, mix the coconut milk and sugar. Bring to a boil and remove from heat.

5. Peel and slice mangoes into ½-inch strips. Discard the pits. Refrigerate until ready to serve.

6. Add the coconut syrup to cooked rice. Stir slowly and bring to a boil. Remove from heat, cover, and let stand for 10 to 15 minutes until the syrup is well absorbed. Fluff the rice with a fork.

7. To serve, place ½ cup rice on a serving plate, and garnish with coconut flakes and mango slices.

NUTRITION INFORMATION PER SERVING:
Calories: 281; Total Fat: 6 g (Saturated Fat: 4 g);
Carbohydrate: 58 g; Protein: 2 g; Fiber: 2 g;
Sodium: 8 mg

Royal Sweet Toast

Shahi-Tukra

PREP: 10 minutes

COOK: 10 minutes

MAKES: 6–8 servings

SERVING SIZE: 5 pieces

Don't get fooled by the name "toast" in this dish. I grew up eating this dessert and still crave it. It's easy but I would rarely make it, for the bread was deep-fat fried and I felt guilty eating it. But one day I had a craving for *Shahi-Tukra*. So, I decided to bake the bread and see if I would be satisfied. The result was amazingly good. Now I eat it with twice the pleasure and no guilt.

¾ cup water

1 cup sugar

Pinch of saffron

¼ teaspoon cardamom

8 slices firm white bread

3 tablespoons canola or ghee

2 tablespoons sliced almonds, roasted

1 tablespoon pistachios, chopped

1. Preheat oven to 350°F.

2. In a medium pan, combine water, sugar, saffron, and cardamom. Bring to a boil on medium-high heat. Reduce heat to medium and simmer for about 6 minutes. Remove from heat and cool for about 10 minutes.

3. Remove the crust from all sides of bread. Using a pastry brush, brush both sides of bread with oil. Place on a baking sheet. Bake the toast in preheated oven for 3 to 5 minutes, until medium brown and toasted on both sides. Cool slightly and cut each toast into 4 equal pieces.

4. Add 6 to 8 pieces of toast to the warm syrup. Let soak for about 1 minute. Remove from the syrup and place in a large strainer. Repeat to soak all pieces. Discard the remaining syrup (you'll have about 1/2 cup syrup left).

5. Place drained pieces in a single layer in a serving dish. Garnish with almonds and pistachios.

TIPS: The temperature of the syrup should be warm (about 150°F). If it's too hot, the bread will become soggy, and if it's cold, the syrup will not soak in.

NUTRITION INFORMATION PER SERVING:
Calories: 222; Total Fat: 8 g (Saturated Fat: 0.5 g); Carbohydrate: 36 g; Protein: 2 g; Fiber: 1 g; Sodium: 97 mg

Sugar-Coated Pastry Strips
Shakker-Parre

PREP: 10 minutes
COOK: 45 minutes
MAKES: 32 servings
SERVING SIZE: ¼ cup (about 12 pieces)

When my kids were little, my mother would bring her homemade *Shakker-Parre* every time she visited us. The children loved them and came to expect them. According to them, *Nani* (which means "maternal grandmother") makes the best *Shakker-Parre*. There are a number of variations sold at snack shops in India—long strips, squares, or round balls. They can be sugar coated or made of sweet dough. Here is *Nani's* best.

DOUGH

3 cups all-purpose flour

⅓ cup canola or vegetable oil

⅞–1 cup water

Canola oil for frying

SYRUP

1½ cups sugar

½ cup water

1. In a medium mixing bowl or food processor, mix all-purpose flour and oil until the flour becomes crumbly and well coated with oil. Gradually add water and make a stiff dough. The dough should come together into a smooth ball. Divide the dough into 2 parts and flatten each into a large disk. Cover with a dry cloth and let sit for 10 minutes.

2. Place a pastry sheet or a large wooden board on a flat surface. Roll out each ball into a 12-inch circle (flour for dusting should not be needed). With a sharp knife, cut the dough lengthwise into strips, about ⅓ inch apart, then cut crosswise 1½ inches apart, making thin strips.

3. Heat 3 inches oil in a wok/*karahi* on medium heat, or in an electric pan to 250°F. To check if the oil is hot enough, drop 1 pastry strip into the oil. It should rise to the top in a few seconds. Using a thin flat spatula, lift several pastry strips at a time and carefully drop them into the hot oil. Based on the size of your fryer, you should be able to fry all the strips from one circle at a time. Fry on medium heat for 12 to 14 minutes, until the strips are light brown.

4. Drain on a paper towel. Cool completely.

5. Combine sugar and water in a 4- to 6-quart skillet. Bring to a boil over medium-high heat and cook for 5 minutes (the syrup should be very thick). Remove from heat. Add all the pastry strips into the syrup at once. Using a large spatula, coat all the strips with syrup. Continue to stir occasionally in a lifting motion for 5 to 7 minutes, until the syrup starts to set. Separate any strips that clump together. The strips will become white as the sugar crystallizes.

6. Cool completely. Store in an airtight container.

NUTRITION INFORMATION PER SERVING:
Calories: 115; Total Fat: 4 g (Saturated Fat: 0.5 g); Carbohydrate: 18 g; Protein: 1 g; Fiber: 0 g; Sodium: 0 mg

Recipe List

Index

Blackened Spicy Chickpeas (Chole),
5, 121–22
Black-Eyed Peas and Potatoes (Aloo-
Lobhia), 125
Black Gram and Bengal Gram Dal
(Ma Cholia Di Dal), 126
Coconut-Vegetable Sambhar
(Nariyal-Subji Sambhar),
133–34
cooking dals, 8–9, 116
Dal-Vegetable Stew (Dhan-Saak),
129–30
digestive aids, 3, **14**, **17**, **20**, 34–35,
116, 119
Garlic-Flavored Mixed Dal
(Lehsun Wali Dal), 131
gas (intestinal), reducing, 3, **14**, **17**, **20**,
34–35, 116, 119
Ginger-Spinach Pink Lentils
(Adrak-Palak Dal), 131–32
Glossary of Dals, **117–18**
Indian vegetarian diet and, 2
intestinal gas, reducing, 3, **14**, **17**, **20**,
34–35, 116, 119
Mixed-Bean Cakes (Masala Vadas),
66–67
Mixed Three Dals (Milli Dal), 129
Mung Bean–Tomato Dal (Sabut
Mung–Tamatar Dal), 135
nutrients in, 32, **33**, 34, **40**, 42,
115
Pigeon Peas (Toor Dal, Arhar Dal),
118, 119
pressure cooker for, 8–9, 116
Quick Chickpea Curry (Kabuli Chane
Ki Subji), 122
Quick Kidney Beans (Rajmah), 120
reducing intestinal gas, 3, **14**, **17**, **20**,
34–35, 116, 119
seasoning process (chounk), 11, **18**,
116, 119
Spinach Bengal Gram Dal (Palak Chana
Dal), 128
Spinach Sambhar (Palak Sambhar),
132–33
stocking the pantry, 27–28
superfood, 43
washed dal (dhulli dal), 116, 119
Zucchini-Tomato Dal (Torai-Tamatar
Dal), 136
See also specific beans and legumes
bean wafers (papad/pappadam), **21**
Spicy Papad (Masala Papad), 56–57
*Becoming Vegan: The Complete Guide to
Adopting a Healthy Plant-Based Diet*
(Davis and Melina), 45
Beet-Kohlrabi Salad (Chukunder-Ganth
Gobhi Salad), 191–92

bengal gram (chana), **117**
Bengal Gram and Bottle Gourd
(Chana-Lauki Dal), 127–28
Black Gram and Bengal Gram Dal (Ma
Cholia Di Dal), 126
Spinach Bengal Gram Dal (Palak Chana
Dal), 128
beverages (drinks), 52–53
Almond Spicy Drink (Thandai), 53,
181
coffee, 53
Cumin-Mint Drink (Jal Jeera), 52, 76
Green Mango Drink (Panna), 75–76
Lemonade (Neembu Pani, Shikanji), 74
Mango Lemonade (Aam Neembu
Pani), 73
Mango Yogurt Drink (Aam Lassi),
174, 182
Spiced *Chai* Latte (Masala Chai),
181–82
yogurt drink (lassi), 53
See also snacks, chaat, and beverages; tea
Bitter Melons, Stuffed (Bharva Karele),
111–12
Black Bean Pilaf (Kalli Khichri), 143
Black Chickpea Curry (Kaale Chane),
123–24
Blackened Spicy Chickpeas (Chole), 5,
121–22
black-eyed peas (lobhia), **117**
Black-Eyed Peas and Potatoes (Aloo-
Lobhia), 125
Black-Eyed Pea Dip (Sukha Lobhia),
55–56
black gram (urad dal), **118**
Black Gram and Bengal Gram Dal (Ma
Cholia Di Dal), 126
black peppercorn (kali-mirch), **15**
black salt (kala namak), **15**
blender, 10
Blossom Pastries, Crunchy (Chirote, Khaja),
197–98
Bottle Gourd and Bengal Gram (Chana-
Lauki Dal), 127–28
bowls, little (katori), 3–4
brain damage, 38
braised vegetables (sukhi subji), 92
breakfast, importance of, 45
breakfast and light meals, 77–90
Bean Burgers (Dal-Vada Burgers),
81–82
Bean-Rice Pancakes (Adai), 84–85
Buckwheat-Zucchini Pancakes (Kuttu
Cheele), 81
Cracked Wheat Pilaf (Uppama), 78–79
light meals, 77–78
Mung Bean Crepes (Passhirattu Dosa),
83–84

pretzel-shaped dessert in syrup (jalebi),
77, 196, 197
pudding (halwa, kheer), 77, 195–96, 197
Quick Rice Dumplings (Quick Idli),
85–86
Stuffed Mung Bean Pancakes (Bharva
Cheele), 80
Veggie Noodles (Savai Uppama), 79
Veggie Sloppy Joe Sandwiches (Pav-
Bhaji), 82–83
See also crepes (dosas); deep-fried
flatbread (puri); dumplings (idlies);
pancakes (adai, cheele, pude); pan-fried
flatbread (parathas); pilafs; soups
breakfast to lunch to dinner meals, 49
British, 195
broccoli, **40**
Brown Basmati Rice (Bhure Basmati
Chawal), 140
brown rice, 138
buckwheat
buckwheat flour (kuttu), 156
Buckwheat Pilaf (Kuttu Pulao), 138,
150
Buckwheat-Potato Fritters (Kuttu
Pakora), 65–66
Buckwheat-Zucchini Pancakes (Kuttu
Cheele), 81
Burgers, Bean (Dal-Vada Burgers), 81–82
B vitamins, 38, 39

cabbage
Cabbage-Peanut Salad (Bund Gobhi-
Mungfali Salad), 189
Cabbage Mixed Vegetables (Bund Gobhi
Milli Subji), 108
Soy Granules and Cabbage Snack (Soy-
Gobhi Uppama), 178–79
cakes
Indian Funnel Cakes (Instant Jalebi),
200–201
Instant Steamed Cakes (Instant
Dhokla), 60
Mixed-Bean Cakes (Masala Vadas),
66–67
Sorghum-Zucchini Cakes (Muthia),
68–69
calcium, 4, 31, 34, 39–41, **40**, 45
cancer, 2, 33, 37
canned foods, 28, 92–93
canola oil, **21**, 35, **36**, 37, 43
caram seeds (ajwain), **14**
carbohydrates, 32, 33–35
cardamom (elaichi), **16**
Cardamom Cookies (Naan-Khatai),
195, 203
Carrots and Turnips (Gajar-Shalgum), 109
Cashews, Spicy (Masala Kaju), 54

cauliflower, 43
  Cauliflower and Peppers *(Gobhi-Mirch Subji)*, 93
  Stuffed Cauliflower *(Bharva Gobhi)*, 94–95
cayenne pepper *(lal-mirch)*, 16
ceci beans. *See* chickpeas *(kabuli chana)*
celiac disease, 5
cereal
  fortified, 38, 39
  Hot-Spicy Cereal Mix *(Chivra)*, 52, 57–58
chaat, 52
  See also snacks, chaat, and beverages
"chaatori hai," 52
chai, 44, 53
  Chai Masala, **17**, 181, 182
  Spiced Chai Latte *(Masala Chai)*, 181–82
  See also tea
chana dal, **117**
cheese boiled in syrup *(rasagulla)*, 197
cheese *(paneer)*, 173
chickpea flour *(besan)*, **15**
chickpeas *(kabuli chana)*, 40, **117**
  Black Chickpea Curry *(Kaale Chane)*, 123–24
  Blackened Spicy Chickpeas *(Chole)*, 5, 121–22
  Chickpea-Potato Snack *(Chana-Aloo Chaat)*, 72–73
  Chickpea Salad *(Kabuli Chana Salad)*, 190
  Chickpeas and Rice Noodles *(Chane Aur Savai)*, 149
  Quick Chickpea Curry *(Kabuli Chane Ki Subji)*, 122
chile peppers, **16**
Chinese parsley. *See* cilantro *(dhania patta)*
Chips, Pita, 56
chocolate, 195
cholesterol, 36, 42, 44
chutneys, 184–89
  Cilantro Chutney *(Dhania Chutney)*, 185
  Coconut Chutney *(Nariyal Chutney)*, 185–86
  Cran-Apple Chutney *(Cranberries-Sev Chutney)*, 184, 188–89
  Instant Sweet-and-Sour Chutney *(Amchur Chutney)*, 187
  Mango Chutney *(Aam Chutney)*, 184, 187–88
  Tamarind Chutney *(Imli Chutney)*, 184–85
  Tomato-Coconut Chutney *(Tamatar-Nariyal Chutney)*, 186–87
  See also salads

cilantro *(dhania patta)*, 17, 18
  Cilantro Chutney *(Dhania Chutney)*, 185
  Cumin-Cilantro Edamame *(Hare Soy Ki Subji)*, 180
cinnamon *(dalchini)*, 17
clay oven *(tandoor)*, 7, 155
cloves *(laung)*, 17
Cocktail Peanuts *(Mungfali Chaat)*, 54
cocoa butter, 36
coconut *(nariyal)*, 17, 36, **36**
  Coconut Chutney *(Nariyal Chutney)*, 185–86
  Coconut-Cream Bananas *(Nariyal Kela)*, 201
  Coconut Curry *(Nariyal Subji)*, 102
  Coconut Green Beans *(Sem-Nariyal)*, 105–6
  Coconut-Mango Rice *(Nariyal-Aam Ke Chawal)*, 206
  Coconut-Vegetable Sambhar *(Nariyal-Subji Sambhar)*, 133–34
  Tomato-Coconut Chutney *(Tamatar-Nariyal Chutney)*, 186–87
coconut oil, 36
coffee, 53
coffee grinder, 10
complete proteins, 32
complex carbohydrates, 33
conversions and measurements, 8, 225
cookies
  Cardamom Cookies *(Naan-Khatai)*, 195, 203
  Whole Wheat Cookies *(Atte-Ke Biscuits)*, 195, 196, 202–3
cooking, getting ready for, 7–28
  beans, legumes, and pulses (dals), 8–9, 116
  canned foods, 27, 92–93
  conversions and measurements, 8, 225
  curry powder, 14
  deep-fat frying, 8, 11
  equipment, 7–10
  flatbread, 153–55
  flour *(atta)*, using the right, 27, 153, 154, 155–56
  freezing extras, 12
  frozen foods, 27
  frying, 8, 11
  grocery list, keeping a running, 12
  herbs and fresh seasonings, 27
  ingredients, 5, 7–8, 10–11, 225
  mail-order sources for spices and other ingredients, 29
  measuring ingredients, 7–8, 10–11, 225
  pantry, stocking the, 12, 27–28

preparing food for cooking, 10
rice and other grains, 27, 138–39
roasting *(bhun-na)*, 11
sauce *(rasa)* preparation, 11
saving time in the kitchen, 12–13
seasoning process *(chounk)*, 11, **18**, 116, 119
simmering, 11
stocking the pantry, 12, 27–28
substitutions, 3, 13–14
techniques, 10–11
temperature for cooking, 11
time (preparation and cooking), 5, 12–13
vegetables, 12, 91–93
  See also Indian vegetarian diet; masalas (spice blends); spices
copper absorption, reduced, 42
coriander *(dhania)*, **18**
coriander leaves. *See* cilantro *(dhania patta)*
corn *(makka)*, 153, 156
  Corn Flatbread *(Makka Roti)*, 171
  Grilled Corn *(Bhutta)*, 101
corn oil, 35
Couscous, Curried Spinach *(Palak Couscous)*, 138, 150–51
cowpeas. *See* black-eyed peas *(lobhia)*
Cracked Wheat Pilaf *(Uppama)*, 78–79
crackers
  Stick Crackers *(Nimki)*, 59
  Whole Wheat Crackers *(Atte Ki Matri)*, 58–59
Cran-Apple Chutney *(Cranberries-Sev Chutney)*, 184, 188–89
Creamy Mushroom Curry *(Khumb Ki Subji)*, 103–4
Creamy Vegetable Stew *(Subji Korma)*, 102–3
crepes *(dosas)*, 77, 137
  Mung Bean Crepes *(Passhirattu Dosa)*, 83–84
crispy fried breads *(pani pun)*, 52
Crumble, Green Pepper *(Besan Wali Shimla Mirch)*, 96
Crunchy Blossom Pastries *(Chirote)*, 198–99
cucumbers
  Cucumber-Tomato Salad *(Kheera-Tamatar Salad)*, 193
  Cucumber-Yogurt Sauce *(Kheere Ka Raita)*, 174, 180
cuisineofindia.com, 45
cumin *(jeera)*, **18**
  Cumin-Cilantro Edamame *(Hare Soy Ki Subji)*, 180
  Cumin-Mint Drink *(Jal Jeera)*, 52, 76
  Cumin Rice *(Jeera Chawal)*, 141
  Roasted Cumin Powder, 18, 25

Measurements and Conversions

F OR ALL PRACTICAL purposes, if you use an 8-ounce (240-milliliter) cup and a standard set of measuring spoons to measure the ingredients in this book, you will be able to duplicate the recipes with ease. Some basic measurements and metric conversions are listed below:

ABBREVIATIONS

g   grams

mg   milligrams

MEASUREMENT CONVERSIONS

3 teaspoons   = 1 tablespoon

4 tablespoons = ¼ cup

8 tablespoons = ½ cup

IMPERIAL vs. METRIC VOLUME (ml=milliliter)

½ teaspoon	2 ml
1 teaspoon	5 ml
1 tablespoon	15 ml
¼ cup (4 tablespoons)	60 ml
⅓ cup	80 ml
½ cup	120 ml
1 cup	240 ml
4¼ cup	1 liter

WEIGHTS (These are approximate, but are fine for cooking.)

1 ounce	28 grams
8 ounces (½ pound)	227 grams
16 ounces (1 pound)	454 grams
2.2 pounds	1 kilogram

LINEAR MEASUREMENTS (cm=centimeter)

½ inch	1 cm
1 inch	2.5 cm
8 inches	20 cm

TEMPERATURES

Fahrenheit	Celsius
350	175
375	190
400	205
450	230

Images by Ngaire

Born in India, **Madhu Gadia**, M.S., R.D., is a registered dietician and the author of *New Indian Home Cooking*. She lives with her husband in Ames, Iowa.

Madhu is a leading authority on Indian cooking and a nutrition consultant, writer, and speaker. She teaches the art and science of Indian cuisine around the country. She has been a guest on TV cooking shows and has written numerous articles for consumer magazines such as *Diabetic Living*, *Vegetarian Journal*, and *Diet*. She has given several presentations and has been a guest on radio both as a nutrition expert and an author.

With her health and cooking experience, Madhu has been able to combine the exotic and alluring tastes of India with the health and practical demands of today's lifestyle. Her expertise lies in homestyle, healthy, and authentic Indian cooking. She emphasizes that healthy and tasty foods go hand in hand. For more information, see www.cuisineofindia.com.